ISBN 978-0-266-26517-7
PIBN 11045651

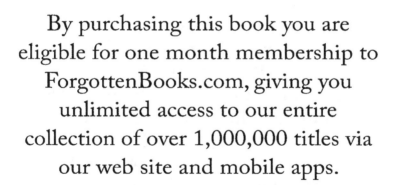

Historic, archived document

Do not assume content reflects current
scientific knowledge, policies, or practices.

Seed Annual
1905

TABLE OF CONTENTS

JOHN BORNMAN & SON, PRINTERS, DETROIT, MICH.

THIS is an age of progress in gardening as well as in other professions. There is an increasing demand for better vegetables and flowers. Improved methods of fertilization and cultivation and multiplied facilities for marketing are contributing much to satisfy this demand. Nevertheless, no amount of care in cultivation or other after-skill will count if you start wrong. If inferior or worthless seeds are planted failure will be the outcome.

The successful gardener, before ordering his supply of seeds for the season, makes a careful study of one or more reliable seed catalogues. He has probably learned from experience that there are two classes of seedsmen represented more or less accurately by their respective catalogues.

One class offer each year, in bewildering numbers, novelties from the four quarters of the globe which they claim are destined to eclipse all similar varieties heretofore known. Such catalogues the gardener must regard humorously if he considers them at all, their misstatements cannot be taken seriously. Only those who enjoy being humbugged buy seeds thus described.

There is another class of seedsmen, dealers who are constantly on the lookout for something of value to add to their lists. By their successful efforts to improve certain varieties they have become specialists and they keep closely in touch with experts in this and in foreign countries. New varieties of proven and distinct merit are promptly included in their lists. Their constant and untiring efforts are also directed to maintaining in purity and type the many well known standard varieties on which the gardener must rely for his principal crops. Their catalogues are not exciting reading but the information given is valuable because it is true. It has always been the aim of D. M. Ferry & Co. that no catalogue in this class should rank higher than their Seed Annual. Accuracy in description, faithfulness in illustration and careful attention to each subject treated make it a valuable guide and book of reference to the progressive gardener. If he is wise he will plant Ferry's seeds and insure success.

OUR TERMS ARE STRICTLY CASH WITH THE ORDER. We do not send C. O. D., as the cost of collecting return charges is quite an unnecessary item of expense, and the prices being given, we can conceive of no necessity to warrant goods being so sent.

HOW TO SEND MONEY. Remittances may be made AT OUR RISK by any of the following methods, viz.; POSTAL MONEY ORDER, DRAFT ON NEW YORK OR CHICAGO, OR EXPRESS COMPANY'S MONEY ORDER.

The rates charged for Postal Money Orders and Express Money Orders are now so low that these are the best ways to remit. We will bear the expense of sending money in either of these ways. Deduct the cost of the order from amount sent. Express Money Orders can be obtained at ALL offices of the principal Express Companies. They are CHEAP and ABSOLUTELY SAFE.

When Money Orders cannot be obtained letters containing money should always be registered. Money in ordinary letters is *unsafe*. If currency is sent by express, the charges should be prepaid, and **if local checks are used, they must be certified.**

FREE OF POSTAGE OR EXPRESS CHARGES. PACKETS, OUNCES, TWO OUNCES, QUARTER POUNDS OR POUNDS, ordered at list prices, will be sent free by mail or express.

Customers ordering enough for a freight shipment, 100 pounds or more, or desiring to pay their own express charges, may deduct 10 cents per pound from prices of this catalogue on all seeds quoted by the pound or less.

PINTS AND QUARTS. PINTS, QUARTS and FOUR QUARTS, ordered at list prices, FIFTEEN CENTS PER QUART, TEN CENTS PER PINT, must be added for postage or express charges, and they will then be sent free.

ONE-FOURTH BUSHEL, BUSHEL AND HUNDRED POUND LOTS. Where ONE-FOURTH BUSHEL, BUSHEL OR HUNDRED POUND lots are ordered, we deliver free at depot or express office in Detroit, Mich., the freight or express charges to be paid by the party ordering.

☞ Where perishable or other goods are ordered to be sent by freight or express to such great distances that the cost of transportation will nearly or quite equal the value of the goods, we must decline to ship unless purchasers remit us, in addition to the price of goods, sufficient funds to prepay transportation charges. When this requirement is not complied with, we reserve the right of declining the order and returning money to the person ordering.

SEEDS BY MEASURE. ONE-FOURTH BUSHEL and over sold at BUSHEL RATES; FOUR QUARTS and over up to ONE-QUARTER bushel sold at FOUR-QUART RATES; less than FOUR QUARTS sold at QUART OR PINT RATES.

SEEDS BY WEIGHT. We supply HALF POUND and over at POUND RATES; less than HALF POUND lots are charged at OUNCE, TWO-OUNCE or QUARTER-POUND RATES; 25 LBS. and over at 100 LB. RATES WHEN QUOTED.

BAGS. To every order for one-quarter bushel and upwards, to the amount of two bushels, 20 CENTS must be added for a new bag in which to ship.

SEEDS IN PACKETS. We offer the following inducements to those wishing to purchase seeds in packets. Select packets to the value of $1.15 and send us $1.00; for $2.35 send $2.00; for $3.60 send $3.00; for $4.85 send $4.00; for $6.15 send $5.00; for $12.50 send $10.00; for $26.00 send $20.00. The seeds will be sent by mail, postpaid; but these low rates apply *to seeds in PACKETS ONLY, and at CATALOGUE PRICES, and NOT to seeds by weight or measure.*

NAME AND ADDRESS SHOULD ALWAYS BE GIVEN. We frequently receive letters containing money and orders, which we cannot fill because the sender has FAILED TO SIGN HIS NAME OR THE P. O. ADDRESS is omitted, and the post mark being blurred, we are unable to fill the order, no matter how much we desire to do so. Use our Order Sheet and Envelope whenever you can, filling out the blank and signing your name and you will have no cause to censure us.

GUARANTEE. Complaints made that seeds are not good, should quite as often be attributed to other causes as to the quality of the seeds. There are hundreds of contingencies continually arising to prevent the best seeds always giving satisfaction, such as sowing too deep, too shallow, in too wet or too dry soil; insects of all descriptions destroying the plants as soon as or before they appear; wet weather, cold weather, frosts, chemical changes in the seeds induced by temperature, etc. For the above reasons it is impracticable to guarantee seeds under all circumstances.

We give no warranty, express or implied, as to description, purity, productiveness, or any other matter of any seeds we send out, and we will not be in any way responsible for the crop. If the purchaser does not accept the goods on these terms they are at once to be returned.

D. M. Ferry & Co.

DETROIT, MICH., January 1, 1905.

CORN: Oakview Early Market

A variety originating on our Oakview seed farm. Similar in general character to our Mammoth White Cory, but with decidedly larger ears which mature fully as early. It is of especial value to market gardeners, as in early corn the largest ears usually control the market. The plant is about four feet high; the ears, twelve to fourteen-rowed, with white square grains. We have on the opposite page a reproduction of ears grown on our trial grounds. **Pkt. 10c; Pt. 15c; Qt. 25c; 4 Qts. 75c; Bushel $4.50**

CORN: Ferry's Early Evergreen

This splendid variety has been proven both on our trial grounds and as a field crop to come into fit condition for use much earlier than Stowell's Evergreen and to remain in condition fully as long. The ear is large and in quality is fully the equal of the older and later Evergreen varieties. The plants average from six and one-half to seven feet high. *For full description see page 29.* **Pkt. 10c; Pt. 15c; Qt. 25c; 4 Qts. 75c; Bushel $4.00**

PEA: Thomas Laxton

This is a splendid pea. The pods are nearly as large as those of Gradus, maturing in about the same time, while in productiveness the Thomas Laxton excels all other extra early wrinkled sorts. Vines similar to that of Gradus but darker in color. Pods large, long, with square ends, similar to those of Champion of England but much larger and darker. Although only recently introduced this variety has come rapidly into favor with market gardeners. Our stock has been carefully selected. The most critical growers will be pleased with the results obtained from planting the seed we offer. As a very superior pea we unreservedly recommend the Thomas Laxton. *See colored page 45.* **Pkt. 10c; Pt. 30c; Qt. 50c; 4 Qts. $1.75; Bushel $10.00**

If Corn or Peas are wanted by mail or express, prepaid, add 10 cents per pint, 15 cents per quart for charges.

CELERY: French's Success

Our extensive trials have proven that for late keeping French's Success is the best celery yet introduced. It does away with the difficulty experienced in the past by all celery growers in preserving even the best late varieties for the attractive prices of the spring markets. On account of its exceptional qualities in this respect French's Success will be found invaluable. *See colored page 26 and further description page 27.* **Pkt. 5c; Oz. 35c; 2 Oz. 60c; ¼ Lb. $1.00; Lb. $3.50**

RADISH: Crimson Giant Turnip

An exceptionally valuable radish in that it attains great size without any sacrifice of quality. From our extensive trials we recommend it unreservedly both for outdoor planting during the entire season and for forcing when a handsome radish of largest size is desired, rather than extreme earliness. The flesh is always excellent, remaining solid, crisp and mild flavored. *The actual size and beautiful color of the variety are shown on page 26.* **Pkt. 5c; Oz. 10c; 2 Oz. 15c; ¼ Lb. 25c; Lb. 75c.**

TOMATO:
Chalk's
Early Jewel

When this tomato was first introduced we found it in our trial gardens to be of the same general character as Early Michigan, a little larger in size but, unfortunately, some later in maturing.

We have now succeeded in obtaining a strain which is distinctly earlier, besides being, if not superior, at least fully equal in size, color and quality to Early Jewel as first offered.

The vine is vigorous, very productive and with somewhat open foliage. The fruit is of a deep scarlet-red color, smooth and of medium to large size, which it holds remarkably well throughout the season. We recommend our strain of this variety as a large, smooth, early tomato of excellent quality. *(See cut).* **Pkt. 10c; Oz. 40c; 2 Oz. 75c; ¼ Lb. $1.25; Lb. $4.00**

WATER MELON:
Ferry's Iceberg

King of shipping melons. Introduced by us in 1902. Similar to Kolb's Gem in size and shape, but darker green in color; flesh sweet, tender and deep red in color, extending very near to the firm, hard rind, which is yellow where it touched the ground, elsewhere dark green. *See further description page 40.* **Pkt. 5c; Oz. 10c; 2 Oz. 15c; ¼ Lb. 20c; Lb. 60c.**

CHALK'S EARLY JEWEL TOMATO.

RUTA BAGA: Perfection White

The ordinary ruta baga is not very highly esteemed for the table. But in Perfection White we offer a variety so highly bred in respect to fine, tender grain and sweet flavor, that we believe it will soon be recognized as a most desirable addition to our table vegetables, is entirely neckless as is shown by cut on page 61. On account of its productiveness and ability to withstand adverse conditions it will also be found very profitable for stock feeding. *Further description page 61.* **Pkt. 5c; Oz. 10c; 2 Oz. 15c; ¼ Lb. 20c; Lb. 60c.**

OAKVIEW
EARLY MARKET
THE LARGEST EXTRA EARLY
SWEET CORN.

FERRY'S
EARLY EVERGREEN
EARLIEST AND BEST
EVERGREEN SWEET CORN.

PETUNIA SUPERBISSIMA

This magnificent strain of Petunias attains a size and a richness of coloring which are truly remarkable, especially in a class of plants so easily grown in almost any soil. The immense petals of velvety texture overlap each other and with frilling and undulation of margin, give the flower a charmingly graceful appearance. A distinctive characteristic of the Superbissima is the dark violet-brown network of veining which deeply marks the widely expanded throat and then spreads over the greater portion of the petals. The Petunia can be had in bloom continuously during summer and fall until cut down by frost. *See page 82 for cultural directions and list of the varieties we offer.* **Pkt. 25c.**

NICOTIANA SANDERÆ

This beautiful hybrid Nicotiana is the very successful introduction of a well known firm of English plant specialists. Wherever exhibited the past season it has been spoken of as the most strikingly beautiful novelty of the year. The plant is described as being about two feet high, hardy, gracefully branching, and producing a wonderful abundance of most handsome carmine-red flowers. Unlike the well known Nicotiana Affinis, this plant is in flower all day and while its fragrance is not so powerful, still it is deliciously sweet. Like the Petunia, it is very easily grown and if started in doors early in spring and planted out in May it will afford a continuous bloom during summer and autumn. The seed may also be sown out of doors as early as warm weather permits. Nicotiana Sanderæ is accorded such enthusiastic praise by competent floral experts that it will doubtless soon be a general favorite. *(See cut).* **Pkt. 25c.**

ROYAL PINKS *(Dianthus Heddewigi nobilis)*

Our recent trials have convinced us that this is a very superior mixture of finely formed, single Pinks of largest size. The flowers are not only distinctly larger but also afford a wider range of colors than we find in other very good mixtures. The petals, deeply cut and fringed, are richly colored in many of the best shades from deep blood-red to carmine and pink, and even white. We are confident that Royal Pinks is a most desirable addition to our list of easily cultivated and graceful annuals. *See other Pinks listed on page 85.* **Pkt. 10c.**

Ruby ... Mignonette

This novelty, introduced by us last year, is attracting very general attention, and is especially appreciated by florists who find in this variety a Mignonette of the most improved type. Our best expectations for the Ruby are realized in that it surpasses all other strains of the Machet class in compactness of form and large size of flower spike, also in splendid depth of color. It can be grown sucessfully either in the greenhouse or out of doors. *See further description on page 80.* **Pkt. 15c.**

Trailing Nasturtium

(Tropaeolum Lobbianum)

We wish to call special attention to the covers of this SEED ANNUAL. The Nasturtium design was executed in natural colors from plants growing in our trial grounds the past season. Our mixture represents in well considered proportions the best shades of color known in the named sorts of this class. We are confident that results from planting any of the Trailing Nasturtiums listed on *page 81* will prove highly satisfactory.

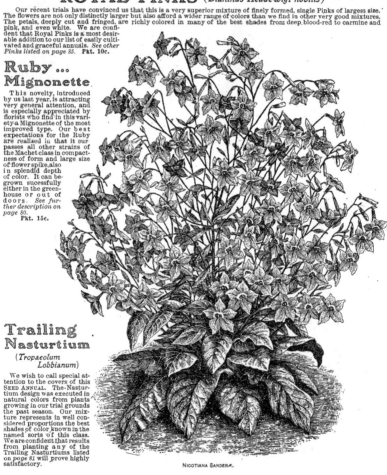

NICOTIANA SANDERÆ.

SUPERBISSIMA
PETUNIAS

5

SEE
PAGE 82.

New Beans
of Special Merit

Golden Carmine Horticultural A pole bean strikingly handsome in shape and color of pod. Superior in quality as snaps or when shelled either green or dry. Excels also in earliness and productiveness. The pods when of size for snaps are a beautiful golden yellow. Later while maturing for green shells they become splashed and mottled with an unusually bright carmine red. The pods are then six to eight inches long, straight, very broad and wonderfully handsome. The quality is so good, the shape and color so attractive that this bean must become a favorite Horticultural variety. (See cut). Further description page 14. **Pkt. 10c; Pt. 30c; Qt. 50c; 4 Qts. $1.75; Bushel $10.00**

Tennessee Green Pod This dwarf snap bean, although new to the seed trade, has for several years been grown in the south and wherever known is freely spoken of in terms of highest praise. Vine prolific; foliage dark green with leaves large and crumpled; pods long, flat, very irregular in shape, bright green and of most excellent quality. Seed of medium size, oval, flat, yellowish brown in color. After careful selection we have developed a uniformly true stock of the variety which we know will give splendid satisfaction. **Pkt. 10c; Pt. 25c; Qt. 40c; 4 Qts. $1.50; Bushel $8.00**

Round Pod Kidney Wax Uniformly perfect in shape; stringless and of excellent quality. We consider this bean desirable especially for the home market. The pods are round, long, slightly curved and very white. Further description page 10. **Pkt. 10c; Pt. 35c; Qt. 55c; 4 Qts. $2.00; Bushel $11.00**

If Beans are ordered by mail or express, prepaid, add 10 cents per pint, 15 cents per quart, for charges.

Squashes
of High Excellence

Mammoth White Bush Scallop We introduced this splendid strain in 1895 and have yet to find any white scalloped squash more handsome than our own selection. The fruit is a beautiful, clear, waxy-white instead of the yellowish white so often seen in the old White Bush Scallop and is much superior in size and appearance. **Pkt. 5c; Oz. 10c; 2 Oz. 15c; ¼ Lb. 25c; Lb. 90c.**

Mammoth Summer Crookneck We have succeeded in establishing a strain of this squash which produces fruit fully twice the size of the old Summer Crookneck. Its color is of a deeper yellow and its surface is more warty. This splendid size and fine color having been attained without any sacrifice of quality. Our stock has become very popular with market gardeners. **Pkt. 5c; Oz. 10c; 2 Oz. 15c; ¼ Lb. 25c; Lb. 90c.**

The two squashes described above are shown in natural colors on page 55, the original fruits having been grown last season on our Oakview seed farms.

The Delicious This new squash, which we first listed in 1903, is undoubtedly of very superior quality. It is an autumn or winter sort of medium size with thick, bright yellow flesh which is dry, fine grained and of most excellent flavor. The shell is bluish green, smooth, moderately hard and very thin. This squash, when mature, is unsurpassed in quality and even earlier it is very good. See cut on page 54. **Pkt. 5c; Oz. 15c; 2 Oz. 25c; ¼ Lb. 40c; Lb. $1.50**

GOLDEN CARMINE HORTICULTURAL BEAN.

Pumpkin

Sugar, or New England Pie We are confident that in this pumpkin of small size, but very fine quality, we are offering a variety of surpassing excellence. The skin is of a beautiful, deep orange color; the flesh rich yellow; very sweet, fine grained and unsurpassed for pies. **Pkt. 5c; Oz. 10c; 2 Oz. 15c; ¼ Lb. 20c; Lb. 60c.**

OUR SEED WAREHOUSE "A," 300 X 120 FEET

THE ESSENTIALS TO THE PRODUCTION OF

GOOD VEGETABLES
and Beautiful Flowers

Good Soil A rich, sandy loam is the best, but a fair degree of success may be secured from any soil which can be made rich and friable. Vegetables of the best quality cannot be grown on barren sand, a cold, hard, lumpy clay, nor in the shade of orchard or other trees.

Liberal Manuring A soil which does not need enriching in order to produce the best results is rarely found and very often success is in proportion to the liberality with which fertilizers have been used. Well decomposed stable manure where straw bedding has been used is the best; manure where sawdust has been used for bedding is not so good. Often wood ashes at the rate of one peck up to one bushel to the square rod will be of great benefit. Commercial fertilizers are excellent and may be used at the rate of 4 to 12 pounds to the square rod and the more concentrated forms, such as Nitrate of Soda, Guano, Dried Blood and Potash Salts, at the rate of one to six pounds to the rod. A mass or lump of any of the commercial fertilizers, even if it is but a quarter of an inch in diameter, is liable to kill any seed or young plant which comes in contact with it, so it is very important if such fertilizers be used that they be thoroughly pulverized and mixed with the soil.

Thorough Preparation Rich soil and liberal manuring will avail little without thorough preparation. The soil must be made friable by thorough and judicious working; if this is well done all that follows will be easy; if it is neglected, only partial success is possible, and that at the cost of a great deal of hard work. The garden should be *well* plowed or dug to a good depth, taking care, if it is a clay soil, that the work is not done when it is too wet. If a handful from the furrow moulds with slight pressure into a ball which cannot be easily crumbled into fine earth again, the soil is too wet and if stirred then will be hard to work all summer, The surface should be made as fine and smooth as possible with the harrow or rake. It is generally desirable to plow the whole garden at once, and to do this in time for the earliest crops, but the part which is not planted for some weeks should be kept mellow by frequent cultivation.

Good Seeds Properly Planted There is no more prolific source of disappointment and failure among amateur gardeners than hasty, careless or improper sowing of the seed. A seed consists of a minute plant enclosed in a hard and more

or less impervious shell with a sufficient amount of food stowed in or around the germ to sustain it until it can expand its leaves, form roots and provide for itself. Moisture, heat, and a certain amount of air are necessary to secure germination. The first steps are the softening of the hard, outer shell and the leaves of the plant from the absorption of water, resulting in the changing of the plant food from the form of starch to that of sugar. In the form of starch the food is easily preserved unchanged, but the plant cannot use it. While in its sugary condition it is easily appropriated but perishable and if not used it speedily decays and the plant is destroyed. A dry seed may retain its vitality and remain unchanged for years, but after germination has commenced, a check of a day or two in the process may be fatal. There is no time in the life of a plant when it is so susceptible of injury, from the over-abundance or want of sufficient heat and moisture, as at the period between the commencement of germination and the formation of the first true leaves. It is just then that the gardener should aid in securing favorable conditions. These are :

First—A proper and constant degree of moisture. The soil should always be moist, never wet. This is secured by making the surface of freshly dug soil so fine and by pressing it over the seed so firmly with a roller or the back of the hoe, that the degree of moisture remains as nearly uniform as possible.

Second—A proper degree of heat, secured by sowing the seed when the temperature of the soil is that most favorable to the germination of the seed of that particular plant. Too high a temperature is often as detrimental as one too low. The proper temperature for each sort may be learned from a careful study of the following pages and the experience of the most successful gardeners in your vicinity.

Third—Covering the seed to such a depth that while a uniform degree of heat and moisture is preserved, the necessary air can readily reach the germinating seed and the tiny stem push the forming leaves into the light and air. This depth will vary with different seeds and conditions of the soil; and can be learned only from practical experience. In general, seeds of the size of the turnip should not be covered with more than half an inch of earth, pressed down, while corn may be an inch, beans an inch to two inches and peas one to three inches deep.

Fourth—Such a condition of soil that the ascending stem can easily penetrate it and the young suitable food. We can usually secure this by thorough preparation of the ground, and taking care *not when the ground is wet*. Occasionally a heavy or long continued rain followed by a bright sun will so surface that it is impossible for the young plant to find its way through it, or a few days of strong v surface that the young plants will be killed. In such cases the only remedy is to plant again.

Judicious Cultivation Not only should every weed be removed as soon as it appears, but the after a rain should be broken up and the ground stirred as soon as it is mit it. The more frequently and deeply the soil is stirred while the plants are young, the better, but a the roots occupy the ground, cultivation should be shallower until it becomes a mere stirring of the surf hundreds of acres of vegetables where the yield and quality have been materially lowered by injudicio cultivation after the roots of the plants had fully occupied the ground. A very small garden, well ct for, will give larger returns and be in every way more satisfactory than a much larger one poorly prepa

How to Build and Manage Hotbed

For early vegetables, some provision for starting certain plants earlier than can be done in the open air is desirable; for this purpose nothing is better than a good hotbed, and its construction is so simple and the expense so slight that every garden should have one. A hotbed proper not only protects the plants from the cold, but supplies *bottom heat*. By this term the gardener means that the soil is constantly kept several degrees warmer than the air above, that being the condition, so far as heat is concerned, which is most favorable for rapid and vigorous growth, and gardeners usually secure it by making a compact pile of some fermenting material and covering it with the earth in which the plants are to grow.

Heating Material The best heating material that is easily available is *fresh* horse manure, containing a liberal quantity of straw bedding. Such manure, if thrown into a loose pile, will heat violently and unevenly and will soon become cold. What is wanted in the hotbed is a steady and moderate but lasting heat. To secure this, the manure should be forked over, shaken apart, and if dry, watered and allowed to stand a few days and then be forked over again, piled and allowed to heat a second time, the object being to get the whole mass into a uniform degree of fermentation, and as soon as this is accomplished it is fit for use.

Sash Some gardeners use sash made especially for hotbeds and glazed with small lights cut from odds and ends and so furnished at very low rates. Such sash can usually be procured in any of our large cities, and costs much less than if made to order. For garden use, however, we much prefer a smaller sash that can be easily handled, and the use of larger and better glass. We recommend that for home gardens the sash be about two and one-half by four or five feet, and that the glass be not less than 10x14, laid with not more than one quarter inch lap. In giving the order to one unaccustomed to the work, it would be well to state what they are to be used for, and that they need to be made like skylight sash.

The Frame This may be made of sound one-inch lumber, the back twelve to fourteen inches high, the front ten to twelve. It should be well fitted to the sash so as to leave as little opening as possible and yet allow the sash to be easily moved up and down, even when the frame is quite wet.

The Soil This should be *light, rich, friable*. Any considerable amount of clay in it is very objectionable. If possible, it should be unfrozen when put into the bed; for this reason it is much better to prepare it the fall before, and cover the pile with enough coarse manure or straw to keep out the frost.

Making the Bed This requires careful attention, as future success depends largely upon the manner in which this work is done. Having cleared away snow and ice, build a rectangular bed one foot larger each way than the frame to be used, carefully shaking out and spreading each forkful and repeatedly treading down the manure so as to *make the bed as uniform as possible in solidity, composition and moisture*. It is of the *utmost importance* that this shaking apart and evenly pressing down of the manure should be carefully and thoroughly done; unless it is, one portion will heat quicker than the other, and the soil will settle unevenly, making it impossible to raise good plants. The proper depth of the bed will vary with the climate, season and the kind of plants to be raised. A shallow bed will quickly give a high temperature which will soon subside; a deeper one, if well made, will heat more moderately, but continue much longer. For general purposes, a bed about two feet deep will be best.

The bed completed, the frame and sash may be put on and fresh manure carefully packed around the outside to the very top (if the weather is at all severe, this outside banking should be replenished as it settles). The bed should then be allowed to stand with the sash partially open for a day or two to allow the steam and rank heat to pass off. The earth should then be evenly distributed over the surface of the bed and carefully leveled. The earth should not be shoveled or dumped in one or more places in the bed and then leveled; if this is done uneven settling of the bed invariably results. Care should be taken that the soil is dry and friable. If wet or frozen soil must be used, it should be placed in small piles until well dried out before spreading. The heat at first will be quite violent, frequently rising to

120 degrees; but it soon subsides, and w degrees the seed may be planted. The i dry soil and allowing the first rank hea great. Every season thousands of ho results from these causes, and seedsmen ure resulting from overheat, or wet, sog

Management of the Bed The cess form degree of heat and moisture; keel times a few degrees warmer than the "hardening off" (by exposure to the air supply of water) of the plants before tra open air. Simple as these may seem to difficulties in the way of securing them which is overheating the air under a br experience one would scarcely believe h perature inside of a well-built hotbed v degrees upon a still, sunny day, even wh outside is far below freezing, or how qu ture will fall to that outside, if upon s the sash is left open ever so little. A ru over the plants is far more injurious than ture when the air is still. Again, in clo will go several days without watering, b hour when open on a sunny day. The ment, however, must be learned by expe easily acquired by one who gives the m tion, keeping constantly in mind the esse

A Cold Frame is a simple constru wintering over you Lettuce, Cauliflower, Brocoli, etc., and useful to protect and harden off plants f or hotbed before fully exposing them in

Select a dry, southern exposure, form to six feet wide and as long as required be fourteen to eighteen inches high, and twelve, with a cross-tie every three fee be covered with sash or cloth. Seeds be wintered, sown in open border early be ready to plant in cold frames about The soil should be well prepared and sm planting. Admit air freely on pleasant in severe weather.

These frames are particularly usef may be covered more cheaply with cl sash. The shades are made as follow strong wooden frames to fit over the be receive some common brand of cotto may be unbleached and should be s securely tacked to the frames. We hav Bed Cloth, which we have for sale, is nary cloth for this purpose.

Transplanting In transplanting, tl regarded are: ca plants so as to avoid injury to the roots as possible to prevent the air coming roots, setting firmly so as to enable the p hold of the soil, and shading to preven withering and blighting the leaves. W growth of tops has been made in hot desirable to trim off some of the larger up to transplant so that evaporation la In transplanting from a hotbed, harde ting them get quite dry a day or two abundance of water a *few hours* befor It is most apt to be successful if don immediately before or during the first the worst time being just *after* a rai being wet it is impossible to sufficiently plant without its baking hard. If wa should be used freely, and the wet covered with dry soil.

Watering The best time to water morning or in the eveni given to the roots at any time, but shou over the leaves while they are exposed If watering a plant has been commence it as it is needed, or more injury than what has been given. One copious wa many scanty sprinklings. The groun stirred with a hoe or rake before it be to cake or crack.

VEGETABLE SEEDS
With General Directions for Cultivation

Artichoke

CULTURE—Sow in hotbeds in February or March and transplant so as to give plenty of room until danger of frost is over. Then set in very rich, well drained soil in rows four feet apart and two feet apart in the row. The plants can be raised in seed beds out of doors, but in that case will not be likely to produce heads the first year. The seed we offer is that of the true artichoke which is a very popular vegetable in Europe. In it the edible portion is the thickened scales at the base of the flower heads or buds. The plant is very different from what is known in America as Artichoke, or Jerusalem Artichoke, in which the edible portion is the tuber. Late in the fall cut off the old tops and thoroughly protect the crowns with leaves or straw, to prevent severe freezing. The second year thin the starting shoots to three of the best, which will commence to form heads about July 1st. The plants may also be blanched like Cardoons. This is accomplished by cutting back the stems close to the ground in July, the rapidly growing shoots which then start up may be tied and blanched like celery. As Artichoke plants do not yield satisfactorily after three or four years it is best to start a new plantation at least as often as once in three years.

Large Globe, or Paris The best sort for general use. Buds large, nearly round; scales pale green, shading to violet at the base, very thick and fleshy. Pkt. 5c; Oz. 40c; 2 Oz. 75c; ¼ Lb. $1.25; Lb. $4.00

Asparagus

CULTURE—Beds are usually formed by setting plants one or two years old, which can be procured of us. If you wish to grow plants from the seed yourself, pour hot, but not boiling, water on the seed and let stand until cool; pour it off and repeat two or three times with fresh hot water. Then sow in drills one foot apart and two inches deep in light, rich soil. When the plants are well up, thin to about one inch apart and give frequent and thorough cultivation during the summer. If this has been well done, the plants will be fit to set the next spring. The permanent beds should be prepared by deep plowing or spading and thoroughly enriching the ground with stable manure or other fertilizer; a moist, sandy soil is best. If the subsoil is not naturally loose and friable, it should be made so by thoroughly stirring with a subsoil plow or spade. Set the plants about four inches deep and one to two feet apart in rows four to six feet apart. After the plants are well started, give frequent and thorough cultivation. Early the next spring spade in a heavy dressing of manure, and about one quart of salt and double the quantity of fresh wood ashes to each square rod and cultivate well as long as the size of the plants will permit, or until they begin to die down. The next season the bed may be cut over two or three times, but if this is done, all the shoots, no matter how small, should be cut. After the final cutting, give a good dressing of manure, ashes and salt. Cultivate frequently until the plants meet in the rows. In autumn after the tops are fully ripe and yellow, they should be cut and burned. A bed 15x50 feet, requiring about one hundred plants, if well cultivated and manured, should give the following season an abundant supply for an ordinary family and continue productive for eight or ten years.

CONOVER'S COLOSSAL. A mammoth, green sort of the largest size and of good quality. Pkt.5c; Oz.10c; 2 Oz.15c; ¼ Lb.20c; Lb.50c. Strong roots $1.00 per 100, postpaid. Large two year old roots, 60 cents per 100 by freight or express, not prepaid.

Columbian Mammoth White This most distinct and valuable asparagus was introduced by us in 1893 and was the result of patient work and careful selection by the originator, thus obviating the necessity of earthing up to produce the white shoots which are so much sought for. The immense shoots are clear white and in favorable weather remain so until three or four inches above the surface. The crown or bud of the young stalk is considerably smaller than the part just below it, thus further distinguishing the variety. All but a very few of the seedlings will produce clear white shoots, and the green ones can be readily distinguished and rejected when setting the permanent bed.

Pkt. 5c; Oz. 10c; 2 Oz. 15c; ¼ Lb. 20c; Lb. 60c.

Strong roots $1.25 per 100, postpaid.

Large two year old roots, 75 cts. per 100 by freight or express, not prepaid.

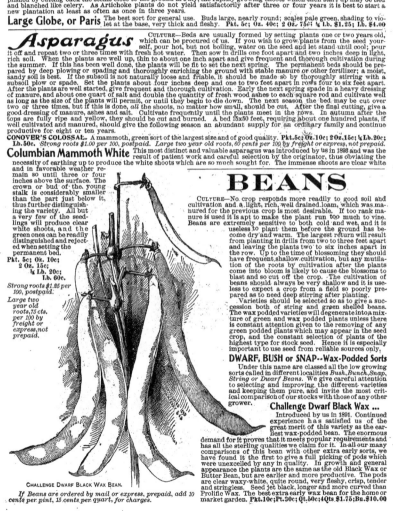

CHALLENGE DWARF BLACK WAX BEAN.

If Beans are ordered by mail or express, prepaid, add 10 cents per pint, 15 cents per quart, for charges.

BEANS

CULTURE—No crop responds more readily to good soil and cultivation and a light, rich, well drained loam, which was manured for the previous crop is most desirable. If too rank manure is used it is apt to make the plant run too much to vine. Beans are extremely sensitive to both cold and wet, and it is useless to plant them before the ground has become dry and warm. The largest return will result from planting in drills from two to three feet apart and leaving the plants two to six inches apart in the row. Up to the time of blossoming they should have frequent shallow cultivation, but any mutilation of the roots by cultivation after the plants come into bloom is likely to cause the blossoms to blast and so cut off the crop. The cultivation of beans should always be very shallow and it is useless to expect a crop in a field so poorly prepared as to need deep stirring after planting.

Varieties should be selected so as to give a succession both of string and green shelled beans. The wax podded varieties will degenerate into a mixture of green and wax podded plants unless there is constant attention given to the removing of any green podded plants which may appear in the seed crop, and the constant selection of plants of the highest type for stock seed. Hence it is especially important to use seed from reliable sources only,

DWARF, BUSH or SNAP-Wax-Podded Sorts

Under this name are classed all the low growing sorts called in different localities Bush, Bunch, Snap, String or Dwarf Beans. We give careful attention to selecting and improving the different varieties and keeping them pure, and invite the most critical comparison of our stocks with those of any other grower.

Challenge Dwarf Black Wax ...

Introduced by us in 1891. Continued experience has satisfied us of the great merit of this variety as the earliest wax-podded bean. The enormous demand for it proves that it meets popular requirements and has all the sterling qualities we claim for it. In all our many comparisons of this bean with other extra early sorts, we have found it the first to give a full picking of pods which were unexcelled by any in quality. In growth and general appearance the plants are the same as the old Black Wax or Butter Bean, but are earlier and more productive. The pods are clear waxy-white, quite round, very fleshy, crisp, tender and stringless. Seed jet black, longer and more curved than Prolific Wax. The best extra early wax bean for the home or market garden. Pkt.10c; Pt.30c; Qt.50c; 4Qts.$1.75; Bu.$10.00

BEANS Dwarf, Bush or Snap—Wax Podded Sorts, Cont'd

REFUGEE WAX. We have taken especial pains with this variety which, as we grow it, is one of the very best in cultivation. The stock we offer is much superior to that commonly sold, being very early. Every plant can be depended upon to produce thick, fleshy, wax-like pods of fine quality and of a clear creamy white color, none of the plants being green podded. Seed yellowish drab, heavily splashed with a bluish black. Pkt. 10c; Pt. 30c; Qt. 45c; 4 Qts. $1.50; Bushel $9.00

D. M. Ferry & Co's Golden Wax This bean was introduced by us in 1876, and its ever increasing popularity has led to the introduction of several "Improved" Golden Wax beans which have been sent out with the claim that they were superior sorts. However, extended and careful tests have convinced us that none of these so-called improved strains are equal in general excellence to the original D. M. Ferry & Co's Golden Wax. The constantly increasing demand for our old stock gives evidence that discriminating growers have found it unequaled by any other. It is an early and very productive sort, the pods being long, nearly straight, broad, flat, golden yellow, very fleshy and wax-like, with short, green points; cooking quickly as snaps, shelling well when green, and of the highest quality used in either way. Seed medium sized, oval, white, more or less covered with two shades of purplish-red. The amount and shade of color on this and all parti-colored beans will be affected greatly by conditions of soil and ripening. Pkt. 10c; Pt. 30c; Qt. 50c; 4 Qts. $1.75; Bushel $10.00

GRENELL RUST PROOF. Vine a little more upright and hardier than the Golden Wax, and the pods are broader, flatter, but slightly inferior in quality. Seed, in color and size, similar to our Golden Wax, but darker. A very popular sort with some gardeners. Pkt. 10c; Pt. 30c; Qt. 50c; 4 Qts. $1.75; Bushel $10.00

Keeney's Rustless Golden Wax Early in the season this seems to be a pole bean, but the runners are short and soon become self-supporting. The pods, which are produced in abundance, are stringless, white, wax-like and handsome. Seed similar to a light colored Golden Wax. Pkt. 10c; Pt. 30c; Qt. 50c; 4 Qts. $1.75; Bushel $10.00

Valentine Wax Our experience has proved this bean to be remarkably early. The pods are thick and fleshy, with but very little string; the plant is vigorous and productive, and it is a popular sort wherever known. *Crop failed.*

D. M. Ferry & Co's Detroit Wax The very hardy, productive, erect-growing plants bear their pods near the center of the vine. Pods straight, broad and flat. We think this variety the least likely to rust of any, and the fact that seedsmen sometimes offer it under other names as absolutely rust-proof, is evidence that they have found it as nearly rust-proof as any wax bean. Seed white, with more or less irregular dark brown or black markings about the eye. Pkt. 10c; Pt. 30c; Qt. 50c; 4 Qts. $1.75; Bushel $10.00

Wardwell's Kidney Wax The very strong growing vines of this variety yield a large crop of long, nearly straight, broad, creamy white, handsome pods. These are of good quality and always command a ready sale, making the variety one of the most profitable for the market gardener. It matures a little later than the Golden Wax. Seed large, kidney-shaped, white, with dark markings about the eye. Pkt. 10c; Pt. 35c; Qt. 55c; 4 Qts. $2.00; Bushel $11.00

Round Pod Kidney Wax A new sort and we think very desirable especially for the home garden. The vine is dwarf, spreading and very productive. The exceedingly beautiful pods are long, cylindrical, slightly curved, very white and wax-like, and of the best quality. They are uniformly perfect, an ill-shaped one being rarely seen. Seed long, cylindrical, nearly white, with a little dark marking about the eye. Pkt. 10c; Pt. 35c; Qt. 55c; 4 Qts. $2.00; Bu. $11.00

Davis Wax This is the most hardy and productive wax podded bush bean in cultivation. The pods are invariably long, white, straight and handsome. The vine is rustless and very vigorous, bearing its pods near the center in clusters. When young, the pods are brittle, crisp and tender. Seed kidney-shaped, clear white and excellent for baking. One of the best for shipping as snap beans and of the greatest value as a market variety. The length, uniformly perfect shape and fine color of the pods and the clear white seed, make this one of the best for canners. It is just what they want, a long, straight, clear white pod which does not discolor in canning. *Sold out.*

Currie's Rust Proof Wax It has been claimed that this variety is absolutely rust-proof, and we have found it like the Detroit Wax, as nearly rust-proof as any good wax podded bean can be. Vine very vigorous, hardy and productive. Seed kidney-shaped, purplish black. Pkt. 10c; Pt. 30c; Qt. 50c; 4 Qts. $1.75; Bu. $10.00

Golden Crown Wax This dwarf and medium early bean is a cross between the Yosemite Wax and the Ivory Pod Wax, and combines the good qualities of each, while eliminating their defects. The vine is vigorous growing, with large leaves, and is very productive. The beautiful, golden colored pods are as large as, and even better in quality than those of the Yosemite, and are wonderfully well filled and perfect in shape. Seed white. Pkt. 10c; Pt. 35c; Qt. 60c; 4 Qts. $2.00; Bushel $12.00

PROLIFIC GERMAN WAX. *Black seeded.* We are so thoroughly satisfied with this improved strain of Black Wax that we have discarded the old stock altogether, this being more vigorous and far more productive, with a longer, whiter, more fleshy pod. Vines medium sized, very vigorous and hardy. Pods medium length, borne well up from the ground, curved, cylindrical, fleshy, and of a clear, creamy white color, with slightly curved points; remain a long time in condition for use as snaps. Beans small, oblong, jet black. No one can afford to plant the old Black Wax or Butter Bean, as this is much better in every respect. Pkt. 10c; Pt. 30c; Qt. 50c; 4 Qts. $1.75; Bushel $10.00

If Beans are ordered by mail or express, prepaid, add 10 cents per pint, 15 cents per quart, for charges.

D.M. FERRY & CO'S GOLDEN WAX BEAN.

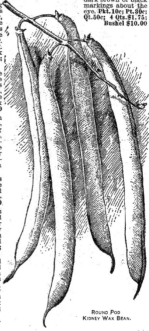

ROUND POD KIDNEY WAX BEAN.

BEANS Dwarf, Bush or Snap—Wax Podded Sorts, Cont'd

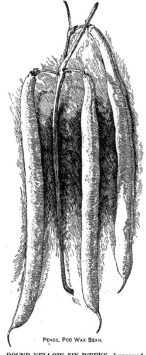

PENCIL POD WAX BEAN.

Pencil Pod Wax Particularly handsome, this new wax podded bean is also medium early, hardy, very prolific and of excellent quality. Pods are long, straight, round like a pencil, fleshy and of a bright yellow color. Tender, brittle and absolutely stringless, they are produced during a long season. Seed long, round, rather small; color black. **Pkt. 10c; Pt. 35c; Qt. 55c; 4 Qts. $2.00; Bushel $11.00**

SCARLET FLAGEOLET WAX. This variety seems to do especially well in the south, and is a favorite with many truck farmers. The large, strong growing and erect vines produce very long, flat, rather coarse, but beautifully wax-like pods, which, though often curved and twisted, are always handsome. Seed large, flat, red. *Sold out.*

VIOLET FLAGEOLET WAX. Known also as Perfection Wax. Plant very large, with large, light green leaves. Pods very long and large, being longer than those of the Scarlet Flageolet Wax, also more twisted. When well grown it is one of the most showy of wax beans. The pods are a little later in coming into use than the Scarlet Flageolet. A favorite with southern market gardeners. Seed large and of a dark violet color. *Sold out.*

CRYSTAL WHITE WAX. Distinct but not strictly a wax bean. Very desirable for pickles. Vines large, spreading, very productive. Pods greenish-white, short, curved, round or thicker than wide, with crease in the back, very fleshy and brittle. Seed small, oval, white. **Pkt. 10c; Pt. 30c; Qt. 50c; 4 Qts. $1.75; Bushel $10.00**

Green Podded Sorts

Extra Early Refugee A very early, green podded kind, furnishing an oval, fleshy pod of fine quality. The vines are a little smaller and more upright growing and the leaves a little larger than those of the late Refugee, though the seed is much the same in shape and color. Our stock has been selected with great care and is uniform, all the vines ripening their pods well together and long before those of the Refugee are in condition for use. Seed long, drab, nearly covered with dark purple blotches. **Pkt. 10c; Pt. 25c; Qt. 40c; 4 Qts. $1.50; Bushel $7.50**

Extra Early Round Pod Red Valentine For snaps there is nothing superior to this variety among the green podded sorts and many prefer it to the wax varieties. Vine erect, with coarse, dark green leaves; pods medium length, curved, cylindrical, with crease in back, very fleshy, crisp and tender; seed long; of medium size and unsymmetrical in shape, pink, marbled with red. Lack of symmetry in the seed of this variety is an indication of superior fleshiness and good quality in the pods. We know of no stock of Red Valentine which can be compared with that we offer in uniformly high quality of pod. Many different strains of Valentine are offered under slightly varying names, each claiming to be a great and distinct improvement. We have carefully tested a great many strains claimed to be improvements, both in trials and in large fields, and have found none that we are willing to substitute for our old stock which combines in the highest degree all the good qualities of the sort. **Pkt. 10c;**
Pt. 25c; Qt. 35c; 4 Qts. $1.25; Bushel $7.00

ROUND YELLOW SIX WEEKS, Improved Round Pod. While this variety does not differ from the Early Yellow Kidney Six Weeks in size or general appearance of the vine, the pods are shorter, very much thicker and more fleshy. Moreover, while retaining the vigor and hardiness of the old sort, it is fully one week earlier. Seed round, light yellow, with slightly darker marking about the eye; much shorter than Kidney Six Weeks. **Pkt. 10c; Pt. 25c; Qt. 35c; 4 Qts. $1.25; Bushel $6.50**

BEST OF ALL. The hardy, vigorous vine produces an abundance of very straight, handsome pods which when fit for use as snaps, are very brittle and of a very deep green color. As the pods mature they become lighter in color and splashed with bright red. When fit for use as green shelled, the beans are large, mottled with red, tender and of fine quality. One of the hardiest and best of the green-podded varieties. Seed large, kidney-shaped, flesh colored and nearly covered with splashes of bright red. **Pkt. 10c; Pt. 15c; Qt. 25c; 4 Qts. 75c; Bushel $4.50**

DWARF HORTICULTURAL. Vine very productive, compact, upright, with large leaves. Pods medium length, cylindrical, curved, with splashes of bright red on a yellowish ground. They become fit for use as green shelled beans very early, and in this condition the beans are very large, easily shelled and are about equal to the Lima in quality, although of quite different form. Seed large, oval, plump, flesh colored and nearly covered with splashes of bright red. *Sold out.*

Improved Goddard Vines large, much branched, erect, forming a large bush; leaflets large, crimped, bright green; pods large, long, flat, usually curved, with long, curved points; green when young, but as the beans become fit for use are splashed and striped with crimson. Green beans very large, splashed with red and of fine quality. Seed marked like Dwarf Horticultural and of the same color, but longer and much larger, making them more desirable for market use. The green beans are almost as large, though different in shape and quite as good in quality as those of the Large Lima. **Pkt. 10c; Pt. 15c; Qt. 25c; 4 Qts. 75c; Bu. $4.50**

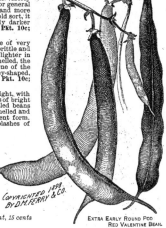

COPYRIGHTED 1898
BY D.M.FERRY & CO.

EXTRA EARLY ROUND POD
RED VALENTINE BEAN.

If Beans are ordered by mail or express, prepaid, add 10 cents per pint, 15 cents per quart, for charges.

BEANS Dwarf, Bush or Snap–Green Podded Sorts, Cont'd

Stringless Green Pod A most valuable addition to our green
podded sorts. The vine is vigorous,
spreading and very productive. The pods are larger and a little
coarser in texture than those of the Red Valentine, but are quite as
fleshy, of equally high quality and remain crisp and tender longer.
They mature a little later; seed yellowish-brown in color. Pkt. 10c;
Pt. 25c; Q_t. 40c; 4 Qts. $1.50; Bushel $8.00

Tennessee Green Pod This dwarf, snap bean, although new to
the seed trade, has for several years
been grown in the south, and wherever known is freely spoken of in
terms of highest praise. Vine prolific; foliage dark green, with leaves
large and crumpled; pods very long, flat, irregular in shape, bright
green and of most excellent quality. Seed of medium size, oval, flat,
yellow in color. After careful selection we have developed a uniformly true stock of the variety which we know will give splendid
satisfaction. Pkt. 10c; Pt. 25c; Q_t. 40c; 4 Qts. $1.50; Bushel $8.00

EARLY YELLOW KIDNEY SIX WEEKS. Vines large, vigorous,
branching, productive, with large leaves; pods long, straight,
handsome and when young, of good quality; seed long, kidney-
shaped, light yellow, with darker marks about the eye. Pkt. 10c;
Pt. 20c; Qt. 30c; 4 Qts. $1.00; Bushel $6.00

EARLY MOHAWK. This sort is so much hardier than the others that
it can be planted earlier and often will furnish beans fit for use before
any other kind. Vines large, stout, with large, coarse leaves; pods
long, straight, coarse, flat, with long, tapering points; seed long,
kidney-shaped, variegated with drab, purple and brown. This
variety is much in favor for forcing under glass, as it matures quickly
and carries a good weight of long, large pods. Pkt. 10c; Pt. 25c;
Q_t. 35c; 4 Qts. $1.25; Bushel $6.50

Refugee, or Thousand to One Vines large, spreading, exceedingly hardy, with small,
smooth leaves; very late and esteemed for late planting and for use
as pickles; pods long, cylindrical, green, becoming white, streaked
with purple as they mature; of good quality as snaps; seed long,
light drab, thickly dotted and splashed with purple. Pkt. 10c;
Pt. 25c; Qt. 35c; 4 Qts. $1.25; Bushel $7.00

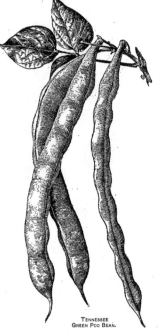

TENNESSEE
GREEN POD BEAN.

☞ *The following four Bush, or Snap Sorts, are
also extensively planted as field beans:*

ROYAL DWARF KIDNEY. Plant large, branching,
with large, broad leaves; pods medium sized, dark
green, coarse; seed large, white, kidney-shaped,
slightly flattened and of excellent quality, green
or dry. Pkt. 10c; Pt. 15c; Q_t. 25c; 4 Qts. 75c;
Bushel $4.00

LARGE WHITE MARROW, OR MOUNTAIN. Vines
large, slender, spreading, with short runners and
small leaves; very prolific; pods broad, green, changing to yellow; seed large, ovoid, clear white, cooking very dry and mealy. Pkt. 10c; Pt. 15c; Q_t. 25c;
4 Qts. 75c; Bushel $4.00

EARLY MARROW PEA, OR DWARF WHITE NAVY.
A variety developed in western New York. Is a sure
cropper, and not only more prolific than the common white bean, but also of better quality. Vine
large, spreading, with small, thin leaves, and occasional runners; ripening its crop early and all at
once. Pods straight, short, small, but usually containing six beans; beans small, oval, white, handsome
and of superior quality. Pkt. 10c; Pt. 15c; Q_t. 20c;
4 Qts. 60c; Bushel $3.75

VINELESS MARROW. A splendid bean for field
culture. Plant large, strong and vigorous, but compact and without runners, bearing its crop in the
center and well up from the ground. The dry beans
are very large, very white, and of the best quality.
A wonderfully prolific and valuable sort. *Sold out.*

STRINGLESS GREEN POD BEAN.

*If Beans are ordered by mail or express, prepaid, add
10 cents per pint, 15 cents per quart, for charges.*

BEANS—DWARF LIMA

This comparatively new class of beans cannot be recommended too highly. They can be grown and gathered much more easily than the pole Limas, and are fully as good in quality. Every home garden should have at least one planting of these beans.

Wonder Bush Lima

A fine new bean introduced by Dreer. It is similar to Dwarf Large White Lima, but the pods are larger, borne more in the center of the vine and mature a little earlier. The vine also is less inclined to form an occasional runner and we think is more productive. Green beans and the seeds like those of Dwarf Large White Lima. **Pkt. 10c; Pt. 25c; Qt. 35c; 4 Qts. $1.25; Bushel $7.00**

Dwarf Large White Lima

A bush form of the true Large Lima. Plants uniformly dwarf, but enormously productive. The pods are as large as those of the Large Lima and contain from three to five very large, flat beans of the best quality. While not quite as early as the Dwarf Sieva, this is considered by many to be of better quality, fully equaling in this respect the Large White Lima. Any one who has tried this variety will wish to plant it again. Seed of medium size, flat, white. **Pkt. 10c; Pt. 25c; Qt. 35c; 4 Qts. $1.25; Bu. $7.00**

BUSH LIMA, OR DWARF SIEVA. (HENDERSON'S.) A dwarf form of the Small Lima, and valuable because of its extreme earliness. Vines are without runners, but continue to grow and set pods until stopped by frost; leaves small and very dark green; borne in clusters and often above the foliage; pods short, flat, and containing two to four beans, which are of excellent quality either green shelled or dry. Seed small, flat and white. **Pkt. 10c; Pt. 25c; Qt. 35c; 4 Qts. $1.25; Bushel $7.00**

KUMERLE BUSH LIMA. A dwarf form of the Challenger Lima, having the same thick pods and large, thick beans which have made the Challenger so popular. The plant, while fully as dwarf, is hardier and matures its crop earlier than the Dwarf Large White Lima. Many people consider this sort the best of the Dwarf Limas. **Pkt. 10c; Pt. 25c; Qt. 35c; 4 Qts. $1.25; Bushel $7.00**

WONDER BUSH LIMA BEAN.

BEANS—Pole or Running

CULTURE—Pole Beans are even more sensitive to cold and wet as well as to droughts and hot winds than the dwarf varieties, but are of superior quality and productiveness. After settled warm weather set poles four to eight feet long and slanting slightly toward the north, in rows four feet apart and extending north and south, the poles being three feet apart in the row. Set in this way the vines climb better and the pods are straighter and more easily seen. Around each stake plant five to eight beans two inches deep and when well started thin to four plants. It is a natural habit of all vines to climb around a pole always in one direction and they will not do well if an attempt is made to train them to run in the opposite direction. Another plan is to plant in rows thickly enough so that there will be one plant to eight or ten inches. Set posts five feet high firmly at each end of the rows and drive stakes made of 2x2 lumber at intervals of about sixteen feet along the rows. Stretch a wire, size No. 10 or 12, between the posts along each row, and fasten it to the tops of the stakes with wire staples; run a lighter wire or twine along the bottom about six inches from the ground fastening likewise to the posts and stakes. Between these two horizontal wires stretch a wire or twine pe en icul wherever there is a plant; the vines will run up these until they reach the top wire, when they will care for themselves. Another way is to omit the bottom wire and stick small stakes two to six inches in the soil and fasten to top wire.

White Crease Back

This variety is especially valuable for its extreme earliness and its habit of perfecting all of its pods within a short time. Vines small to medium, but vigorous, and in good soil wonderfully productive, bearing round, quite fleshy pods in clusters of from four to twelve. Pods medium length, silvery-green, of the best quality as snaps and stand shipping better than most sorts. The beans are too small to be of much value when shelled green, but are of very superior quality baked. Seed small, oval, white and hard. **Pkt. 10c; Pt. 20c; Qt. 30c; 4 Qts. $1.00; Bu. $6.00**

Early Golden Cluster Wax

A well known, early and very beautiful sort. Vines large, strong growing, vigorous, hardy; leaflets large, light green, crimped; pods six to eight inches long, borne in abundant clusters, each containing from three to six pods, varying in color from golden yellow to creamy white. They are broad, thick and fleshy, deeply creased along the edge to which the beans are attached, of the very best quality, and stay in condition for use a long time. Seed flattened, oval, dull white in color. **Pkt. 10c; Pt. 25c; Qt. 40c; 4 Qts. $1.50; Bu. $8.00**

EARLY GOLDEN CLUSTER WAX BEAN.

If Beans are ordered by mail or express, prepaid, add 10 cents per pint, 15 cents per quart, for charges.

BEANS—Pole or Running—Continued

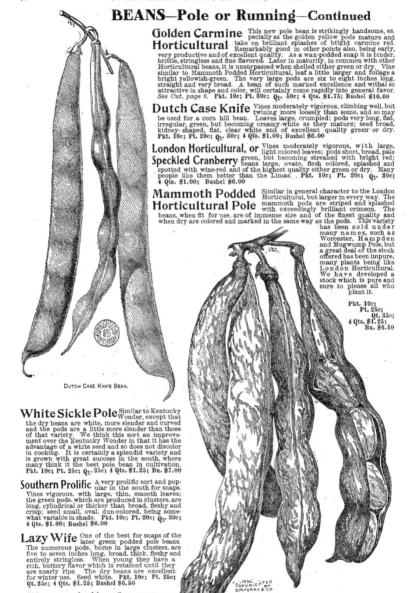

Golden Carmine Horticultural

This new pole bean is strikingly handsome, especially as the golden yellow pods mature and take on brilliant splashes of bright carmine red. Remarkably good in other points also, being early, very productive and of excellent quality. As a wax-podded snap it is tender, brittle, stringless and fine flavored. Later in maturity, in common with other Horticultural beans, it is unsurpassed when shelled either green or dry. Vine similar to Mammoth Podded Horticultural, leaf a little larger and foliage a bright yellowish-green. The very large pods are six to eight inches long, straight and very broad. A bean of such marked excellence and withal so attractive in shape and color, will certainly come rapidly into general favor. See Cut, page 6. Pkt. 10c; Pt. 30c; Qt. 50c; 4 Qts. $1.75; Bushel $10.00

Dutch Case Knife

Vines moderately vigorous, climbing well, but twining more loosely than some, and so may be used for a corn hill bean. Leaves large, crumpled; pods very long, flat, irregular, green, but becoming creamy-white as they mature; seed broad, kidney-shaped, flat, clear white and of excellent quality green or dry. Pkt. 10c; Pt. 20c; Qt. 30c; 4 Qts. $1.00; Bushel $6.00

London Horticultural, or Speckled Cranberry

Vines moderately vigorous, with large, light colored leaves; pods short, broad, pale green, but becoming streaked with bright red; beans large, ovate, flesh colored, splashed and spotted with wine-red and of the highest quality either green or dry. Many people like them better than the Limas.. Pkt. 10c; Pt. 20c; Qt. 30c; 4 Qts. $1.00; Bushel $6.00

Mammoth Podded Horticultural Pole

Similar in general character to the London Horticultural, but larger in every way. The mammoth pods are striped and splashed with exceedingly brilliant crimson. The beans, when fit for use, are of immense size and of the finest quality and when dry are colored and marked in the same way as the pods. This variety has been sold under many names, such as Worcester, Hampden and Mugwump Pole, but a great deal of the stock offered has been impure, many plants being like London Horticultural. We have developed a stock which is pure and sure to please all who plant it.

Pkt. 10c; Pt. 25c; Qt. 35c; 4 Qts. $1.25; Bu. $6.50

DUTCH CASE KNIFE BEAN.

White Sickle Pole

Similar to Kentucky Wonder, except that the dry beans are white, more slender and curved and the pods are a little more slender than those of that variety. We think this sort an improvement over the Kentucky Wonder in that it has the advantage of a white seed and so does not discolor in cooking. It is certainly a splendid variety and is grown with great success in the south, where many think it the best pole bean in cultivation. Pkt. 10c; Pt. 25c; Qt. 35c; 4 Qts. $1.25; Bu. $7.00

Southern Prolific

A very prolific sort and popular in the south for snaps. Vines vigorous, with large, thin, smooth leaves; the green pods, which are produced in clusters, are long, cylindrical or thicker than broad, fleshy and crisp; seed small, oval, dun-colored, being somewhat variable in shade. Pkt. 10c; Pt. 20c; Qt. 30c; 4 Qts. $1.00; Bushel $6.00

Lazy Wife

One of the best for snaps of the later green podded pole beans. The numerous pods, borne in large clusters, are five to seven inches long, broad, thick, fleshy and entirely stringless. When young they have a rich, buttery flavor which is retained until they are nearly ripe. The dry beans are excellent for winter use. Seed white. Pkt. 10c; Pt. 25c; Qt. 35c; 4 Qts. $1.25; Bushel $6.50

If Beans are ordered by mail or express, prepaid, add 10 cents per pint, 15 cents per quart, for charges.

MAMMOTH PODDED HORTICULTURAL BEAN.

BEANS—Pole or Running—Continued

Kentucky Wonder

This splendid variety, introduced by us in 1885, has since been offered as Seek-No-Further and was introduced in 1891 as a novelty under the name of Old Homestead. Vine vigorous, climbing well and very productive, bearing its pods in large clusters; pods green, very long, often reaching nine or ten inches, nearly round and very crisp when young, becoming very irregular and spongy as the beans ripen. Seed long, oval, dun-colored. An early and very prolific sort, with showy pods which are most excellent for snaps. It is sometimes catalogued as being the same as Southern Prolific but this is an error, as the latter is two weeks later and has shorter pods. **Pkt. 10c; Pt. 25c; Qt. 35c; 4 Qts. $1.25; Bushel $7.00**

Red Speckled Cut Short, or Corn Hill

An old variety, very popular in the central and southern states for planting among corn and it will give a good crop without the use of poles. Vines medium sized, twining loosely, with dark colored, smooth leaves; pods short, cylindrical and tender; seed nearly oblong, cut off diagonally at the ends, white, covered at one end and slightly over the whole surface with reddish-brown dots. **Pkt. 10c; Pt. 20c; Qt. 30c; 4 Qts. $1.00; Bushel $6.00**

BEANS—Pole Lima

Seibert's Early Lima

Introduced by us in 1895. Practical value has been the object aimed at in the development of this grand variety. It is the outcome of the labors of a skilful market gardener who selected for several years the largest green beans from the thinnest and most easily opened pods. The vine is very productive and continues so from the very first to the last of the season, so that although the pods rarely contain more than four beans the total yield is enormous. The green shelled beans are of immense size and are tender and succulent. They shrink in drying to about the size of the Large White Lima. In earliness, ease of shelling, size, beauty and quality of the green beans, this variety is far in advance of all other sorts. It is recognized as the best of all the Limas for either the garden or market. **Pkt. 10c; Pt. 25c; Qt. 35c; 4 Qts. $1.25; Bu. $7.00**

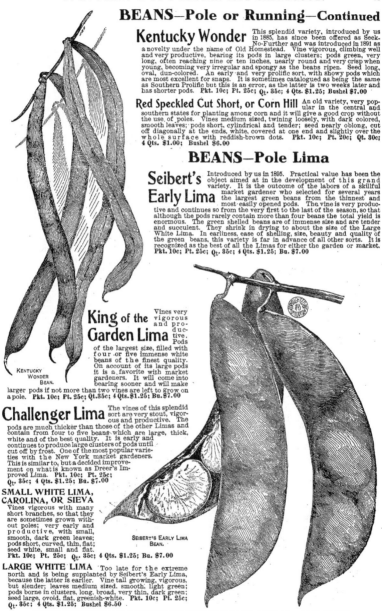

Kentucky Wonder Bean.

King of the Garden Lima

Vines very vigorous and productive. Pods of the largest size, filled with four or five immense white beans of the finest quality. On account of its large pods it is a favorite with market gardeners. It will come into bearing sooner and will make larger pods if not more than two vines are left to grow on a pole. **Pkt. 10c; Pt. 25c; Qt.35c; 4 Qts.$1.25; Bu.$7.00**

Challenger Lima

The vines of this splendid sort are very stout, vigorous and productive. The pods are much thicker than those of the other Limas and contain from four to five beans which are large, thick, white and of the best quality. It is early and continues to produce large clusters of pods until cut off by frost. One of the most popular varieties with the New York market gardeners. This is similar to, but a decided improvement on what is known as Dreer's Improved Lima. **Pkt. 10c; Pt. 25c; Qt. 35c; 4 Qts. $1.25; Bu. $7.00**

SMALL WHITE LIMA, CAROLINA, OR SIEVA

Vines vigorous with many short branches, so that they are sometimes grown without poles; very early and productive, with small, smooth, dark green leaves; pods short, curved, thin, flat; seed white, small and flat. **Pkt. 10c; Pt. 25c; Qt. 35c; 4 Qts. $1.25; Bu. $7.00**

Seibert's Early Lima Bean.

LARGE WHITE LIMA

Too late for the extreme north and is being supplanted by Seibert's Early Lima, because the latter is earlier. Vine tall growing, vigorous, but slender; leaves medium sized, smooth, light green; pods borne in clusters, long, broad, very thin, dark green; seed large, ovoid, flat, greenish-white. **Pkt. 10c; Pt. 25c; Qt. 35c; 4 Qts. $1.25; Bushel $6.50**

If Beans are ordered by mail or express prepaid, add 10 cents per pint, 15 cents per quart, for charges.

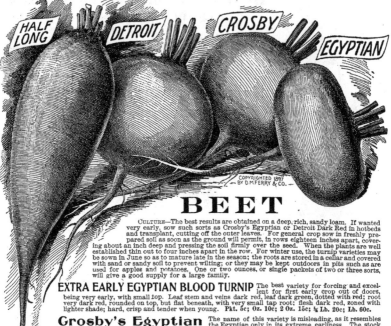

COPYRIGHTED 1897
BY D. M. FERRY & CO.

BEET

CULTURE—The best results are obtained on a deep, rich, sandy loam. If wanted very early, sow such sorts as Crosby's Egyptian or Detroit Dark Red in hotbeds and transplant, cutting off the outer leaves. For general crop sow in freshly prepared soil as soon as the ground will permit, in rows eighteen inches apart, covering about an inch deep and pressing the soil firmly over the seed. When the plants are well established thin out to four inches apart in the row. For winter use, the turnip varieties may be sown in June so as to mature late in the season; the roots are stored in a cellar and covered with sand or sandy soil to prevent wilting; or they may be kept outdoors in pits such as are used for apples and potatoes. One or two ounces, or single packets of two or three sorts, will give a good supply for a large family.

EXTRA EARLY EGYPTIAN BLOOD TURNIP
The best variety for forcing and excellent for first early crop out of doors, being very early, with small top. Leaf stem and veins dark red, leaf dark green, dotted with red; root very dark red, rounded on top, but flat beneath, with very small tap root; flesh dark red, zoned with lighter shade; hard, crisp and tender when young. Pkt. 5c; Oz. 10c; 2 Oz. 15c; ¼ Lb. 20c; Lb. 60c.

Crosby's Egyptian
The name of this variety is misleading, as it resembles the Egyptian only in its extreme earliness. The stock we offer is of a distinct vermilion color which is very attractive not only in the beets as pulled, but after they have been cooked. They are also more spherical than the Extra Early Egyptian and we think of better quality. One of the best for early planting out of doors. It becomes fit for use sooner than any other variety but it is not as well suited as the Egyptian for forcing in hotbeds or for transplanting. Pkt. 5c; Oz. 10c; 2 Oz. 15c; ¼ Lb. 20c; Lb. 70c.

Detroit Dark Red Turnip
Long experience has shown this variety of our own introduction to be the best deep red turnip beet, not only for market gardeners, but for home use. It is also by far the best for canning, making a strikingly handsome product, much superior to that obtained from any other variety. Its small, upright-growing top, early maturing, and the splendid shape and color of the root make it popular with every one who plants it. Top small, upright-growing, so that the rows may be close together; leaf stem and veins dark red, blade green; root globular or ovoid and very smooth; color of skin dark blood-red; flesh deep vermilion red, zoned with a darker shade, very crisp, tender and sweet, and remaining so for a long time. We believe that the stock of this variety which we offer will produce a crop more uniform in shape, color and quality than any other beet seed obtainable. Pkt. 5c; Oz. 10c; 2 Oz. 15c; ¼ Lb. 20c; Lb. 70c.

EARLY ECLIPSE
Top small, dark purplish-green. Root nearly globular, with a small tap and very small collar. Flesh bright red, zoned with a lighter shade, very sweet, crisp and tender, especially when young. Pkt. 5c; Oz. 10c; 2 Oz. 15c; ¼ Lb. 60c.

EDMAND'S EARLY BLOOD TURNIP
Top small, spreading; ribs and short leaf stalks dark red; blade of leaf bright green, with wavy edge; root dark red, interior color purplish-red, with little zoning; crisp, tender, sweet, and an excellent keeper. Pkt. 5c; Oz. 10c; 2 Oz. 15c; ¼ Lb. 20c; Lb. 60c.

EARLY BLOOD TURNIP (Improved). An extra selected stock of Blood Turnip, having larger, coarser top and root than the Detroit Dark Red, and requiring a considerably longer time to mature. Excellent for summer and autumn use. Pkt. 5c; Oz. 10c; 2 Oz. 15c; ¼ Lb. 20c; Lb. 55c.

BASTIAN'S EARLY BLOOD TURNIP. Top small; stem purplish-pink; leaf bright green; root with medium sized tap, turnip-shaped, bright red. Flesh light purplish-pink, zoned with white; crisp, tender, very sweet and of good quality. Pkt. 5c; Oz. 10c; 2 Oz. 15c; ¼ Lb. 20c; Lb. 55c.

DEWING'S BLOOD TURNIP. Top medium sized; leaf stem and veins dark red; leaf green; root dark red, turnip-shaped, with large tap; flesh carmine red, zoned with lighter shade; tender, sweet, and a good keeper. Pkt. 5c; Oz. 10c; 2 Oz. 15c; ¼ Lb. 20c; Lb. 65c.

EARLY TURNIP BASSANO. Top large; leaf stems light red; leaf light green; root large, round, turnip-shaped; flesh pink, zoned with white; very sweet and tender when young. An excellent sort to plant for use as "greens." Pkt. 5c; Oz. 10c; 2 Oz. 15c; ¼ Lb. 20c; Lb. 50c.

D. M. FERRY & CO'S HALF LONG BLOOD
This is an entirely distinct variety and we consider it by far the best for winter and spring use. The root is deep red, very symmetrical, two or three times as long as thick and always smooth and handsome. The flesh is rich, dark red, very sweet, crisp and tender, never becoming woody even in portions above the ground; it retains its good quality longer than other sorts. Pkt. 5c; Oz. 10c; 2 Oz. 15c; ¼ Lb. 20c; Lb. 70c.

LONG DARK BLOOD
A standard late variety keeping well through the winter. It is of good size, long, smooth, growing half out of the ground, with few or no side roots. Skin dark purple, almost black; flesh dark red, very tender and sweet. Pkt. 5c; Oz. 10c; 2 Oz. 15c; ¼ Lb. 20c; Lb. 50c.

SWISS CHARD, OR SEA KALE BEET. Although little known in America, this vegetable is worthy of a place in every garden. The leaf and the leaf stems are the parts used and they are much superior to those of other beets to use as greens. Later in the season the broad, flat, beautiful, wax-like leaf stems are cooked as a salad or pickled. Pkt. 5c; Oz. 10c; 2 Oz. 15c; ¼ Lb. 20c; Lb. 60c.

SUGAR BEET

Sugar Beets are desirable not only for the manufacture of sugar, but are invaluable for stock feeding and table use. They are deservedly popular both on the farm and in the small garden. No one who raises beets of any kind should fail to plant at least a trial bed. Our list comprises the best strains on the market.

SOIL—The best soil for Sugar Beets is a rich, friable, sandy or clayey loam. They cannot be profitably grown on a tenacious wet clay or a very sandy or excessively hard and stony soil. Rich, mucky soils will often give an immense yield of roots which though excellent for feeding are of little value for sugar making. Most farm lands capable of producing a good crop of corn or wheat can be made to grow a good crop of beets.

MANURE—Sugar Beets do much better when the soil has been made rich for a preceding crop than when the fertilizers are applied the same season. The use of rank, undecomposed manures, or such as contain a large amount of nitrogen, will result in large, coarse roots of little value for sugar making. If the condition of the ground necessitates the use of a fertilizer the current season, the greatest care should be taken to have it evenly and thoroughly mixed with the surface soil.

SEED—There is no crop where the quality of the seed used is of greater importance than this. If inferior seed be planted, no matter how rich the soil or how skillful the cultivation, the yield will be unsatisfactory and unprofitable. A great deal of most patient and skillful labor has been expended in establishing and developing strains of beets which are adapted to sugar making. *It is only by the use of the best seeds that profitable sugar making is possible.*

PLANTING AND CULTIVATING—The great secret of successful and economical culture of beets is thorough preparation of the soil before planting. The seed should be planted as soon as the soil can be gotten into good condition, which is not likely to be before the middle of April, but the seed should be in before the last of May. We plant in drills twenty to thirty inches apart, dropping from twelve to twenty seeds to the foot. This will require from ten to fifteen pounds of seed to the acre. It is very important that the seed be well covered with not to exceed one inch of soil pressed firmly over it. As soon as the young plants have started sufficiently to make the rows visible they should be cultivated and the field should receive constant attention so as to keep the surface soil loose and destroy the starting weeds. When the beets are about two or three inches high they should be thinned so as to stand six to ten inches apart in the row, and cultivation should be discontinued as soon as the roots have commenced to form. Often a crop is injured by late cultivation which starts the plants into fresh growth when they should be maturing and developing sugar. Sugar beets ripen and become fit for harvesting as distinctly as do potatoes or corn, and they indicate that they are approaching this condition by the outer leaves turning yellowish and the top seeming to decrease in size owing to the curling of the central leaves. They should be gathered and stored when ripe or mature, for if left they may start into fresh growth which lessens the proportion of sugar. The successful cultivation of beets rich in sugar requires rotation of crops, however rich and good the soil may appear to be.

Jaensch's Victrix Sugar Beet Seed

The latter part of the 19th century has been made notable for the earnestness with which scientific men have investigated and studied the problem of how to raise larger farm crops at less cost.

No plant has been more carefully studied in this respect than the Sugar Beet, and as a result the improvements in it have been marvelous. Instead of crops yielding 10 per cent or less as was the common average twenty years ago, we now have those yielding, under most favorable conditions.

18 to 20 Per Cent Sugar.

This increase has been brought about not so much by improved methods of fertilization and culture, though these have been factors, as by

Improvement in Seed.

The profitableness of a crop, even under the same conditions of soil and culture, is largely determined by the quality of the seed used which affects the total weight of roots harvested, the amount of tare (or proportion of the root which has to be removed in topping) and above all in the proportion of sugar the roots contain. A factory which will lose money when run on beets giving but barely 12 per cent of sugar, may be made to give a good profit when supplied with beets yielding 14 per cent or more. A farmer who will lose money on a crop of roots so ill-shaped that it is necessary to remove a large portion in trimming, will **do well** on a crop in which, because of the use of better seed, there is a small amount of tare, and for which he gets an extra price because of the large sugar content. A difference of a few cents in the price of the seed is of no importance as compared with the question of quality.

Jaensch's Victrix is Unquestionably the Best Strain of Sugar Beet.

It is grown by the most successful Sugar Beet experts in the world, Gustav Jaensch & Co. This firm has worked for many years in the midst of the best Sugar Beet growers and factories in Germany, and Mr. Jaensch himself has devoted years of careful study to determining what a Sugar

JAENSCH'S VICTRIX
SUGAR BEET.

Beet should be and how it may be produced. His facilities and knowledge being unequaled, it is not surprising that the result should be so satisfactory. Jaensch & Co., not only by most careful examination and analysis of thousands of specimens, select each year a few of the best, but from these they select those which show the greatest power to perpetuate their good qualities, rejecting those, no matter how good in themselves, whose descendants are not superior. Having obtained a superior beet, the seed of which produces beets of superior quality, they skillfully increase the stock and are able to offer seeds by the ton, every one of which is the direct descendant in the second or third generation of a single beet. Such seed has a special value, since it gives greater

Uniformity of Product

which is of great importance to both the manufacturer and farmer. Beets of uniform quality can be more economically worked than those differing greatly in sugar content. Roots from the same field, or even from the same load, are not apt to show precisely the same per cent of sugar, and when this difference is great, the farmer is quite likely to be dissatisfied with his crop and refuse to contract another year. Much of this dissatisfaction can be avoided by using seed of uniform quality. Not only do Jaensch & Co. produce the best seed grown in Europe, but before sending it out they submit it to a process by which the

Germinating Power

is conserved and its ability to resist the attacks of insects and diseases increased. Often this special treatment enables growers to get a good stand when all other seeds fail.

We have been appointed sole agents for the sale of Jaensch's Victrix in America, and urge every Sugar Beet factory to make a trial of it; every Sugar Beet grower should procure at least enough for an acre or two, and compare the product with that of other seed. He cannot afford to do otherwise.

Jaensch's Victrix Sugar Beet Seed

Per Lb. 35c., postpaid. Lots of 5 lbs. to 25 lbs. by express, at purchaser's expense, 25c. per lb.
Original sealed sacks, weighing about 110 lbs. each, $17.50 per sack f. o. b. Detroit.

Sugar Beet
Continued

KLEIN WANZLEBEN
SUGAR BEET.

VILMORIN'S
IMPROVED
SUGAR BEET.

Klein Wanzleben

A little larger than Vilmorin's Improved and containing about the same amount of sugar. Its yield of beets is from twelve to eighteen tons per acre. The beet grows below the surface. The green leaves are rather large and spreading, with wavy edges. A little hardier and easier grown than Vilmorin's Improved. Probably the best sort for the experimenter to use. Pkt. 5c; Oz. 10c; 2 Oz. 10c; ¼ Lb. 15c; Lb. 35c.

Vilmorin's Improved

In general the most desirable beet for the sugar factory is the one containing the largest percentage of sugar. In this variety we have one of the richest sorts in cultivation, and moreover it will do better on new lands than any other variety, suffer less from an excess of nitrogen and will keep the best. In size it is medium or a little below, yielding from ten to sixteen tons per acre, and containing, under favorable conditions, as high as eighteen per cent of sugar. The beet grows below the surface. The green leaves are smooth edged and spreading. Pkt. 5c; Oz. 10c; 2 Oz. 10c; ¼ Lb. 15c; Lb. 35c.

Beets for Stock Feeding

Giant Feeding Sugar Beet, or Half Sugar Mangel

The investigations of scientific men and the experience of practical stock feeders have established that a ration of some appetizing green food is of such great importance as to be practically essential to the profitable winter feeding of stock. In the northern states a supply of such food can only be obtained from some root crops. Of these Mangel Wurzel is popular because of the immense yield, but is not fully satisfactory because of the low nutritive value. By the same system of careful selection and breeding which has accomplished so much with the Sugar Beet, there has been established in the GIANT FEEDING SUGAR a strain of beets which, while giving nearly as large a yield of easily grown and harvested roots as a crop of Mangels, supplies a food of very much *higher nutritive value*, the roots for feeding purposes being really more valuable, pound for pound, than those of the very best strains of Sugar Beet, and the yield under equally favorable conditions being more than double. The roots grow partly out of the ground and because of this and their shape the crop can be harvested and stored *at less expense* than any other root crop. We are certain that every one who plants this variety and grows it with care will be much pleased with the crop. Every farmer should try it. Pkt. 5c; Oz. 10c; 2 Oz. 10c; ¼ Lb. 15c; Lb. 35c.

French White Sugar Red Top

Previous to the introduction of Giant Feeding Sugar, this was the sort most largely grown for stock feeding in Europe, where the superior feeding value of the Sugar Beets over the coarse Mangel Wurzels is generally recognized. This sort is so rich in sugar that it is sometimes grown for sugar factories. We do not recommend it for this purpose, but do as a most profitable crop for feeding stock. The numerous green leaves are quite erect, and the elongated, egg-shaped root is tinged with red at the top. It is very hardy and productive, yielding about twenty tons to the acre. Pkt. 5c; Oz. 10c; 2 Oz. 10c; ¼ Lb. 15c; Lb. 35c.

FRENCH WHITE SUGAR
RED TOP BEET.

French Yellow Sugar

Grows to a large size; root half long, yellow and sweet. Excellent for stock feeding. Pkt. 5c; Oz. 10c; 2 Oz. 10c; ¼ Lb. 15c; Lb. 40c.

GIANT FEEDING SUGAR BEET, OR HALF SUGAR MANGEL.

MANGEL WURZEL
.. BEET ..

LONG RED A large, long variety grown for stock feeding. The root stands up well above the surface; color light red; flesh white and rose colored. Pkt. 5c; Oz. 10c; 2 Oz. 10c; ¼ Lb. 15c; Lb. 35c.

D. M. Ferry & Co's Improved Mammoth Long Red An improvement on the old variety. The root is very large, uniformly straight and well formed, comparatively thicker and deeper colored than the common sort and with smaller top. We know our stock of this variety will produce the largest and finest roots which can be grown and that it is vastly superior to many strains of the same sort offered under other names, such as Norbitan Giant, Colossal, Monarch, etc. Pkt. 5c; Oz. 10c; 2 Oz. 10c; ¼ Lb. 15c; Lb. 35c.

YELLOW GLOBE A large, round, orange-colored variety of excellent quality, producing a better crop on shallow soil than the Long Red. The roots often keep better than those of the long varieties, as they can be more easily handled without injury. Pkt. 5c; Oz. 10c; 2 Oz. 10c; ¼ Lb. 15c; Lb. 35c.

Orange Globe We think this one of the best varieties of Mangel Wurzel grown for stock feeding. It has an exceedingly small top and few leaves; leaf stalk and blade green; root medium sized, uniformly globe shaped, having a very small tap and few side roots; color of skin deep orange-yellow; flesh white and of excellent quality. The root grows almost entirely above g un , making it admirably adapted to shallow soil and very easy to harvest. Pkt. 5c; Oz. 10c; 2 Oz. 10c; ¼ Lb. 15c; Lb. 35c.

GOLDEN TANKARD MANGEL WURZEL.

Yellow Leviathan Root long, olive-shaped, growing over one-half out of the ground; flesh white, sweet and tender; top green, comparatively small; neck small, short. We think this is perhaps the best of the yellow field beets, because its fine flesh never becomes woody and its root grows so well out of the ground that the crop is easily harvested. Pkt. 5c; Oz. 10c; 2 Oz. 10c; ¼ Lb. 15c; Lb. 35c.

Golden Tankard Top comparatively small, with yellow stems and mid-ribs; neck very small; root large, ovoid, but filled out at top and bottom so as to approach a cylindrical form. Flesh yellow, zoned with white. Pkt. 5c; Oz. 10c; 2 Oz. 10c; ¼ Lb. 15c; Lb. 35c.

Red Globe Similar to Yellow Globe, except in color, which is a light red or pink. Pkt. 5c; Oz. 10c; 2 Oz. 10c; ¼ Lb. 15c; Lb. 35c.

YELLOW OVOID, or INTERMEDIATE Root ovoid, intermediate between the long and globe varieties; flesh solid, nearly white, zoned with yellow; hardy, vigorous and productive. Pkt. 5c; Oz. 10c; 2 Oz. 10c; ¼ Lb. 15c; Lb. 35c.

D. M. FERRY & CO'S IMPROVED MAMMOTH LONG RED MANGEL WURZEL.

ORANGE GLOBE MANGEL WURZEL.

BROCOLI

Although originating from a very distinct type, the modern improved sorts of Brocoli can scarcely be distinguished from cauliflower; the points of difference being that they are generally taller and the heads more divided. The culture is the same as that given for cauliflower.

Early Large White French The best variety. Heads white, very compact and hard, continuing firm for a long time. A hardy, vigorous, easily grown sort. Pkt. 5c; Oz. 45c; 2 Oz. 85c; ¼ Lb. $1.50

Brussels Sprouts

Improved Half Dwarf. The plants which are very hardy, grow two or three feet high, and produce from the sides of the stalk numerous little sprouts which resemble very small cabbages, one or two inches in diameter. The leaves should be broken down in the fall to give the little heads more room to grow. They should be treated in all respects like winter cabbage or kale. We offer a carefully grown strain, very hardy, and giving compact, round sprouts of large size and good quality. Pkt. 5c; Oz. 15c; 2 Oz. 25c; ¼ Lb. 40c; Lb. $1.50

BRUSSELS SPROUTS.

EARLY LARGE WHITE FRENCH BROCOLI.

Cabbage

For many years cabbage seed has been a leading specialty with us. Our cabbage seeds are all grown from approved stock seeds which are largely of our own development on our Oakview Seed Farm; they are all grown under our personal inspection and supervision. There is no seed more reliable, nor can any be more implicitly depended upon to give planters uniformly satisfactory results.

CULTURE—The requisites for complete success are: *First*, good seed; in this crop the quality of the seed used is of the greatest importance; no satisfactory results can possibly be obtained when poor seed is planted. *Second*, rich, well prepared ground. A heavy, moist and rich loam is most suitable. *Third*, frequent and thorough cultivation. The ground should be highly manured and worked deep. Cabbage is grown all over the country and specific directions regarding the time and methods of planting applicable to all localities cannot be given. In general, north of the 40th parallel the *early sorts* should be sown very early in hotbeds, hardened off by gradually exposing them to the night air and transplanted as early as the ground is in good condition, setting eighteen to thirty-six inches apart, according to size of variety. South of the 40th parallel, sow about the middle of September, or later according to latitude, transplanting into cold frames if necessary to keep through winter and setting in open ground as early as possible in the spring.

The late autumn and winter varieties may be sown from the middle to the last of spring and transplanted when four to six inches high. If the weather and soil is dry the late sowings should be shaded and watered in order to hasten germination, but it is important that the plants should not be shaded or crowded in the seed bed, or they will run up weak and slender and will not endure transplanting well.

One of the most successful eastern market gardeners recommends sowing cabbage for family use as follows: at the desired time sow the seed in hills, six to twelve seeds in a place, and after the plants are of sufficient size, thin to a single plant to the hill, and cultivate as usual. This is a very simple method and in some cases is very successful.

Cabbages should be hoed every week and the ground stirred as they advance in growth, drawing up a little earth to the plants each time until they begin to head, when they should be thoroughly cultivated and left to mature. Loosening the roots will sometimes retard the bursting of full grown heads.

Of late years many crops of early cabbages have been destroyed by maggots at the roots. The best remedy seems to be to remove the earth from around the stem and apply an emulsion of kerosene made as follows: add one quart of kerosene oil to two quarts of *boiling* soft soap which has been thinned to the consistency of cream. Stir the oil thoroughly by churning or other method until it has united with the soap and forms a cream-like substance. Then dilute with five times as much water. Tobacco dust, ashes, slacked lime and coal dust are also recommended as preventives, and with us have proved valuable in the order named. These are scattered about the plants, leaving one here and there untreated for the flies to congregate around and deposit their eggs upon, when that plant should be pulled up and destroyed.

The cabbage worms which destroy the leaves and heads later may be killed by dusting with pyrethrum powder, slug shot or Paris green. The last two are poisonous and should not be used in large quantities, or late in the season; however, should their use be necessary, care should be taken to remove the outside leaves before the heads are used.

If the disease called club root should get a foot-hold, do not plant the land with any of the cabbage family for a year or two. This is usually an effective remedy.

To preserve cabbages during winter, pull them on a dry day, and turn them over on the heads a few hours to drain. Set them out in a cool cellar, or bury them in long trenches in a dry situation, covering with boards or straw so as to keep out frost and rain.

A great many of the varieties of cabbages are simply strains rather than *distinct* sorts, and are *really* the same as some old, and better known kinds. We do not know of a single variety offered in this country which we have not seen, both in trial and in fields, and we are confident that every good quality can be found in a greater degree in the varieties we offer than in any other kinds.

FIRST EARLY SORTS

Early Jersey Wakefield

The earliest and hardest heading of first early cabbages. Most gardeners depend upon it for the bulk of their extra early crop. Its exceeding hardiness not only to resist cold but other unfavorable conditions, insures the greatest likelihood of profitable and satisfactory results. Our stock is grown and selected with the greatest care; there is none better and there are few as good. Head conical, very compact, solid and of excellent quality. The thick, stout leaves and compact habit make it the best sort for wintering over or for very early setting. Pkt. 5c; Oz. 20c; 2 Oz. 35c; ¼ Lb. 60c; Lb. $2.00

EARLY JERSEY WAKEFIELD CABBAGE.

Extra Early Express

A first early sort in which the plant is compact, with round, thick leaves forming an oval head astonishingly large for the size of the plant. Head comparatively thicker, less pointed and only slightly later than that of Early Jersey Wakefield and while somewhat softer it stands shipment better, hence is extensively grown in the south for northern markets. Pkt. 5c; Oz. 15c; 2 Oz. 25c; ¼ Lb. 40c; Lb. $1.50

Very Early Etampes

Similar to the well known Jersey Wakefield. The plant is lighter colored, but not quite so hardy. The head is fully as large, not quite so hard, but of excellent quality. Sold also as "Earliest of All," "Wonderful," etc. Pkt. 5c; Oz. 15c; 2 Oz. 25c; ¼ Lb. 40c; Lb. $1.50

Charleston or Large Wakefield

A strain in which the plant is larger and a little later than Early Jersey Wakefield, the head being not so pointed and much larger. Exceedingly hardy and on account of the fine solid head, with market gardeners and shippers it is deservedly a very popular sort to follow Jersey Wakefield. Pkt. 5c; Oz. 20c; 2 Oz. 35c; ¼ Lb. 60c; Lb. $2.00

Early Spring

The earliest flat headed variety. A wonderfully compact plant, with few outer leaves, so that a great number of fine, solid heads can be produced on an acre. Although it does not come to full maturity as early as Jersey Wakefield, it becomes solid enough for use about as early, and is by far the best early sort for markets that demand a large, flat cabbage. The plant is vigorous, with short stem. The leaves are large, broad, and of peculiar light green color. The head is oval, and very large for the size of the plant, nearly equaling those of the later kinds. Pkt. 5c; Oz. 25c; 2 Oz. 40c; ¼ Lb. 75c; Lb. $2.50

CABBAGE—Second Early or Summer Sorts

Henderson's Early Summer An early, large-heading cabbage; plants strong growing, with large, spreading outer leaves. Head flat or slightly conical and keeps longer without bursting than most of the early sorts. Valuable for both family and market. This may be called an improvement on the Newark Flat Dutch, which it has superseded. **Pkt. 5c; Oz. 20c; 2 Oz. 35c; ¼ Lb. 60c; Lb. $1.75**

All Head Early The strain of All Head Early which we offer is of especial value because of the uniformity and close adherence to the type in habit of growth and the shape and quality of the head. The plant is more compact, the leaf smoother and thicker and the head larger and a little more round than the Early Summer. We consider this one of the best second early sorts on our list and recommend it for both the market and home use. **Pkt. 5c; Oz. 20c; 2 Oz. 35c; ¼ Lb. 60c; Lb. $2.00**

Early Dwarf Flat Dutch Continued experience confirms our belief that this is a most valuable second early sort. The plant is short stemmed, upright and having comparatively few and short leaves, the rows can be set close together. Head large, solid, crisp and tender, maturing with Early Summer. Every plant will form a hard head fit for market and will mature much earlier than the Late Flat Dutch or other sorts usually grown for market and shipping. Our carefully selected strain should not be confounded with the inferior, later stocks frequently offered as Early Flat Dutch. **Pkt. 5c; Oz. 20c; 2 Oz. 35c; ¼ Lb. 60c; Lb. $1.75**

ALL HEAD EARLY CABBAGE.

All Seasons One of the earliest of the second early sorts. Head very large, round, often nearly spherical but usually somewhat flattened; very solid and of the best quality, keeping as well as the winter sorts. Plant very vigorous and sure heading; leaves large, smooth, with dense bloom. Remarkable for its ability to stand the hot sun and dry weather. Our trial has shown that heads which were fit for market by July 10th were still salable September 10th, the only change being increased size and density. One of the very best sorts for general cultivation, for if planted for fall crop and stored, it remains in fine condition until late in spring. **Pkt. 5c; Oz. 20c; 2 Oz. 35c; ¼ Lb. 60c; Lb. $1.75**

Succession A sure heading, long keeping variety, very similar to All Seasons and producing well shaped heads having few and small outer leaves. Our seed is from carefully grown, selected stock and is the best that can be procured. **Pkt. 5c; Oz. 20c; 2 Oz. 35c; ¼ Lb. 60c; Lb. $2.00**

Fottler's Early Drumhead
or Brunswick Short Stem

In many sections, particularly in the east, this is the most Popular cabbage grown, and it certainly is one of the very best second early sorts in cultivation, especially for the home garden. It keeps well both under the sun and during the winter and we think has proved one of the best all seasons cabbage in cultivation. Head large, flat, compact, solid and of fine quality. We have taken pains to have our stock free from the longer stemmed, coarse plants often seen in inferior stocks of this variety. **Pkt. 5c; Oz. 20c; 2 Oz. 35c; ¼ Lb. 60c; Lb. $1.75**

EARLY DWARF FLAT DUTCH CABBAGE.

Early Drumhead Plant very hardy, compact, with thick, dark green leaves covered with a dense bloom. Head flat, very solid and of good quality. **Pkt. 5c; Oz. 15c; 2 Oz. 25c; ¼ Lb. 40c; Lb. $1.50**

Early Winnigstadt One of the best for general use, being very hardy and sure to head. Owing to its compact and upright habit of growth and peculiar texture of short, thick leaf the variety seems to suffer less from the cabbage worm than most other sorts. Head regular, conical, very hard, and keeps well both summer and winter. It is the hardiest, not only as regards frost, but will suffer less from excessive wet, drought, insects or disease, than any other second early sort. This is one of the oldest varieties in cultivation and one whose reputation has suffered through the sale of degenerated and inferior stock. We have devoted a great deal of time and labor to the development of the strain we offer and send it out confident that it is one of the best and purest stocks of Winnigstadt in the country. **Pkt. 5c; Oz. 15c; 2 Oz. 25c; ¼ Lb. 40c; Lb. $1.50**

ALL SEASONS CABBAGE.

CABBAGE—Late or Autumn and Winter Sorts

Mammoth Rock Red This is the best, largest and surest heading red cabbage yet introduced and much better than the stock offered as Red Drumhead. No one should plant the latter as long as our strain of Mammoth Rock Red can be obtained. The plant is large, with numerous spreading leaves. The head is large, round, very solid and of deep red color. Nearly every plant will form an extra fine head. Pkt. 5c; Oz. 20c; 2 Oz. 35c; ¼ Lb. 60c; Lb. $2.00

Acme Flat Dutch An early and very desirable strain of Flat Dutch, in which the plant is very compact, few leaved and short stemmed. The head is large, nearly round and very solid. Pkt. 5c; Oz. 15c; 2 Oz. 25c; ¼ Lb. 40c; Lb. $1.50

The Warren, or Improved Stone Mason We think this is one of the most desirable for fall and winter use, being the best in quality of any of the smooth leaved kinds. The stock we offer is much superior to that usually sold under this name. Plant medium sized, with only a moderate number of leaves; head medium sized to large, round or slightly flattened, very solid, crisp and tender, without being coarse or strong flavored. It will certainly give the greatest satisfaction both to the amateur and market gardener and ought to be planted largely by both. Pkt. 5c; Oz. 20c; 2 Oz. 35c; ¼ Lb. 60c; Lb. $1.75

Surehead A compact growing, general crop cabbage, having medium sized to large, thick heads and many outer leaves. We assure our customers that our stock is of the best obtainable and will certainly produce fine heads. Pkt. 5c; Oz. 20c; 2 Oz. 35c; ¼ Lb. 60c; Lb. $1.75

Louisville Drumhead A strong and vigorous, but not coarse growing sort of Flat Dutch type. Plant short stemmed and compact, with broad, well rounded, large leaves, very full at base. Head firm, medium sized, slightly flattened, averaging quite deep. Pkt. 5c; Oz. 20c; 2 Oz. 35c; ¼ Lb. 60c; Lb. $1.75

D. M. Ferry & Co's Premium Late Flat Dutch We have taken great pains to maintain and develop the good qualities which have made this sort so popular and offer a very superior strain. A thousand plants can be depended upon to produce from nine hundred and fifty to one thousand large, oval, solid heads of splendid quality, which will keep for a long time in the best condition. Pkt. 5c; Oz. 20c; 2 Oz. 35c; ¼ Lb. 60c; Lb. $1.75

Houseman Late Flat Dutch The largest and best of the late market sorts. A strain of Late Flat Dutch cabbage in which the plant is very vigorous and hardy. The leaves are very large and broad; the stem of moderate height; the head very large and solid. A hardy and very sure heading sort. Always forms a large, handsome head which keeps better than those of most kinds. Particularly desirable for those who wish to raise large quantities of cabbage for fall shipment. Pkt. 5c; Oz. 15c; 2 Oz. 25c; ¼ Lb. 40c; Lb. $1.50

D. M. Ferry & Co's Premium Late Drumhead We recommend this sort for markets that require a very large, solid head. A sure heading sort which in good, rich soil, will grow to an enormous size and on poorer soils will give good sized heads which are very compact, solid and of excellent flavor. Pkt. 5c; Oz. 20c; 2 Oz. 35c; ¼ Lb. 60c; Lb. $1.75

Marblehead Mammoth Drumhead The largest cabbage known, weighing, in some instances, over *fifty pounds*. Under good cultivation acres have been grown where the heads would *average* thirty pounds each. The plant is very large and late in maturing and the seed should be planted earlier than that of most sorts. Pkt. 5c; Oz. 20c; 2 Oz. 35c; ¼ Lb. 60c; Lb. $1.75

HOLLANDER, OR DANISH BALL HEAD CABBAGE.

Hollander, or Danish Ball Head This variety is very hardy, very handsome, very solid, of fine quality, and one of the best keepers. It is one of the best for growing for distant markets or for late spring use. The plant is vigorous, rather compact growing, with a longer stem than most American sorts and exceedingly hardy, not only in resisting cold but also dry weather; it matures its head a little later than the Flat Dutch. The leaves are large, very thick, bluish-green covered with whitish bloom. The head is round, of less diameter than that of the Flat Dutch, but very solid. The leaves of the head are very thick, white and tender and not only overlap or pass by each other more than those of most sorts, but are so tightly drawn as to form an exceedingly solid head which stands shipment better and arrives at its destination in more attractive shape than those of any other late sort. In quality it is one of the best, being very white, crisp and tender. We have given a great deal of attention to this variety and offer seed of our own growing which we believe will produce a crop of more uniformly typical heads than can be grown from other stocks. Pkt. 5c; Oz. 25c; 2 Oz. 40c; ¼ Lb. 75c; Lb. $2.25

Green Glazed A late variety, extensively grown in the south, as it is not affected by the heat as much as most sorts. Head large but rather loose and open. Enjoys comparative immunity from the attacks of worms and insects. Pkt. 5c; Oz. 20c; 2 Oz. 35c; ¼ Lb. 60c; Lb. $2.00

HOUSEMAN LATE FLAT DUTCH CABBAGE.

Savoy Cabbages

The English prize the Savoy cabbages because of their sweet and delicate flavor, and as they become better known in this country they are growing rapidly into favor with discriminating buyers.

EARLY DWARF ULM SAVOY. One of the earliest and sweetest of the Savoys. Head round, solid; leaves small, thick, fleshy, of fine deep green color and of most excellent quality. Pkt. 5c; Oz. 20c; 2 Oz. 35c; ¼ Lb. 60c; Lb. $1.75

IMPROVED AMERICAN SAVOY. The best of all the Savoys either for home use or the market and the surest to head. The head is larger, more solid and in every way better than the sorts called Perfection, Green Globe, or Drumhead Savoy. The plant is vigorous, and even more densely and uniformly curled than the Early Dwarf Ulm Savoy; the head being globular, larger and more solid. Pkt. 5c; Oz. 20c; 2 Oz. 35c; ¼ Lb. 60c; Lb. $1.75

-- CARROT --

The Carrot is one of the most wholesome and nutritious of our garden roots deserving to be more extensively used for culinary purposes and we urge our readers to give some of the early table sorts a trial. For feeding stock, especially horses and milch cows, the carrot cannot be surpassed and it should be more largely grown by farmers for this purpose.

CULTURE—While a sandy loam made rich by manuring the previous year is the best soil for the carrot, any good land if thoroughly and deeply worked will produce satisfactory crops. When possible to do so, it is advisable to sow as early in the spring as the ground is fit to work, though good crops may, in this latitude, be grown from sowings as late as June 15, but success from such late planting is uncertain. For table use sow the smaller kinds as early as practicable in rows 16 to 18 inches apart. For field culture, prepare the ground thoroughly and sow in drills 18 to 24 inches apart, using from one and one-half to three pounds of seed to the acre. Cover one-half to one inch deep and see to it that the soil is pressed firmly above the seed. As soon as the plants appear, use the cultivator or wheel hoe. Do not let the weeds get a start. Thin the smaller table sorts to six to eight to the foot and the field varieties to four to six inches apart in the row. For winter use, gather and store like beets or turnips.

EARLY SCARLET HORN CARROT.

EARLIEST SHORT HORN. The earliest variety in cultivation and the best suited for forcing. Tops small, finely divided. The roots are nearly round and of reddish-orange color. When fully matured they are about two inches in diameter but should be used before they are full grown and while young and tender. Pkt. 5c; Oz. 10c; 2 Oz. 15c; ¼ Lb. 25c; Lb. 90c.

Early Scarlet Horn

Excellent for early planting out of doors. Tops small, coarsely divided; roots top-shaped but tapering, abruptly to a medium tap; skin orange-red. Pkt. 5c; Oz. 10c; 2 Oz. 15c; ¼ Lb. 25c; Lb. 80c.

EARLY HALF LONG SCARLET CARENTAN. Tops very small; roots cylindrical with remarkably small necks; very handsome deep orange in color, with scarcely any core and of the best quality. They can be sown very thick and are well adapted for forcing. Pkt. 5c; Oz. 10c; 2 Oz. 15c; ¼ Lb. 25c; Lb. 80c.

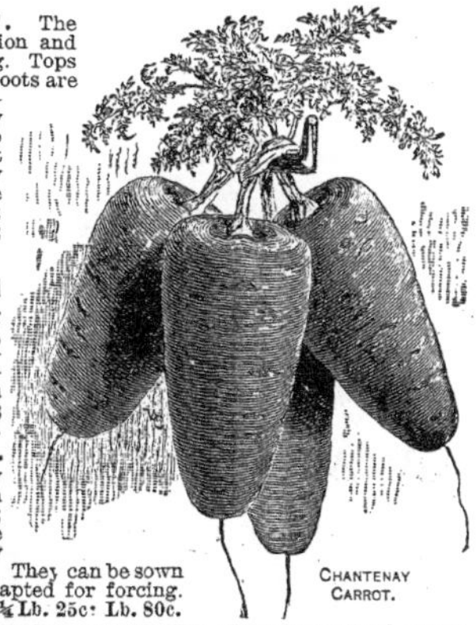

CHANTENAY CARROT.

HALF LONG SCARLET NANTES, STUMP ROOTED. Tops small; roots cylindrical, smooth, bright orange; flesh orange, becoming yellow in center but with no distinct core. Of the finest quality and one of the most symmetrical and handsome of the medium sized sorts; excellent for the market or home garden. Pkt. 5c; Oz. 10c; 2 Oz. 15c; ¼ Lb. 25c; Lb. 75c.

CHANTENAY
Tops medium sized; necks small; roots tapering slightly but uniformly stump rooted and smooth; color deep orange-red; flesh very crisp and tender. Although this is a medium early sort, it furnishes roots of usable size as early as any, is a heavy cropper and undoubtedly is one of the best for both the market and private garden, while its great productiveness makes it very desirable as a field sort. Pkt. 5c; Oz. 10c; 2 Oz. 15c; ¼ Lb. 25c; Lb. 75c.

EARLY HALF LONG SCARLET, STUMP ROOTED. Excellent for early market or for field culture. Of medium size; flesh bright scarlet, brittle and of fine flavor. Pkt. 5c; Oz. 10c; 2 Oz. 15c; ¼ Lb. 20c; Lb. 70c.

Guerande, or Ox Heart
Tops small for the size of the roots which are comparatively short, but often reach a diameter of five inches, terminating abruptly in a small tap root. Flesh bright orange, fine grained and sweet. This variety is especially desirable for soil so hard and stiff that longer rooted sorts would not thrive in it. When young, excellent for table use and when mature, equally good for stock. Pkt.-5c; Oz. 10c; 2 Oz. 15c; ¼ Lb. 25c; Lb. 75c.

DANVERS
Grown largely on account of its great productiveness and adaptability to all classes of soil. Tops of medium size, coarsely divided. The smooth and handsome roots are deep orange, of medium length, tapering uniformly to a blunt point; flesh sweet, crisp, tender and of a deep orange color. Although the roots of this variety are short, they produce as large a bulk as the longer field sorts and are more easily harvested. Pkt. 5c; Oz. 10c; 2 Oz. 15c; ¼ Lb. 25c; Lb. 75c.

GUERANDE, OR OX HEART CARROT.

Improved Long Orange
An improvement obtained by years of careful selection of the best formed and deepest colored roots of the old Long Orange, and of the older sorts for farm use the most popular on mellow soil. Roots shorter, thicker and smoother than those of the Long Orange, but so uniform and true that the bulk of the crop will be greater. Pkt. 5c; Oz. 10c; 2 Oz. 15c; ¼ Lb. 25c; Lb. 75c.

D. M. Ferry & Co's Improved Short White
We think this distinct variety is destined to take first rank as a field carrot, owing to its enormous productiveness and the ease with which it can be harvested. Roots half long, smooth, very heavy at the shoulder but tapering regularly to the point; color light green at the crown, white below; flesh white, solid, crisp and of excellent quality. This variety is a real acquisition as a heavy yielding, easily harvested, white carrot, and is the best of this class. Pkt. 5c; Oz. 10c; 2 Oz. 15c; ¼ Lb. 20c; Lb. 60c.

LARGE WHITE BELGIAN. Grows one-third out of the ground. Root white, green above ground with small top. Flesh rather coarse. The roots are of large size and the variety is extensively grown for stock feeding. Pkt. 5c; Oz. 10c; 2 Oz. 15c; ¼ Lb. 20c; Lb. 50c.

IMPROVED LONG ORANGE CARROT.

Cauliflower

The Cauliflower, although one of the most delicious vegetables, is but little grown except by professional gardener because of the erroneous notion that it is so difficult to grow that only skilled gardeners can produce it. Any one will " reasonably certain of success with this most desirable vegetable if he carefully follows the cultural directions given belo

CULTURE—For spring and early summer crop, sow in March or early in April, in hotbed and transplant to cold fran when sufficiently large to handle. As soon as danger of hard freezing is over set in the open ground in rows two and o half feet apart and eighteen inches apart in the row. The plants will endure a light frost. The soil for cauliflower sho be like that for cabbage, but it is better if made richer than is ordinarily used for that crop. Plenty of good manu must be well incorporated with the soil and the latter be brought into the highest state of tilth. No application, howev can be more necessary or more useful than that of cultivator and hoe. For late crop, sow at same time as for late c bage and treat in the same manner. It should be borne in mind that cauliflower *will not* head up well in hot, dry weath and hence the sowings need to be so timed as to bring the heads to maturity either before the hot summer weather se in or not until the cooler weather of the fall. If it receive at this time a liberal supply of water, the size and quality the heads will be greatly improved. After the head begins to form, draw the leaves over and tie them together to pr tect it from the sun and to keep it white. The heads should be cut for use while the "curd" is compact and hard, as the soon become much impaired in quality and appearance after they open and separate into branches. Of the enemies of th crop, none is more formidable than the cabbage root maggot. This seems to have a special liking for the cauliflower. Probably the best and most surely effective protective measure is enveloping each plant with a tight fitting collar of tarred felt. Plant lice are another serious pest of this crop. Effective remedies are dusting with fine tobacco dust, or spraying with strong tobacco tea or kerosene emulsion.

Our cauliflower trials for several years included samples of seeds from some of the most skillful American growers, and while their stocks produced hardy, vigorous plants the heads formed were uniformly more open in the curd and matured a little later than those grown from the best imported seed. All the cauliflower seed we offer is produced by the most experienced growers in Europe, in such localities as are best suited to its proper development and the greatest care is taken to save seed from perfectly developed plants only.

Early Snowball

Admirably adapted for forcing or wintering over for early crop, and the most popular sort for these purposes. It is also one of the best sorts for late summer and fall crop, and with reasonably favorable conditions every plant will form a large, solid head of fine quality. The plants are compact, with few narrow, upright leaves and are well suited for close planting. The heads are solid, compact, round, very white and curd-like and are developed earlier than those of any other sort.

In our recent comparative trials of samples from the best known growers and prominent seedsmen in Europe and America our stocks of Early Snowball were unsurpassed by any in earliness. They also gave the highest percentage of well formed heads.

We are in position to supply the most critical trade with seed which can be depended upon as the very best. **Pkt. 25c; ¼ Oz. 75c; Oz. $2.50; 2 Oz. $4.75; ¼ Lb. $9.00**

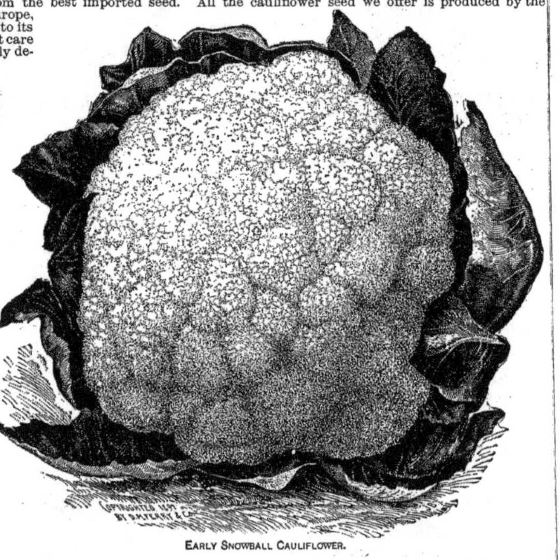

EARLY SNOWBALL CAULIFLOWER.

Extra Early Dwarf Erfurt

Similar in all respects to Early Snowball and nearly as early. It will give excellent results either in the home garden or for market use and is superior to most seed sold at higher prices. **Pkt. 25c; ¼ Oz. 75c; Oz. $2.25; 2 Oz. $4.25; ¼ Lb. $8.00**

Early Favorite

This is very early, exceedingly hardy, easily grown and perhaps the best sort for the inexperienced grower, as it will head under conditions in which many sorts would fail. The plants are large and form large heads which, although inclined to be open, are crisp, tender and of fine quality. It keeps in condition for use a long time. Many years' experience has convinced us that it is one of the hardiest sorts in cultivation. We urge you to try it. **Pkt. 5c; Oz. $1.00; 2 Oz. $1.50; ¼ Lb. $2.50**

Early Erfurt

One of the best for general cultivation. Heads large, close, compact and very white. **Pkt. 5c; Oz. $1.25; 2 Oz. $2.25; ¼ Lb. $4.00**

Early London

This is a well known variety and of value where a succession is desired, since its heads mature just after those of the extra early sorts and before the late varieties are fully developed. Heads are tender and good for general use. **Pkt. 5c; Oz. 40c; 2 Oz. 75c; ¼ Lb. $1.25**

LeNormand's Short Stem

Plant hardy, compact growing, sure heading and producing many leaves which protect the close, solid curd, keeping it well blanched. **Pkt. 5c; Oz. 75c; 2 Oz. $1.25; ¼ Lb. $2.25**

Large Algiers

A valuable late sort, sure to head, of excellent quality and popular with market gardeners. Plant large but of upright growth, the leaves protecting the heads so that they will endure uninjured a frost that would ruin most other sorts. One of the very best of the late varieties. **Pkt. 5c; Oz. 80c; 2 Oz. $1.50; ¼ Lb. $2.50**

Veitch's Autumn Giant

A distinct and valuable late variety. The heads are very large, extremely white, firm and compact and being well protected by foliage, remain a long time fit for use. The plants should be started and transplanted early in the season to insure their full development. **Pkt. 5c; Oz. 50c; 2 Oz. 90c; ¼ Lb. $1.50**

:: CELERY ::

CULTURE—Sow the seed (which is slow to germinate) in shallow boxes indoors or in a finely prepared seed bed out of doors, in straight rows, so that the small plants may be kept free from weeds. See to it that the seed is not covered too deep and that the bed is kept m₀is₀, almost wet, until the seeds germinate, as plenty of moisture is essential to get a satisfactory growth. The seed will not germinate well if planted in a hotbed or where subjected to a temperature above 60° Fah. When the plants are one to two inches high, thin out and transplant so that they may stand three inches apart each way. When they are four inches high, cut off the tops, which will cause the plants to grow stocky.

The crop is usually made to succeed some earlier one, but in order to grow good celery the soil must be made as rich as possible, the essentials to success being very rich soil and plenty of water. If good plants are used, they may be set out as late as the middle of August, but the best results are usually obtained from setting about the middle of June or first of July. The most desirable time will depend upon local climate and is that which will bring the plants to maturity during cool, moist weather. In setting, prepare broad trenches about six inches deep and four to six feet apart, in which the plants should be set six inches apart, cutting off the outer leaves and *pressing the soil firmly about the roots*. When the plants are nearly full grown they should be "handled," which is done by gathering the leaves together while the earth is drawn about the plant to one-third its height, taking care that none of it falls between the leaves, as it would be likely to cause them to rust or rot. After a few days draw more earth about them and repeat the process every few days until only the tops of the leaves are visible. Or it may be blanched by pressing the leaves together with two wide boards held in place by stakes or by wire hooks at the top. This is the method commonly used by market gardeners, but celery so blanched is more likely to become pithy than that blanched with earth. Care should be taken that the plants are not disturbed while they are wet or the ground is damp; to do so increases the liability to injury from rust.

A part of the crop may be simply "handled" and then at the approach of severe freezing weather taken up and set out compactly in a dark cellar or an unused cold frame, where the temperature can be kept just above the freezing point and it will then gradually blanch so that it may be used throughout the winter. Should the plants begin to wilt, water the roots without wetting the stalks or leaves, and they will revive again.

Celery is sometimes grown by what is termed the new process, which consists in making a spot as rich as possible and there setting the plants six to eight inches apart each way. If the soil is very rich and there is an abundance of water, the plants will blanch each other and the product will be very white and handsome, but we think it is inferior in quality to that grown by the old method.

Golden Yellow Self Blanching

This is the best celery for early use. Critical gardeners depend upon our stock of this sort to produce their finest early celery. Plants of a yellowish-green color, but as they mature the inner stems and leaves turn a beautiful golden yellow, which adds much to their attractiveness and makes the work of blanching much easier. The handsome color, crispness, tenderness, freedom from stringiness and fine nutty flavor of this variety make it only necessary to be tried in order to establish it as the standard of excellence as an early sort. Pkt. 5c; Oz. 45c; 2 Oz. 85c; ¼ Lb. $1.50; Lb. $4.50

Rose Ribbed Paris

Very attractive and of splendid quality. In general character this sort resembles the Golden Yellow Self Blanching from which it originated, but the plant is more compact, the stalks a little larger and the upper portions, particularly of the heart stems, are a richer, deeper yellow, beautifully blended with pink. The stalks are a very rich and wax-like yellow. The plant is stout and vigorous and as self-blanching as any variety in cultivation. The leaves are broad, the outer ones dark green, but becoming more yellow toward the center until those of the heart are deep yellow. Though the ribs are prominent the large, thick stalks are practically stringless and wonderfully crisp, tender and good flavored. We have carefully tested this sort and we believe it to be one of the most valuable kinds in cultivation both for the home garden and those markets which demand vegetables of high quality. No celery grower or market gardener should fail to grow it extensively. Pkt. 5c; Oz. 25c; 2 Oz. 40c; ¼ Lb. 75c; Lb. $2.50

GOLDEN YELLOW SELF BLANCHING CELERY.

CRIMSON
GIANT
TURNIP
RADISH.

FOR
DESCRIPTIONS
SEE
OPPOSITE PAGE.

FRENCH'S SUCCESS CELERY.

THE
LONGEST
KEEP
VARIET

CELERY— CONTINUED

White Plume
While we are fully aware that this variety has great merit as an early market sort, being as early as any and very attractive when fit for use, yet we do not think that it compares favorably with the Golden Yellow Self Blanching either in flavor or solidity, or that it will remain in condition for use as long after it is earthed up. Plants light yellowish-green with tips of leaves almost white. As they mature, the inner stems and leaves turn white and require to be earthed up but a short time before they are in condition for use. Where a fine appearing celery at a minimum amount of labor is the object, this variety will give entire satisfaction. An *Improved* White Plume with longer stems is being offered, but careful comparison with our stock shows that it is not equal in quality or so desirable as that we offer. Pkt. 5c; Oz. 20c; 2 Oz. 35c; ¼ Lb. 60c; Lb. $2.00

DWARF WHITE SOLID. An erect, compact growing variety. Stalks moderately thick and distinctly ribbed, solid, crisp and of excellent quality. This variety is also sold as *Large Ribbed Kalamazoo* and *Kalamazoo*. Pkt. 5c; Oz. 15c; 2 Oz. 25c; ¼ Lb. 40c; Lb. $1.50

PERFECTION HEARTWELL. A medium green, second early variety. The plants are taller than Dwarf White Solid and a little later in maturing, being one of the earliest green leaved sorts. The stalks are of medium size, round, very solid, crisp, tender, white and of fine flavor. Pkt. 5c; Oz. 15c; 2 Oz. 25c; ¼ Lb. 40c; Lb. $1.50

SEYMOUR'S WHITE SOLID. A large sized, vigorous growing variety; stalks white, round, very crisp; perfectly solid and of superior flavor. Matures a little earlier than Giant Pascal. Pkt. 5c; Oz. 15c; 2 Oz. 25c; ¼ Lb. 40c; Lb. $1.50

Giant Pascal
This is a green leaved variety developed from the Golden Yellow Self Blanching, and is an excellent sort for fall and winter use. It blanches to a beautiful yellowish-white color, is very solid and crisp and of a fine nutty flavor. The stalk is very thick, the upper portion nearly round but broadening and flattening toward the base. With rich soil and high culture this variety will be wholly satisfactory if a large growing, medium late celery of excellent quality is desired. Especially recommended for the south where it is prized more than almost any other kind. Pkt. 5c; Oz. 20c; 2 Oz. 35c; ¼ Lb. 60c; Lb. $1.75

Evan's Triumph
As grown by us this is one of the best late sorts. The variety produces a very strong and vigorous plant with large, very white, crisp, tender and fine flavored stalks. It is late and requires the whole season to develop but will keep well for a very long time and has proven to be one of the most popular late varieties. When it is properly grown a dozen plants trimmed for market will weigh nearly twice as much as the same number of some smaller and earlier sorts. Pkt. 5c; Oz. 20c; 2 Oz. 35c; ¼ Lb. 60c; Lb. $2.00

GIANT PASCAL CELERY.

French's Success
Keeps the best of any celery yet introduced. Growth compact and short in stem so that plants may be well earthed up for blanching while growing close together. Foliage dark green; heart large, solid and formed early; stalks white, thick, yet brittle and without stringiness, and of good quality. It requires more time to mature than some sorts but remains firm, solid and in perfect condition until late in spring. We recommend it as the best variety for the late market. Pkt. 5c; Oz. 35c; 2 Oz. 60c; ¼ Lb. $1.00; Lb. $3.50 (*See opposite page*).

SOUP, OR CUTTING CELERY. This variety is not suitable for blanching but is adapted to sowing thick in rows and cutting when three or four inches high, to use for soup flavoring. The tops grow very large and rapidly and if cut repeatedly a succession will be furnished throughout the season. Pkt. 5c; Oz. 15c; 2 Oz. 25c; ¼ Lb. 40c; Lb. $1.25

CELERY SEED FOR FLAVORING. Oz. 10c; 2 Oz. 10c; ¼ Lb. 15c; Lb. 30c.

Celeriac or Turnip-Rooted Celery

LARGE SMOOTH PRAGUE CELERIAC.

CULTURE—Sow the seed at the same season and give the same treatment as common celery. Transplant the young plants to moist, rich soil, in rows two feet apart and six inches apart in the row. Give thorough culture. As the roots are the edible portion of this vegetable, it is not necessary to earth up or "handle" it. After the roots have attained a diameter of two inches or over, they will be fit for use. To keep through winter, pack in damp earth or sand and put in the cellar or leave out of doors, covering with earth and straw, like beets or carrots.

Large Smooth Prague
An improved form of turnip-rooted celery, producing large and smooth roots which are almost round and with very few side roots. Plants vigorous, with large, deep green foliage. Pkt. 5c; Oz. 20c; 2 Oz. 35c; ¼ Lb. 60c; Lb. $2.00.

Turnip-Rooted
The root of this celery is turnip-shaped, tender, with sweet taste and rather strong flavor. It is used principally for seasoning meats and soups. Pkt. 5c; Oz. 15c; 2 Oz. 25c; ¼ Lb. 40c; Lb. $1.50.

Crimson Giant Turnip Radish

A variety extraordinary in that, while growing to an unusually large size, it is always tender, crisp and of mild flavor. It remains in perfect condition a remarkably long time, and unlike other forcing varieties, does not become pithy even when twice their size in diameter. Root turnip shaped; color a beautiful crimson-carmine; flesh firm, crisp and tender. While very desirable as a second early forcing variety, we specially recommend it for outdoor planting. *See opposite page.* Pkt. 5c; Oz. 10c; 2 Oz. 15c; ¼ Lb. 25c; Lb. 75c.

Chervil

A hardy annual, worthy of more general use for flavoring and garnishing. The curled variety is even more beautiful than parsley and can be used to great advantage in beautifying dishes of meats and vegetables. The leaves are ready for use in six to ten weeks from sowing the seed. CULTURE—Sow in early spring in rich, well prepared soil and when plants are well established transplant to about one foot apart. **Curled** Greatly superior to the old, plain variety, being earlier, more handsome and having fully as fine fragrance and flavor. **Pkt. 5c; Oz. 15c; 2 Oz. 25c; ¼ Lb. 40c; Lb. $1.25**

Chicory

Large-Rooted, or Coffee Our stock is the improved type, with very much larger, smoother, whiter and proportionately shorter roots than the old kind. The dried and prepared roots are used quite extensively as a substitute or adulterant for coffee. Sow the seed as early in the spring as the ground can be prepared, in a rather light, moderately rich soil, in drills two to two and one-half feet for either garden or field culture. When the plants are sufficiently large, thin four to six inches apart in the row. Keep clear of weeds and in the fall dig the roots, slice them and dry in an apple evaporator or kiln constructed for the purpose. Where the roots are grown in quantity for the manufacturers of "prepared" chicory, they are usually brought to the factory in the "green" state and there dried in kilns constructed for the purpose. **Pkt. 5c; Oz. 10c; 2 Oz. 15c; ¼ Lb. 25c; Lb. 75c.**

Chives

Allium Schoenoprasum An onion-like plant, which by some is highly esteemed for use as a salad, the green stems having a very pleasant onion flavor. Also the plant makes an excellent ornamental garden bed edging, which may frequently be cut, a new growth of leaves appearing soon after each cutting. The seed may be sown in rows in place, or in boxes and transplanted. The plants are productive during two or three years, and may then be taken up, divided and reset. **Pkt. 10c; ⅜ Oz. 25c.**

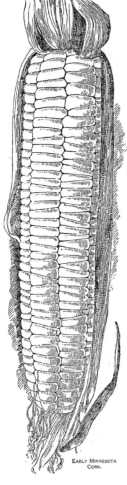

EARLY MINNESOTA
CORN.

Collards

A cabbage, or kale-like plant, known in different sections as "Cole," "Colewort," or simply "Greens." It is extensively used in the south, where it continues in growth and is usable throughout the entire winter.

Georgia, Southern, or Creole We offer the true white or green stemmed sort so extensively used in the south, where it furnishes an abundance of food for the table or for stock. Forms a large, loose, open head, or a mass of leaves on a tall stem. Freezing does not injure but rather improves the quality. Sow thick in drills, in rich ground, transplanting when four inches high; or sow in drills where the plants are to remain and when well started thin to two or three feet apart in the row. In the south, sow from January to May and August to October. **Pkt. 5c; Oz. 10c; 2 Oz. 20c; ¼ Lb. 30c; Lb. $1.00**

Corn Salad

Fetticus, or Lamb's Lettuce This small salad is used during the winter and spring months as a substitute for lettuce and is also cooked and used like spinage. In warm weather the plants will mature in four to six weeks. During August and September sow the seed in shallow drills about one foot apart. If the soil is dry it should be firmly pressed over the seed in order to secure prompt germination. On the approach of severe cold weather, cover with straw or coarse litter. The plants will also do well if the seed is sown very early in the spring and like most salad plants, are greatly improved if sown on very rich soil; indeed, the ground can scarcely be made too rich for them. **Pkt. 5c; Oz. 10c; 2 Oz. 15c; ¼ Lb. 20c; Lb. 60c.**

CORN Sweet or Table ::: Varieties :::

CULTURE—A rich, warm, alluvial soil is best, but excellent sweet corn can be raised on any good, ordinary soil, if it is deeply and thoroughly worked before planting. In the north sweet corn should be planted as early as can be done without risking great loss from frosts or from rotting of the seed in the soil. Give frequent and thorough but shallow cultivation until the tassels appear.

Oakview Early Market A variety originating on our Oakview seed farms. Similar in general character to our Mammoth White Cory, but with decidedly longer ears which mature quite as early. It is of especial value to market gardeners, as in early corn the largest ears usually control the market. The plant is about four feet high; the ears large, twelve to fourteen-rowed, with white, square grains. **Pkt. 10c; Pt. 15c; Qt. 25c; 4 Qts. 75c; Bushel $4.50**

Mammoth White Cory One of the largest and best extra early varieties. The stalks are about four feet high, each generally bearing two large, fine-shaped ears which become fit for use as early as those of any variety in cultivation. They are twelve-rowed, very symmetrical and handsome, seldom with any opening between the rows at the base. The grain is large, broad, very white and of remarkably good quality for such an early sort. The size and beauty of this variety give it ready sale, even when the market is overstocked. **Pkt. 10c; Pt. 15c; Qt. 25c; 4 Qts. 75c; Bushel $4.50**

White Cob Cory The plants are usually about four and one-half feet high and bear two or even three ears which are eight-rowed with large, somewhat coarse but very sweet and tender grain. **Pkt. 10c; Pt. 15c; Qt. 25c; 4 Qts. 75c; Bushel $4.00**

Crosby's Early A most excellent variety of fine quality. Ears of medium size, twelve-rowed or more, with short, nearly square grains which are very white, sweet and tender. Plants about four feet in height. This is the sort so largely grown in Maine for canning, and it is the use of this variety rather than any peculiarity of soil that has given Maine sweet corn its reputation for quality. **Pkt. 10c; Pt. 15c; Qt. 25c; 4 Qts. 75c; Bu. $4.50**

Early Minnesota This old and deservedly popular variety is one of the best early sorts for the market and the private garden. Stalks about five feet high, with no suckers, and bearing one or two ears well covered with husks; ears long, eight-rowed; kernels very broad, sweet and tender, not shrinking much in drying. By careful selection we have developed a stock of this standard variety which is remarkably uniform, and in which all the good qualities that have made this sort so popular are intensified. **Pkt. 10c; Pt. 15c; Qt. 25c; 4 Qts. 75c; Bushel $4.00**

If Corn is wanted by mail or express, prepaid, add 10 cents per pint, 15 cents per quart, for charges.

C O R N — Sweet or Table Varieties — Continued

Early Sweet or Sugar Ears long, slender, eight-rowed. Grain very white, tender and sugary; plant about six feet high, productive, hardy and quite early. An old but excellent table sort. Our stock is distinct and true, and not such a mixture of all sorts of early sweet or sugar corn as is often offered under this name. **Pkt. 10c; Pt. 15c; Qt. 25c; 4 Qts. 75c; Bushel $4.00**

Perry's Hybrid This is a very popular eastern variety. Stalks about six feet high, bearing two large, twelve or fourteen-rowed ears which often have a red or pink cob; grain medium sized, cooking very white and tender. Matures a little later than the Minnesota. **Pkt. 10c; Pt. 15c; Qt. 25c; 4 Qts. 75c; Bushel $4.00**

Moore's Early Concord Stalk about six feet high, bearing near its base large, fourteen to sixteen-rowed ears of short, very white, square grain, similar to that of Crosby's Early and of the same splendid quality. It is an excellent second early sort either for the garden or the canning factory. **Pkt. 10c; Pt. 15c; Qt. 25c; 4 Qts. 75c; Bushel $4.00**

Black Mexican This corn, when in condition for the table, cooks remarkably white, but the ripe grain is black or bluish-black. It is surpassed by none in tenderness and fine quality. For family use it is considered by many the most desirable of the second early sorts. It does especially well for second early in the south. Stalk about six feet high. **Pkt. 10c; Pt. 15c; Qt. 25c; 4 Qts. 75c; Bushel $4.50**

Hickox Hybrid Earlier than Stowell's Evergreen, and forms a long, cylindrical and very attractive ear of very white and handsome grain. It is one of the best varieties for canners' use. By planting it at the same time as Stowell's Evergreen the season will be lengthened considerably, as the Hickox will be about through by the time Stowell's Evergreen comes in. Very prolific; about six and one-half feet high, and ordinarily every stalk will have two large, fully developed ears. *Crop failed.*

Old Colony This variety differs from the Evergreen in that it is a little sweeter and richer in quality, but does not remain so long in condition for use. Stalks about six and one-half feet high, usually bearing two large, sixteen to twenty-rowed ears. The planter may be sure of a great number of marketable ears as great weight of corn per acre as can be produced by any variety. We do not know of any kind of late corn more valuable for the home or market garden than our improved strain of this splendid sort. **Pkt. 10c; Pt. 15c; Qt. 25c; 4 Qts. 75c; Bushel $4.50**

Country Gentleman This variety has a small, white cob, densely covered with irregular rows of very long, slender, white grains which are of excellent quality. Stalks from six and one-half to seven feet high. By many it is regarded as the best of the late varieties. **Pkt. 10c; Pt. 15c; Qt. 25c; 4 Qts. 75c; Bushel $4.00**

Ferry's Early Evergreen We have tested many samples of Evergreen Corn that were claimed to be earlier than Stowell's Evergreen and to be just as good, but we have never found any of them so valuable as the stock of this variety we offer. It has been proven both on our trial grounds and in the field to come into fit condition for use much earlier than Stowell's Evergreen and to remain in condition quite as long. The ears are large, with sixteen to twenty more or less irregular rows with very long grain which is of the very best quality. The plants average from six and one-half to seven feet high and in ear resemble those of Stowell's Evergreen, but differ in earliness and we think are more uniform. **Pkt. 10c; Pt. 15c; Qt. 25c; 4 Qts. 75c; Bushel $4.00**

Stowell's Evergreen The standard main crop variety. It is hardy and productive, very tender and sugary, remaining a long time in condition suitable for boiling. Our stock has been carefully grown and selected to avoid the tendency to a shorter grain and deterioration in the evergreen character of this best known of all late sorts. Height about seven and one-half feet. **Pkt. 10c; Pt. 15c; Qt. 20c; 4 Qts. 60c; Bushel $3.50**

Mammoth This variety produces the largest ears of any sort with which we are acquainted. It is of excellent quality, sweet, tender and delicious, and its only fault is the immense size of the ear. Plant averages about eight feet high. **Pkt. 10c; Pt. 15c; Qt. 25c; 4 Qts. 75c; Bu. $4.50**

FIELD VARIETIES

EXTRA EARLY ADAMS. Very early. The stalk is about four and one-half feet high, without suckers, has a small tassel, and bears a single, very full, *short*, many-rowed ear, often nearly as thick as it is long, and well covered with coarse husks; kernels white, smooth. An extremely hardy variety. **Pkt. 10c; Pt. 15c; Qt. 20c; 4 Qts. 60c; Bushel $3.50**

EARLY ADAMS, OR BURLINGTON. An excellent early, field variety, and often used for table, particularly in the south. Ears about eight inches long, twelve or fourteen-rowed; kernels white, rounded, somewhat deeper than broad and indented at the outer end which is whiter and less transparent than the inner. **Pkt. 10c; Pt. 15c; Qt. 20c; 4 Qts. 60c; Bushel $3.00**

EARLY RED BLAZED. An early flint variety of medium height. Ears long, eight-rowed, well filled, small at base. Grain flinty and of fine quality, bright yellow at base of ears, but red at the tips. It is also known as Smut Nose. **Pkt. 10c; Pt. 15c; Qt. 15c; 4 Qts. 40c; Bushel $2.00**

EARLY GOLDEN DENT, OR PRIDE OF THE NORTH. A very early Dent variety. Stalks small, with broad leaves. Ears short, twelve to sixteen-rowed, well filled. Grain long, yellow, making an extra quality of meal. **Pkt. 10c; Pt. 10c; Qt. 15c; 4 Qts. 40c; Bushel $2.00**

Rice Pop Corn A very handsome and prolific variety. Ears short; kernels long, pointed and resemble rice; color white. Probably no variety of pop corn is superior to this for parching. *We supply lots of four quarts and less, shelled.* **Pkt. 10c; Pt. 15c; Qt. 20c; 4 Qts. 60c; Bushel of Ears $1.50**
If Corn is wanted by mail or express, prepaid, add 10 cents per pint, 15 cents per quart, for charges.

COUNTRY GENTLEMAN CORN.

Cucumber

This is one of the vegetables that can be grown to perfection by any one who can control a few square yards of soil that is fully exposed to the sun. The fruit is so much better when gathered fresh from the vines than it is in the more or less wilted condition in which it is found on the market, that every family should be supplied from its own garden.

CULTURE—In order to obtain the largest yield of cucumbers, the soil should be well enriched with well rotted manure, but an abundance of good fruit can be raised on any rich garden soil. Plant the seed not over an inch deep in hills four to six feet apart each way, dropping fifteen to twenty seeds in a hill. After the plants begin to crowd and danger from the striped beetle is pretty nearly over, thin to three plants to the hill. Give frequent but shallow cultivation, until the plants make runners so long that this is impracticable. In field culture, plow furrows four feet apart and similar ones at right angles to the first. At each intersection drop a shovelful or more of *well rotted* manure which should be *well mixed* with the soil, forming a broad, flat hill four to six inches above the surface. Many growers omit every fourth row, thus forming paths for the distribution of manure and gathering the fruit. In many sections where earliness is very important, market gardeners start plants in boxes made like the ordinary berry box, but without the raised bottom. The boxes are set in hotbeds or cold frames, filled with rich, friable soil and the seed planted. When danger of frost is over, the plants are set in the open ground, the boxes being cut away, so the roots are not disturbed at all.

The plants are liable to attack from the striped cucumber beetles which are so numerous in some cases as to destroy them. These may be kept off by a frequent dusting with air slacked lime, soot or sifted ashes diluted with fine road earth. Care should be taken not to use too much of any of the above materials, for if used too freely they will kill the vines. The best protection against injury is a vigorous and rapid growth of the young plants.

Pick the fruit before it begins to ripen, as the vines will cease setting fruit as soon as any seed begins to mature. In gathering for pickles, cut the stem instead of pulling the fruit off and be careful not to mar the fruit in any way, for if the skin be broken the pickles will not keep so well.

We pay particular attention to growing and selecting the various strains of cucumbers, so as to keep them pure and true to name.

EARLY SHORT GREEN CUCUMBER.

Early Russian
Earliest and hardiest. Vine vigorous and productive. Fruit three to four inches long, thick, oval and covered with fine, small spines. *Crop failed.*

Early Cluster
Vine vigorous, producing the bulk of the crop near the root and in clusters. Fruit short, with uniformly thick end, dark green, but paler at blossom end. A very productive sort. Pkt. 5c; Oz. 10c; 2 Oz. 15c; ¼ Lb. 25c; Lb. 90c.

Early Short Green, or Early Frame
An excellent sort both for table use and for pickling. Plants very vigorous and productive. Fruit straight, handsome, small at each end, bright green, lighter at the blossom end, with crisp, tender flesh and makes excellent pickles. Comes into use a little later than the Early Cluster and keeps green a long time. Our stock is very superior. Pkt. 5c; Oz. 10c; 2 Oz. 15c; ¼ Lb. 25c; Lb. 90c.

Jersey Pickling
Intermediate between the Long and the Short Green, forming a long, slender, cylindrical pickle which is very crisp and tender. Pkt. 5c; Oz. 10c; 2 Oz. 20c; ¼ Lb. 30c; Lb. $1.00

EARLY CLUSTER CUCUMBER.

JERSEY PICKLING CUCUMBER.

CUCUMBER—Continued

Chicago, or Westerfield Pickling Very popular with market gardeners. Fruit medium length, pointed at each end, with very large and prominent spines; color deep green. It is an extremely prolific variety and is one of the best for those who want crisp, coarsely prickled pickles. Pkt. 5c; Oz. 10c; 2 Oz. 20c; ¼ Lb. 30c; Lb. $1.00

Boston Pickling or Green Prolific A distinct and very productive variety, extensively grown for pickles. Fruit medium sized, very smooth, symmetrical, bright green. Pkt. 5c; Oz. 10c; 2 Oz. 20c; ¼ Lb. 30c; Lb. $1.00

Emerald A new, rather late variety of very symmetrical shape and smooth skin. It retains its dark green color until nearly ripe. It is spineless and the flesh is crisp, white and tender. Pkt. 5c; Oz. 15c; 2 Oz. 25c; ¼ Lb. 40c; Lb. $1.25

Bismarck A late variety producing long, very dark green fruit, pointed at each end, very constant in form and color; flesh crisp and tender; excellent either for pickles or slicing. The stock we offer is a great improvement over that usually sold either as Bismarck or Tailby Hybrid, being much better and more uniform in shape, without the distinct neck which was a fault of the old stock. It can be depended upon to produce very symmetrical, handsome, dark green fruits which will hold their color better than those of any other kind. This is one of the best sorts for growing under glass. Pkt. 5c; Oz. 20c; 2 Oz. 35c; ¼ Lb. 60c; Lb. $2.00.

Extra Long, or Evergreen White Spine Beautiful in shape and color and of the finest quality. The fruit is long, cylindrical, dark green, with very white, crisp and tender flesh. An entirely new and distinct sort developed by ourselves through very careful selection, our aim being to secure the best possible table cucumber. The vine is vigorous and productive, and comes into full bearing earlier than the Bismarck. An excellent sort for culture under glass. Pkt. 5c; Oz. 10c; 2 Oz. 20c; ¼ Lb. 30c; Lb. $1.00

Cumberland A new and distinct variety, said to have originated from crossing the Parisian Pickling and the Early White Spine; it certainly has the good qualities of each of these sorts. The fruits are large, symmetrical, dark green, covered with innumerable small, white spines, and are of prime quality for slicing. The vine is vigorous, wonderfully prolific, and continues in bearing much longer than most sorts. Pkt. 5c; Oz. 15c; 2 Oz. 25c; ¼ Lb. 40c; Lb. $1.25

Early White Spine
One of the best sorts for table use. Vines vigorous, fruiting early and abundantly; fruit uniformly straight and handsome, dark green, with a few white spines; flesh tender and of excellent flavor. In this country this variety is used more, we presume, than any other for forcing under glass. Pkt. 5c; Oz. 10c; 2 Oz. 20c; ¼ Lb. 30c; Lb. $1.00

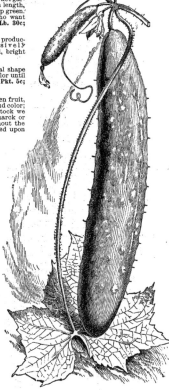

IMPROVED LONG GREEN CUCUMBER.

EXTRA LONG, OR
EVERGREEN WHITE SPINE CUCUMBER.

Arlington A selection from the White Spine, which is more pointed at each end. The young fruits are unusually crisp and tender and are of very dark green color so that the variety is considered by many to be the best for small pickles. Pkt. 5c; Oz. 10c; 2 Oz. 20c; ¼ Lb. 30c; Lb. $1.00

Cool and Crisp A strain of White Spine somewhat like the Arlington, but larger and less symmetrical. The vine is vigorous and the fruit long, cylindrical, dark green, with many white spines. The flesh is peculiarly crisp and tender and it is one of the very best for table use. Pkt. 5c; Oz. 10c; 2 Oz. 20c; ¼ Lb. 30c; Lb. $1.00

Improved Long Green Produced by selection from the Long Green. Vines vigorous and productive, forming fruit fit for the table nearly as early as the shorter sorts; fruit about twelve inches long, firm and crisp. Excellent for pickles; when mature is sometimes used for making sweet pickles. We offer a carefully selected strain, uniformly long, of good form, with the large warts and spines well distributed over the surface instead of being clustered at one end as in inferior stocks. Pkt. 5c; Oz. 15c; 2 Oz. 25c; ¼ Lb. 40c; Lb. $1.50

Small Gherkin (For Pickles). A very small, oval, prickly variety quite distinct from all others and grown exclusively for pickles. It is the smallest of all the varieties and should always be picked when young and tender. The seed is slow to germinate, requiring usually from two to three weeks. Pkt. 5c; Oz. 15c; 2 Oz. 25c; ¼ Lb. 40c; Lb. $1.25

CRESS, CURLED, OR PEPPER GRASS.

CRESS

Curled, or Pepper Grass This small salad is much used with lettuce, to the flavor of which its warm, pungent taste makes a most agreeable addition. **Pkt. 5c; Oz. 10c; 2 Oz. 15c; ¼ Lb. 20c; Lb. 50c.**

CULTURE—The seed should be sown in drills about sixteen inches apart, on very rich ground and the plants well cultivated. It may be planted very early but repeated sowings are necessary to secure a succession. Keep off insects by dusting with Pyrethrum Powder.

Gray Seeded Early Winter A variety that does well on upland and produces a large cluster of leaves quite similar to those of the Water Cress in appearance and quality. It is quite hardy and thrives best in the cool autumn months. **Pkt. 5c; Oz. 10c; 2 Oz. 20c; ¼ Lb. 30c; Lb. $1.00**

CULTURE—Make first sowing as early in spring as the ground can be worked and continue, for succession, every two weeks. Or sow in early autumn in rich, mellow soil, in shallow drills sixteen inches apart, covering one-half inch deep. Thin out as required for use.

True Water This is a distinct variety of cress with small, oval leaves and only thrives when its roots and stems are submerged in water. It is one of the most delicious of small salads and should be planted wherever a suitable place can be found. **Pkt. 5c; Oz. 35c; 2 Oz. 60c; ¼ Lb. $1.00; Lb. $3.50**

CULTURE—The seed should be sown and lightly covered in gravelly, mucky lands, along the borders of small, rapid streams. The plants will need no subsequent culture, as under favorable conditions they increase very rapidly by self-sown seed and extension of the roots. The shoots should be cut, not broken off, for market. In summer it is best to cut them closely, the oftener the better.

DANDELION

Dandelion is native to Europe and Asia but is naturalized in all temperate countries.

CULTURE—Sow early in the spring, on very warm, *rich* soil, in drills eighteen inches apart; thin the young plants to five inches in the row and cultivate well; they will be fit for cutting the next spring. When grown for the roots, sow in September and cultivate well during the fall and the following summer; the roots will be fit to dig in October. Roots are sometimes removed from the field to the hotbed or house for forcing. Roots dug in fall and dried are sold for medicinal purposes.

Cultivated, or French Common This is considered the best by many and is not at all the same as our wild dandelion, being greatly improved by careful selection. **Pkt. 5c; Oz. 20c; 2 Oz. 35c; ¼ Lb. 60c; Lb. $1.75**

Improved Thick Leaved One of the earliest and best greens in cultivation. **Pkt. 5c; Oz. 45c; 2 Oz. 85c; ¼ Lb. $1.50; Lb. $4.50**

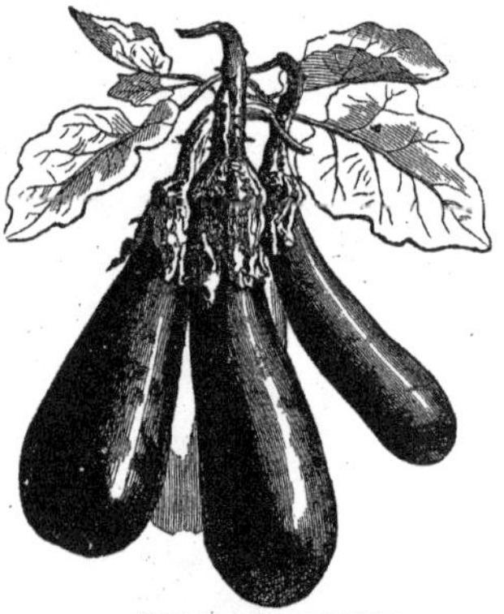

EARLY LONG PURPLE EGG PLANT.

EGG PLANT

CULTURE—Egg Plant seed germinates slowly and should be started in moderately high temperature, for in this, as in all sub-tropical plants, it is of importance to secure a rapid and continuous growth from the first, the plants never recovering from a check received when young. When the plants have formed two rough leaves transplant to three or four inches apart. When the ground is warm and all danger not only from frosts, but from cold nights is past, harden off the plants by gradual exposure to the sun and air, and decreasing the supply of water, then *carefully* transplant into the open ground, setting the plants two and a half feet apart. If needed, shade the young plants and protect them from the potato bug, which will often destroy them. Some seasons egg plants will fail to set fruit or will not begin bearing until too late to mature, no matter how faithfully they may have been cared for. This is especially likely to happen if the summer is cool and rather moist. We know of no certain remedy for it, though pinching off the ends of the branches after the plants begin to bloom and not letting more than two or three fruits set, is a good practice.

BLACK BEAUTY EGG PLANT.

SOIL—Egg Plant will grow on almost any soil in the south but it develops to greater perfection on a rich, deep, loamy land, free from debris. In the clay districts this is not easily obtained but there are often small fields that are sufficiently dry and yet contain enough sand to make egg plant growing profitable. No matter whether clay land, loam or sandy soil be employed for raising this crop, it will be necessary to plow deeply and thoroughly. The land should be drier than that required by cabbage or beets. In fact, it will stand a greater drought than the ordinary vegetables.

Early Long Purple This is a very early maturing and most productive variety; fruit long, dark, rich purple and of fine quality. **Pkt. 5c; Oz. 20c; 2 Oz. 35c; ¼ Lb. 60c; Lb. $2.00**

Black Pekin Nearly as early as the Early Long Purple and nearly as large as the later sorts. Very prolific and desirable for market gardeners' use. Fruit nearly round; skin smooth, black and glossy; flesh white, fine grained and delicate. **Pkt. 5c; Oz. 25c; 2 Oz. 40c; ¼ Lb. 75c; Lb. $2.50**

Black Beauty Fruit large, symmetrical in shape and uniformly of a rich, dark purple color. Fruits mature a little earlier than our Improved Large Purple but are not quite as large. **Pkt. 5c; Oz. 60c; 2 Oz. $1.00; ¼ Lb. $1.75; Lb. $6.00**

EGG PLANT Continued

D. M. Ferry & Co's Improved Large Purple (SPINELESS). This variety is a general favorite both for market and private use. The large size and high quality of its fruit and its extreme productiveness make it the most profitable for market gardeners. Plants large, spreading; foliage light green; fruit very large, oval; color a splendid dark purple. Plants usually ripen four to eight large fruits. **Pkt. 5c; Oz. 40c; 2 Oz. 75c; ¼ Lb. $1.25; Lb. $4.00**

Mammoth Pearl A smooth leaved variety with large, egg-shaped, pure white fruit. The flesh is of fine quality. This sort is also valuable for its peculiar form and color. *Crop failed.*

D. M. FERRY & CO'S IMPROVED LARGE PURPLE EGG PLANT.

ENDIVE

Endive may be grown at any season of the year but is more generally used late in the fall. Sow the seed in June or July, in drills fourteen to twenty inches apart and when well started thin the plants to one foot apart. When nearly full grown tie the outer leaves together over the center in order to blanch the heart of the plant. By covering fresh plants every few days a succession may be kept up. Blanching may also be done by slipping a large sized but short tile or piece of tile over each plant after the leaves are gathered up and held closely together.

Large Green Curled A large, strong-growing Endive which, by tying up, can be made to form finely blanched centers of good quality. Outer leaves well cut and bright, deep green. **Pkt. 5c; Oz. 15c; 2 Oz. 25c; ¼ Lb. 40c; Lb. $1.50**

Ever White Curled A very beautiful sort in which the leaves are very light colored, even the outer ones being nearly white. Plant moderately dense, with divided leaves which are a little coarser than those of the Green Curled. **Pkt. 5c; Oz. 15c; 2 Oz. 25c; ¼ Lb. 40c; Lb. $1.25**

Moss Curled One of the best, autumn, winter or spring salads. Plants compact-growing, forming large, dense clusters of finely divided, green leaves which, when properly blanched, are exceedingly crisp and tender. **Pkt. 5c; Oz. 15c; 2 Oz. 25c; ¼ Lb. 40c; Lb. $1.25**

Broad Leaved Batavian (*Escarolle*). This variety has broad, thick, plain or slightly wrinkled leaves, forming a large head, and is desirable for stews and soups. If the outer leaves are gathered and tied at the top, the inner ones will blanch and may be used for salad. **Pkt. 5c; Oz. 15c; 2 Oz. 25c; ¼ Lb. 40c; Lb. $1.25**

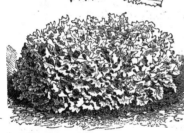

BROAD LEAVED BATAVIAN ENDIVE.

GARLIC

GARLIC A bulbous-rooted plant with a strong, penetrating odor but much esteemed by some for flavoring soups, stews, etc. We frequently receive orders for *garlic seed* but we can supply bulbs only. Prepare the ground the same as for onions and plant the bulbs in drills eight inches apart and four inches apart in the rows, covering two inches deep. When the leaves turn yellow take up the bulbs, dry in the shade and lay them up in a dry loft as you would onions.

Bulbs, ¼ Lb. 15c; Lb. 40c.

HORSE RADISH.

Horse Radish

Horse Radish rarely produces seed but is grown from pieces of the roots.

CULTURE—Mark off the rows two and one-half feet apart in rich, moist, well prepared ground and set the pieces of roots eighteen inches apart in the rows, vertically, the small end down and the top one to three inches below the surface. Cultivate thoroughly until the tops cover the ground, when their shade will keep down the weeds.

SMALL ROOTS—3 for 10c; 25c per dozen, postpaid. By freight or express, at purchaser's expense, **75c per 100.**

LARGE GREEN CURLED ENDIVE.

KALE

Borecole, Kale and German Greens are general terms applied to certain cabbage-like plants which do not form heads, but are used in their open growth. Some of the varieties are the most tender and delicate of any of the cabbage tribe. They are hardy and are not injured by the frost.

CULTURE—As far north as Cincinnati the seed may be sown in September and plants treated like spinage, or planted and grown like late cabbage until very late in the season. In the south kale will live and grow throughout the winter without protection. It is better not to cut or handle the plants when frozen, but if this is unavoidable, thaw them out in cold water. The young shoots which start up in the spring from the old stumps are very tender and make excellent greens.

TALL GREEN CURLED SCOTCH. This is very hardy and is not injured by a moderate frost. About thirty inches tall, with an abundance of dark green leaves which are densely curled and cut, forming a very beautiful plant. It stands the winters in the middle states without any protection. Pkt. 5c; Oz. 10c; 2 Oz. 15c; ¼ Lb. 25c; Lb. 75c.

Dwarf Curled Scotch, or German Greens

Plant low and compact, but with large, bright, deep green leaves, curled and crimped until the whole plant resembles a bunch of moss. It would be well worthy of cultivation simply for its beauty. One of the best sorts for use, and when well grown and cooked is one of the most palatable of vegetables. Pkt.5c; Oz.10c; 2 Oz. 15c; ¼ Lb. 25c; Lb. 75c.

TALL GREEN CURLED SCOTCH KALE.

Siberian
Sometimes called Sprouts and German Greens. In this variety the very large, green leaves are comparatively plain in the center but coarsely cut and frilled on the edge. The plant is low but spreading and very hardy. Pkt. 5c; Oz. 10c; 2 Oz. 15c; ¼ Lb. 20c; Lb. 60c.

Imperial, or Slow Seeder
A strain of Siberian in which the plants are slower to develop their seed stalks and consequently remain longer in condition for use. Pkt. 5c; Oz. 10c; 2 Oz. 15c; ¼ Lb. 20c; Lb. 60c.

GERMAN DWARF PURPLE. Similar to the Dwarf Curled Scotch, but of a rich purple color. Pkt.5c; Oz.10c; 2 Oz. 20c; ¼ Lb. 30c; Lb. $1.00

SIBERIAN KALE.

Kohl Rabi

The Kohl Rabi is a vegetable intermediate between the cabbage and turnip, and combines the flavor of each. The edible part is a turnip-shaped bulb formed by the enlargement of the stem. When used for the table this should be cut when quite small, as it is then very tender and delicate, but if allowed to reach its full size it becomes tough and stringy.

CULTURE—Sow in light, rich soil as early as possible, in drills sixteen inches apart and when well established thin to six inches apart in the row. One or two plantings at intervals of ten days will give a succession until hot weather, when they fail to grow well; plantings may be made the latter part of July for fall use.

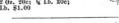

Early White Vienna
(Extra for forcing). Extremely early, with distinctly small tops. Bulbs of medium size, white, handsome and of best quality. Pkt. 5c; Oz. 25c; 2 Oz. 40c; ¼ Lb. 75c; Lb. $2.25

EARLY PURPLE VIENNA. Very early, with small top, the leaf stems being tinged with purple. Bulb bright purple; desirable for forcing and early outdoor planting. Pkt.5c; Oz. 25c; 2 Oz. 40c; ¼ Lb. 75c; Lb. $2.50

LARGE GREEN. Hardy, quite late and used for feeding stock. Bulbs large, weighing eight to ten pounds, whitish-green in color; leaves large and numerous. Pkt. 5c; Oz. 10c; 2 Oz. 20c; ¼ Lb. 30c; Lb. $100.

EARLY WHITE VIENNA KOHL RABI.

Leek

Belongs to the onion family. Sow the seed and care for the young plants as for onions, but they need more room in order to develop. When the young plant is about the size of a goose quill, transplant to a prepared bed in rows about two feet apart and four or five inches in the row. Set the roots deep and draw the earth to them when cultivating, so that they may be well blanched by the time they are fit for use.

LONDON FLAG. This is the variety generally cultivated in this country. It is hardy and of good quality. Pkt. 5c; Oz. 10c; 2 Oz. 20c; ¼ Lb. 30c; Lb. $1.00

LARGE AMERICAN FLAG. A variety which has become very popular with some market gardeners on account of its being larger than the London Flag. Pkt. 5c; Oz. 15c; 2 Oz. 25c; ¼ Lb. 40c; Lb. $1.25

LARGE ROUEN. Stem very large but comparatively short; the leaf is very broad, covered with whitish bloom. Stands a long time in condition for use. Pkt. 5c; Oz. 15c; 2 Oz. 25c; ¼ Lb. 40c; Lb. $1.25

Monstrous Carentan
The largest variety, often three inches in diameter and becoming very white and tender. A hardy and desirable sort. Pkt. 5c; Oz. 15c; 2 Oz. 25c; ¼ Lb. 40c; Lb. $1.50

MONSTROUS CARENTAN LEEK.

LETTUCE

For early outdoor culture in the latitude of Cincinnati and southward the seed may be planted in the fall, protecting the young plants from severe freezing either with frames or coarse litter which may be removed as soon as danger of severe freezing is over.

Lettuce in ground out of doors will stand some freezing, but is killed by prolonged frost or frequent freezing and thawing. North of Cincinnati an early crop may be secured by starting under glass from January to March and hardening off well before setting in ground, which should be done as soon as weather will permit.

CULTURE—Lettuce, to be at its best, should be grown rapidly, hence, the soil should be made as rich and friable as possible by liberal manuring and thorough preparation. For winter, sow under glass from November to February and thin out as necessary to prevent crowding. Keep at a moderate heat and give all the light and air possible. For general crop, sow outdoors as early in the spring as the ground can be worked, in drills eighteen inches apart and thin the young plants to four inches apart in the row. As the plants begin to crowd, thin them out and use as required. In this way a much longer succession of cuttings may be had from the same ground.

Varieties marked A are particularly adapted for culture under glass and for early spring use.

Those marked B are sometimes grown under glass, but are especially desirable for outdoor, summer culture.

Big Boston, Brown Dutch, California Cream Butter and Deacon are very hardy and suited for winter outdoor culture in the south.

Cabbage, or Heading Lettuces

HANSON LETTUCE.

Early Tennis Ball A (Seed black). A first class variety and one of the best head lettuces for forcing under glass or early planting outdoors. Plants medium sized, having thick, dark green leaves and when well grown forming very solid heads, the inner leaves being blanched to a rich creamy-white and exceedingly crisp, tender and rich flavored. Out of doors the variety does not stand hot weather as well as many sorts. It is of fine quality if used when in prime condition.

Pkt. 5c; Oz. 15c; 2 Oz. 25c; ¼ Lb. 40c; Lb. $1.25

Silver Ball A (Seed white). A remarkable variety in that it is an excellent sort both for forcing and outdoor culture. The thick, light green leaves have so much sheen that they actually look silvery-white in some lights. The heads are of good size and of excellent quality.

Pkt. 5c; Oz. 10c; 2 Oz. 20c; ¼ Lb. 30c; Lb. $1.00

BIG BOSTON A (Seed white). A very popular variety with gardeners who want a large heading, forcing sort; also for outdoor winter culture. Plants large, very hardy and vigorous; leaves broad, comparatively smooth but wavy at edge, thin and very hard; color bright, light green; when well grown are quite tender. Indoors this forms a solid head while out of doors it is less distinctively a heading sort. Grown in the south as a winter lettuce.

Pkt. 5c; Oz. 15c; 2 Oz. 25c; ¼ Lb. 40c; Lb. $1.50

SALAMANDER LETTUCE.

California Cream Butter, or Royal Summer Cabbage A (Seed brown). A strong growing sort with large, green leaves marked with scattered brown dashes. It forms a very solid head of rich cream-colored leaves which are very thick, tender and of splendid quality. This sort is very hardy and is sometimes called Winter Lettuce. Pkt. 5c; Oz. 15c; 2 Oz. 25c; ¼ Lb. 40c; Lb. $1.25.

White Summer Cabbage B (Seed white). A bright green, vigorous heading sort which forms a solid head of thick, tender leaves, the inner ones blanched to a beautiful cream-yellow.

Pkt. 5c; Oz. 10c; 2 Oz. 20c; ¼ Lb. 30c; Lb. $1.00

Mammoth Black Seeded Butter B. A strain of large, smooth-leaved, head lettuce, forming very large, solid, cabbage-like heads of thick, brittle leaves, the inner ones beautifully blanched, very crisp, tender and of fine flavor. Pkt. 5c; Oz. 15c; 2 Oz. 25c; ¼ Lb. 40c; Lb. $1.50

CALIFORNIA CREAM BUTTER, OR ROYAL SUMMER CABBAGE LETTUCE.

Market Gardener's Private Stock A (Seed black). A most excellent sort. The leaves are very large, deep, bright green, slightly wrinkled and form a large head which blanches nicely and remains a long time in condition for use. A sort which cannot fail to please those who appreciate fine quality. Pkt. 5c; Oz. 15c; 2 Oz. 25c; ¼ Lb. 40c; Lb. $1.25

SALAMANDER B (Seed black). A very bright green and attractive variety. It forms large, solid heads composed of thick, smooth, very tender leaves, the inner ones finely blanched and all of the finest quality. It remains a long time in head before running to seed. Pkt. 5c; Oz. 15c; 2 Oz. 25c; ¼ Lb. 40c; Lb. $1.25

HANSON B (Seed white). Plant large, forming a large, flat head, resembling that of cabbage and so slow to form a seed stalk that it often fails to seed at all. Outer leaves bright green with prominent, light colored veins; inner leaves white and usually curved and twisted at the base; very tender and sweet. A standard summer heading lettuce. Pkt. 5c; Oz. 15c; 2 Oz. 25c; ¼ Lb. 40c; Lb. $1.25

Hubbard's Market A (Seed white). Similar in type to Tennis Ball, but forms a larger, looser, more showy head and is later to mature.

Pkt. 5c; Oz. 15c; 2 Oz. 25c; ¼ Lb. 40c; Lb. $1.25

LETTUCE, Cabbage or Heading, Continued

Deacon *(Seed white)*. This does not make as large a head as some others but the heads formed are very solid and of excellent flavor and remain in condition for use as long as any variety in cultivation. Plant medium sized with very few outer leaves which are a deep green and very thick. The inner leaves blanch to a bright, rich yellow and are exceedingly well flavored, crisp and tender. This is certainly one of the best in quality of the summer heading sorts. Pkt. 5c; Oz. 15c; 2 Oz. 25c; ¼ Lb. 40c; Lb. $1.25

Buttercup B *(Seed white)*. Plants medium sized, with numerous round, smooth leaves which are of a beautiful yellowish-green color and of very good quality. They form medium sized, fairly solid heads which, when prepared for the table, are exceedingly attractive in appearance. Pkt. 5c; Oz. 15c; 2 Oz. 25c; ¼ Lb. 40c; Lb. $1.25

Brown Dutch *(Seed black)*. An old sort noted for its hardiness. Leaves large, thick, green tinged with brown. It always forms a large, solid head which is somewhat coarse looking, but the inner leaves are beautifully blanched, exceedingly sweet, tender and well flavored. Desirable because of its hardiness and fine quality. May be used in the south as a winter lettuce. Pkt. 5c; Oz. 15c; 2 Oz. 25c; ¼ Lb. 40c; Lb. $1.25

White Chavigne B *(Seed white)*. Forms a very full head made up of large, well rounded, rather dark green leaves which are coarsely savoyed, the inner ones much lighter colored and formed into a compact, solid head. An excellent sort, quick in forming a head and slow in running to seed. Pkt. 5c; Oz. 20c; 2 Oz. 35c; ¼ Lb. 60c; Lb. $2.00

CURLED OR LOOSE LEAVED LETTUCE

Detroit Market A *(Seed white)*. A variety quite similar to the Grand Rapids in general **Gardeners' Forcing** character, but it will stand higher temperature and so can be crowded to maturity a little quicker. The leaves are not quite so tender and brittle as those of the Grand Rapids. Pkt. 5c; Oz. 15c; 2 Oz. 25c; ¼ Lb. 40c; Lb. $1.25

Grand Rapids A *(Seed black)*. As a lettuce for greenhouse forcing, this variety undoubtedly stands at the head of the list, being of quick growth, little liable to rot and standing for some days after being fit to cut. The plant is upright and forms a loose head or cluster of large, light yellowish-green leaves, slightly crimped and blistered and rather thin. It will stand shipping long distances better than most sorts. Pkt. 5c; Oz. 15c; 2 Oz. 25c; ¼ Lb. 40c; Lb. $1.25

Simpson's Early Curled B *(Seed white)*. An early, erect growing, clustering variety. It may be sown thickly and cut when the plants are very young. Leaves broad, often frilled and blistered and formed into a loose head. Light green in color and exceedingly sweet, tender and well flavored. Popular in the New York markets. Pkt. 5c; Oz. 10c; 2 Oz. 20c; ¼ Lb. 30c; Lb. $1.00

Black Seeded Simpson A For those who like a large, thin, exceedingly tender leaf, and for those markets which demand a large, loose cluster of leaves rather than a solid head, this is one of the best varieties, either for forcing or early sowing out of doors. Plant forms a large, loose head, light yellowish-green in color, so that a little wilting is not noticed. Leaves large, thin, slightly ruffled and blistered, even the large outer ones being quite tender. It is attractive, of excellent quality and continues a long time in condition for use. Pkt. 5c; Oz. 10c; 2 Oz. 20c; ¼ Lb. 30c; Lb. $1.00

FERRY'S EARLY PRIZE HEAD LETTUCE.

Ferry's Early Prize Head B *(Seed white)*. This old standard variety is still the best of the large, thin-leaved, clustering sorts for the home garden, but it is not a good kind to ship long distances, as the leaves are so tender that they are easily broken in handling. The leaves are very large, crimped, bright green tinged with brownish-red, and are exceedingly tender, crisp and sweet, forming a large, loose head. Pkt. 5c; Oz. 10c; 2 Oz. 20c; ¼ Lb. 30c; Lb. $1.00

Tilton's White Star B *(Seed white)*. A distinct sort of the Black Seeded Simpson type, but grows larger and more rapidly and its leaves are broader, thicker, darker and less frilled at the edge. It forms a large, loose head, blanches well and is of excellent quality. The plants remain long in condition for use before running to seed. Repeated trials, both for forcing and early planting outdoors, convince us that this is a most valuable sort. Pkt. 5c; Oz. 10c; 2 Oz. 20c; ¼ Lb. 30c; Lb. $1.00

Denver Market B *(Seed white)*. A variety of the same general character of growth as Tilton's White Star but the heads are not quite as large and the leaves are more crimped and cut. Pkt. 5c; Oz. 10c; 2 Oz. 20c; ¼ Lb. 30c; Lb. $1.00

Cos Lettuce The Cos Lettuces are distinct from the preceding sorts, in having long, narrow, spoon shaped leaves, which usually fold into loose, sugar loaf shaped heads, which blanch better by having the outer leaves drawn about them and tied. On account of their exceeding crispness, tenderness and delicate flavor, they are becoming more and more popular in this country.

BLACK SEEDED SIMPSON LETTUCE.

Early White Self-Folding *(Seed white)*. A distinct Cos lettuce which will do better without tying up than most Cos lettuces. The leaves are yellowish-white in color, long, narrow upright, folding into a solid head like that of an Early York Cabbage and very crisp and tender. This is a truly self-blanching lettuce of superior flavor. Sold also as Trianon. Pkt. 5c; Oz. 15c; 2 Oz. 25c; ¼ Lb. 40c; Lb. $1.25

Martynia A strong growing, hardy annual plant with curiously shaped seed pods, which, when young and tender, are highly prized for pickling. The pods are produced in great abundance and should be gathered when less than half grown, as after the hardening of the flesh they are worthless.

Proboscidea The common variety. Sow in rich, warm soil when danger of frost is over, in drills three feet apart, and thin the plants out to two feet in the row. Pkt. 10c; Oz. 30c; 2 Oz. 55c; ¼ Lb. $1.00; Lb. $3.00 *(See also page 79)*.

MUSK MELON

CULTURE—Plant the seed in hills six feet apart each way, dropping ten to twelve seeds in a hill. After the plants begin to crowd and the striped beetles are pretty well gone thin to four of the most vigorous plants in a hill. Give frequent but shallow cultivation, until the plants make runners so long that this is impracticable. Rich earth for the young plants is far better than manure, but if the latter must be used, see that it is well rotted and thoroughly mixed with the soil.

If the plants grow very rank, more and finer fruit will be secured by pinching off the ends of the shoots when they are about three or four feet long. The quality of melons of all varieties is largely dependent upon conditions of growth and ripening. Unhealthy vines or unfavorable weather produces fruit of comparatively poor flavor.

The plants are liable to attack from the striped beetles, which are so numerous in some cases as to destroy them. The beetles may be kept off by frequent dusting with air slacked lime, soot or sifted ashes diluted with fine road earth; care should be taken not to use too much of any of the above materials or the vines will be injured.

GREEN FLESHED VARIETIES

Jenny Lind Fruit small, somewhat flattened, deeply ribbed; flesh green and exceedingly sweet. It ripens early and on account of its size is particularly good for hotel use. Pkt. 5c; Oz. 10c; 2 Oz. 15c; ¼ Lb. 25c; Lb. 90c.

Extra Early Citron A small, round melon, valuable on account of its extreme earliness and great productiveness. The skin is green, becoming yellowish at maturity. The flesh is light green, sweet and of fair quality. Pkt. 5c; Oz. 10c; 2 Oz. 15c; ¼ Lb. 25c; Lb. 90c.

Netted Gem, or Rocky Ford This has become one of the most popular of small or basket melons and is shipped in large quantities from Colorado and Arizona. The fruit is oval, slightly ribbed, densely covered with fine netting. Flesh thick, green, very sweet and high flavored. We offer an exceptionally fine stock of this early sort, the fruit being very uniform in shape and quality. Pkt. 5c; Oz. 10c; 2 Oz. 15c; ¼ Lb. 25c; Lb. 90c.

Extra Early Hackensack We offer under this name distinct stock, very different and much superior to that often sold as Extra Early Hackensack. The fruit is medium sized, nearly round, with deep ribs and very coarse netting. The flesh is green, a little coarse but very juicy and sweet. Pkt. 5c; Oz. 10c; 2 Oz. 25c; ¼ Lb. 45c; Lb. $1.25

SMALL GREEN NUTMEG MUSK MELON.

Small Green Nutmeg Fruit of medium size, slightly ribbed, globular. Skin dark green and nearly covered with broad, shallow netting. Flesh thick, a little coarse, but of fine flavor. This variety is early and in universal demand for both home and market and is a size well suited for hotel and restaurant use. Our stock is carefully grown and selected and will be found first-class in every particular. Pkt. 5c; Oz. 10c; 2 Oz. 15c; ¼ Lb. 25c; Lb. 90c.

Baltimore, or Acme Fruit medium sized, oval, slightly pointed at stem end, slightly ribbed, covered when ripe with coarse netting. Flesh thick, green, very fine flavored and sweet. One of the most uniformly good melons on our list. Pkt. 5c; Oz. 10c; 2 Oz. 20c; ¼ Lb. 30c; Lb. $1.00

Early White Japan A very early, medium sized variety of fine quality. Fruit oval, white, with green flesh which is very sweet and fine flavored. One of the best for the home garden. Pkt. 5c; Oz. 10c; 2 Oz. 20c; ¼ Lb. 30c; Lb. $1.00

Cosmopolitan This variety was introduced by us in 1894, and combining, as it does, the firm, sweet flesh of the French Cantaloupe and the delicious flavor of the American Musk Melon, it is truly cosmopolitan in character. It is the most beautiful of the green fleshed melons. Fruit slightly oval, nearly round without ribs. Color light green, but becoming covered at maturity with dense, silver gray netting. Flesh green, firm, sweet and uniformly high flavored. Pkt. 5c; Oz. 15c; 2 Oz. 25c; ¼ Lb. 40c; Lb. $1.25

NETTED GEM, OR ROCKY FORD MUSK MELON.

Improved Large Green Nutmeg Vines vigorous, hardy, productive; fruit very large, round, slightly flattened at both ends, ribbed, covered with coarse netting; flesh very thick and of the highest flavor. Pkt. 5c; Oz. 10c; 2 Oz. 20c; ¼ Lb. 30c; Lb. $1.00

Hackensack, or Turk's Cap Fruit very large, the diameter much more than the length; ribs large and of irregular width, densely covered with coarse netting; flesh green, thick, coarse, but very sweet and fine flavored. Our stock is true to the "Turk's Cap" type, and after careful comparison with that of other growers we do not hesitate to pronounce it the best in the country. Pkt. 5c; Oz. 10c; 2 Oz. 20c; ¼ Lb. 30c; Lb. $1.00

HACKENSACK MUSK MELON.

Champion Market Fruit large, round or slightly oval, with very shallow depressions and covered with dense netting. Flesh green, of medium texture, very thick and sweet. The variety is an improvement on Montreal and will suit those who like a large, sweet, green fleshed sort. Pkt. 5c; Oz. 15c; 2 Oz. 25c; ¼ Lb. 40c; Lb. $1.50

Bay View Fruit of the largest size, frequently weighing ten to fifteen pounds, long, deeply ribbed and covered with coarse netting; flesh green, thick and of fine flavor. By far the best of the large melons and so hardy as to be the best for inexperienced cultivators. A late variety. Pkt. 5c; Oz. 15c; 2 Oz. 25c; ¼ Lb. 40c; Lb. $1.25

COPYRIGHTED 189_ BY D. M. FERRY & CO.

MUSK MELON—Continued

ORANGE FLESHED VARIETIES

PETOSKEY, or Paul Rose

A yellow fleshed sort of suitable size for a basket melon and of the finest quality. Fruit oval, about five inches in diameter and in general appearance much like the Netted Gem, but a little larger. Flesh orange colored, high flavored, very thick, firm and sweet. Pkt. 5c; Oz.10c; 2 Oz.20c; ¼Lb. 30c; Lb.$1.00

OSAGE,
or Improved Miller's Cream

Fruit medium sized, oval, slightly ribbed, dark green in color, covered more or less with shallow netting. The flesh is deep salmon color and very thick, there being but a slight cavity in the center of even the largest fruit. A favorite variety for the later markets. We have taken a great deal of pains to develop the thick, deep, rich colored and fine flavored flesh of this sort, and careful comparisons on our trial grounds prove it to be unequaled, even by "Special Selected Seed," offered at very high prices. Pkt. 5c; Oz. 15c; 2 Oz. 25c; ¼ Lb. 40c; Lb. $1.25

PETOSKEY, OR PAUL ROSE MUSK MELON.

McCOTTER'S PRIDE
This late variety is the result of long continued skillful breeding and selection, with the purpose of securing a very large melon of spherical shape, with flesh of fine grain and high quality. The fruit is very large, nearly round, evenly and moderately ribbed, dark green in color, partially covered with gray netting. The flesh is orange-red, very thick, sweet and of fine flavor. Pkt. 5c; Oz. 15c; 2 Oz. 25c; ¼ Lb. 40c; Lb. $1.25

Emerald Gem
A splendid variety. Fruit small to medium sized, globular, or slightly flattened at the ends, only slightly notted and ribbed. Skin deep green while young, becoming slightly tinged with yellow as the fruit matures; flesh deep salmon-yellow, thick, ripening close to the rind and exceedingly high flavored. This variety has steadily grown in popular favor, and in many large markets leads all other kinds, because of its sweetness and convenient size. Pkt. 5c; Oz. 15c; 2 Oz. 25c; ¼ Lb. 40c; Lb. $1.50

DEFENDER
A splendid variety, originated and introduced by us. It is one of the very best yellow fleshed sorts and in some respects is far superior to any of this class. The fruit is medium sized, oval in shape, slightly ribbed, covered with gray netting. The flesh is firm, fine grained, rich, deep yellow, darker than that of the Osage and of higher flavor. The flesh extends to the rind and retains its color and quality quite to the outer shell which, though thin, is very hard and firm, so that one can remove the edible portion with a spoon, leaving a rind no thicker than that of an orange. The vine is vigorous and very productive. The fruit, because of the hard, firm rind, keeps and bears shipment remarkably well. We know of no yellow fleshed sort so desirable for either the home or market garden. Pkt. 5c; Oz. 15c; 2 Oz. 25c; ¼ Lb. 40c; Lb. $1.25.

Surprise
This old variety is still very highly esteemed. Vines hardy and productive; fruit oval, not deeply ribbed, covered with slight patches of netting; skin yellowish-white; flesh deep salmon color, very rich and high flavored. Pkt. 5c; Oz. 15c; 2 Oz.25c; ¼Lb. 40c; Lb. $1.25.

Long Yellow
A very large variety; long; oval, deeply ribbed; flesh thick, light salmon colored and of a peculiarly musky flavor. This variety is often used in its green state for mangoes. Pkt.5c; Oz. 10c; 2 Oz.15c; ¼Lb.25c; Lb. 90c.

DEFENDER MUSK MELON.

WATER MELON

Although the Water Melon is a tropical fruit and can be most easily grown in the south on a warm, rich, sandy soil, yet no one need abandon its culture because he has not these conditions, for some of the sweetest melons ever produced have been grown in Michigan, in the latitude of 45 degrees north, and Cuban Queens weighing over 60 pounds have been raised in cold clay soil in northern Ohio.

CULTURE.—In order to get good Water Melons, it is essential that the plants get a good start, and to this end it is important to prepare hills about eight feet apart, by thoroughly working into the soil an abundance of well rotted manure —hen manure, guano, or other forms rich in nitrogen, being most desirable. Over this highly manured soil put an inch or more of fresh earth and plant the seed on this, covering it about an inch in depth. It is important that the seed should not be planted before the ground becomes warm and dry, as the young plants are very sensitive to cold and wet. When the plants have formed the first pair of rough leaves, they should be thinned so as to leave two or three of the strongest and best to each hill. Frequent watering of the plants with liquid manure will hasten the growth, thus diminishing the danger from insect pests.

Phinney's Early A valuable variety for use in the north as it is hardy and a sure cropper. Vines vigorous and productive, fruiting quite early; fruit medium sized, oblong, smooth, marbled with two shades of green; rind thin; flesh pink, tender and crisp. Pkt. 5c; Oz. 10c; 2 Oz. 15c; ¼ Lb. 20c; Lb. 50c.

D. M. Ferry & Co's Peerless
One of the best sorts for private gardens and for market gardeners who deliver direct to consumers. Vine moderately vigorous, hardy, productive; fruit medium sized, oval, bright green, finely mottled; rind thin; flesh bright scarlet, solid to the center, crisp, tender and very sweet. Pkt. 5c; Oz. 10c; 2 Oz. 15c; ¼ Lb. 20c; Lb. 50c.

Gypsy, or Georgia Rattlesnake
One of the largest, oldest and most popular sorts, particularly in the south. Fruit oblong, of light green color, finely marked with a darker shade. Flesh bright scarlet and very sweet. Pkt. 5c; Oz. 10c; 2 Oz. 15c; ¼ Lb. 20c; Lb. 50c.

Sweet Heart This melon was introduced by us in 1894 and it has become very popular as a shipping melon, particularly in the south. Vine vigorous and productive, ripening its fruit early. Fruit large, oval, very heavy; rind thin but firm; flesh bright red, firm, solid but very tender, melting and sweet. Fruit retains its good quality for a long time after ripening. Our stock is the very best. Pkt. 5c; Oz. 10c; 2 Oz. 15c; ¼ Lb. 20c; Lb. 60c.

Kolb's Gem Vines of medium size but remarkably vigorous and healthy. Leaves of medium size, deeply cut with a peculiar frilled edge. Fruit of the largest size, round or slightly oval marked with irregular mottled stripes of dark and light green. Rind exceedingly hard and firm, making it a good sort for shipping long distances. Flesh bright red, solid, a little coarse, but sweet and tender. Pkt. 5c; Oz. 10c; 2 Oz. 15c; ¼ Lb. 20c; Lb. 50c.

SWEET HEART WATER MELON.

Dixie A popular market sort. Vine vigorous, large growing and hardy, ripening its fruits earlier than most of the large sorts; fruit medium sized to large, about one-third longer than thick. Color of skin dark green, striped with a lighter shade; rind thin but tough; flesh bright scarlet, ripens closely to the rind, is of the best quality and free from the hard, coarse center which is so objectionable a feature of many shipping melons. Pkt. 5c; Oz. 10c; 2 Oz. 15c; ¼ Lb. 20c; Lb. 50c.

Triumph A southern variety which has become very popular with shippers. The fruit is uniformly large, nearly round, dark green, often indistinctly striped with a lighter shade and has a thin and firm rind which makes it an excellent shipper; flesh bright red and of good quality. Pkt. 5c; Oz. 10c; 2 Oz. 15c; ¼ Lb. 20c; Lb. 60c.

Monte Cristo, or Kleckley's Sweets A variety unsurpassed for home use or near markets. Vine vigorous and productive; fruit of medium size, oval; color dark green, often showing fine russeting; flesh very bright, rich red, and exceedingly sweet. This variety is so crisp and tender that it will not stand shipping, the fruit bursting open if subjected to even a slight jar, or when the rind is penetrated with a knife. Pkt. 5c; Oz. 10c; 2 Oz. 15c; ¼ Lb. 20c; Lb. 60c.

Florida Favorite A splendid melon of largest size and excellent quality; fruit long, mottled dark green with stripes of lighter shade; rind thin but firm; flesh very bright, deep red; very sweet, tender and excellent. Pkt. 5c; Oz. 10c; 2 Oz. 15c; ¼ Lb. 20c; Lb. 60c.

FLORIDA FAVORITE WATER MELON.

WATER MELON—CONTINUED

Ferry's Iceberg
We introduced this splendid melon in 1902. In general shape, size and appearance it is similar to the well known Kolb's Gem, but is distinctly darker and the skin where the melon rests on the ground is rich yellow instead of white as in that variety. It has a very firm, hard rind and is as good a shipper as the Kolb's Gem, but the flesh is much deeper colored, extends nearer to the rind, is much more tender and sweet. This is much the best dark colored shipping melon yet produced and is superior to all others used for this purpose. Pkt. 5c; Oz. 10c; 2 Oz. 15c; ¼ Lb. 20c; Lb. 60c.

FERRY'S ICEBERG
WATER MELON.

Cuban Queen
Fruit medium sized to large, globular or oval; skin striped light and dark green in sharp contrast; rind medium thick, but stands shipment well. Flesh bright red, solid, very crisp and sugary. Pkt. 5c; Oz. 10c; 2 Oz. 15c; ¼ Lb. 20c; Lb. 50c.

Dark Icing
Fruit large, nearly round, dark green, very indistinctly mottled with lighter shade. Flesh very rich, bright red. Pkt. 5c; Oz. 10c; 2 Oz. 15c; ¼ Lb. 20c; Lb. 50c.

Long Light Icing
Our stock of this sort is much better than that usually offered, and superior to many strains offered as Early Monarch, etc. Repeated trials have demonstrated that we have very fine stocks of Icing melons, each variety being distinct and showing the type well instead of being a mere mixture of white seeded sorts. The melons of the Long Light Icing variety are uniformly long and large and the flesh deep, rich red, and of splendid quality. Pkt. 5c; Oz. 10c; 2 Oz. 15c; ¼ Lb. 20c; Lb. 60c.

Round Light Icing
Fruit medium sized, round, very light green or white, mottled with slightly darker green. Flesh bright, light red, very sweet and tender. Pkt. 5c; Oz. 10c; 2 Oz. 15c; ¼ Lb. 20c; Lb. 60c.

Mountain Sweet
A large, oval variety; rind green and rather thick; flesh scarlet and quite solid to the center, very sweet and delicious. This is an old standard sort and one of the best for the home garden. Pkt. 5c; Oz. 10c; 2 Oz. 15c; ¼ Lb. 20c; Lb. 50c.

Ice Cream
Medium sized, with very sweet, scarlet flesh. A good variety for home market. Pkt. 5c; Oz. 10c; 2 Oz. 15c; ¼ Lb. 20c; Lb. 50c.

Citron
Grows uniformly round and smooth, striped and marbled with light green. Flesh white and solid; seeds red. This variety is not used for eating in the raw state, but for preserves, pickles, etc. Pkt. 5c; Oz. 10c; 2 Oz. 15c; ¼ Lb. 25c; Lb. 75c.

Mushroom
The Mushroom is an edible fungus of a white color, changing to brown when old. The gills are loose, of pinkish-red, changing to liver color. It produces no seed, but instead there is developed a white, fibrous substance in broken threads, called spawn, which is developed and preserved in horse manure, pressed in the form of bricks. Thus prepared it will retain its vitality for years.

Mushrooms can be grown in cellars, in sheds, in hotbeds or sometimes in the open air, the great essential being a uniform degree of temperature and moisture. Fermenting horse manure at a temperature of about 70 degrees, mixed with an equal weight of fresh sod loam, is made into beds the size required and eight to twelve inches deep. See to it that the bed is packed firmly and evenly. In this bed plant the broken pieces about six inches apart; cover the whole with two inches of light soil and protect from cold and rain. One brick will plant eight to ten square feet of bed. The mushrooms will appear in about six weeks. Water sparingly and with lukewarm water.

English Mushroom Spawn, in bricks of about 1 lb., 25c. per pound, prepaid; 5 lbs. for $1.00 prepaid.

French Mushroom Spawn, 3 lb. boxes, $1.50 each, prepaid.

Mustard
Mustard is not only used as a condiment but the green leaves are used as a salad or cut and boiled like spinage. Sow as early in the spring as the ground will permit, in drills about eighteen inches apart, covering one-half inch deep. For succession, sow every few weeks till autumn. Water freely. In the south the seed should be sown in autumn and the plants used early in the spring as a salad and for greens.

WHITE ENGLISH. The leaves are light green, mild and tender when young; seed light yellow. Pkt. 5c; Oz. 10c; 2 Oz. 10c; ¼ Lb. 15c; Lb. 40c.

Southern Giant Curled
This mustard is very highly esteemed in the south, where the seed is sown in the fall and the plants used very early in the spring as a salad. Our stock is the true curled leaf. Pkt. 5c; Oz. 10c; 2 Oz. 15c; ¼ Lb. 20c; Lb. 60c.

Nasturtium
Sow after the ground is warm, in drills one inch deep, by the side of a fence, trellis work, or some other support to climb upon. Nasturtiums will thrive in good ground in almost any situation, but are more productive in a light soil.

TALL MIXED GARDEN. Cultivated not only for ornament but its beautiful orange colored flowers serve as a garnish for dishes and the young leaves are excellent for salads. The green seed pods preserved in vinegar, make a pickle greatly esteemed by many. Pkt. 5c; Oz. 10c; 2 Oz. 15c; ¼ Lb. 25c; Lb. 75c. Other varieties see Flower Seeds, page 81.

Okra, or Gumbo
Cultivated for its young seed pods which are used in soups or stewed and served like asparagus. It is highly esteemed in the south for making the famous gumbo soup. The pods, when young and tender, may be sliced in sections and strung on a thread and hung up in the shade to cure as one would dry apples; in this condition they can be used for soup at any time.

Culture—Plant in hills about four feet apart, putting six to eight seeds in a hill and after the plants are well started, cut out all but two. The dwarf sorts can be planted much closer in hills two to three feet apart or in drills two feet apart thinning the plants to about one foot apart in the row. Gather the pods when quite green and about an inch and a half long.

White Velvet
A great improvement on the old White or the Green. The plant is of medium height, bearing a large crop of white, smooth pods which retain their tenderness until nearly full size. Pkt. 5c; Oz. 10c; 2 Oz. 15c; ¼ Lb. 20c; Lb. 60c.

Perkins' Mammoth Long Pod
Plant dwarf, very early and productive. The pods are long, slender, deep green and remain tender much longer than most sorts. Pkt. 5c; Oz. 10c; 2 Oz. 15c; ¼ Lb. 20c; Lb. 60c.

DWARF WHITE. The longest podded variety; vines two feet high and very productive. Mature pods long, very thick and fleshy. Pkt. 5c; Oz. 10c; 2 Oz. 15c; ¼ Lb. 20c; Lb. 50c.

DWARF GREEN. An early and very productive sort. Pods dark green, thick and fleshy. Pkt. 5c; Oz. 10c; 2 Oz. 15c; ¼ Lb. 20c; Lb. 60c.

⇒ ONION ⇐

The Onion not only contains considerable nutriment and has valuable medicinal properties, but is most useful in counteracting the bad effects of sedentary life. The disagreeable odor it imparts to the breath may be avoided in a great measure by thorough cooking, or by eating a few leaves of parsley.

In onion culture, thorough preparation of the ground, careful sowing and the best of after culture, though essential for a full yield, will avail nothing unless seed of the best quality be used. Given the same care and conditions, the product from two lots of onion seed of the same variety but of different quality may be so unequal in the quantity of merchantable onions, that it would be more profitable to use the good seed though it cost twenty times as much as the other.

Our thorough equipment and long experience in growing onion seed of the very best quality, enables us to say without hesitation that our stock is fully equal to any, and superior in quality to most that is offered.

Although onions are often raised from sets and from division, by far the best and cheapest mode of production is from seed. The facility with which seed is sown, and the superior bulbs it produces, recommend it for general use.

HOW TO RAISE ONIONS

THE SOIL. A crop of onions can be grown on any soil which will produce a full crop of corn, but on a stiff clay, very light sand or gravel, or on some muck or swamp lands, neither a large nor a very profitable crop can be grown. We prefer a rich loam with a slight mixture of clay. This is much better if it has been cultivated with hoed crops, kept clean from weeds and well manured for two years previous, because if a sufficient quantity of manure to raise an ordinary soil to a proper degree of fertility is applied at once, it is likely to make the onions soft. The same result will follow if we sow on *rank*, mucky ground or on that which is too wet.

MANURING. There is no crop in which a liberal use of manure is more essential than in this, and it should be of the best quality, well fermented and shoveled over at least twice during the previous summer to kill weed seeds. If rank, fresh manure is used, it is liable to result in soft bulbs with many scallions. Of the commercial manures, any of the high grade, complete fertilizers are good for ordinary soils and even very rich soils are frequently greatly benefited by fine ground bone and mucky ones by a liberal dressing of wood ashes.

PREPARATION. Remove all refuse of previous crops in time to complete the work before the ground freezes up, and spread the composted manure *evenly* at the rate of about fifty cart loads to the acre. This should first be cultivated in and then the ground ploughed a moderate depth, taking a narrow furrow in order to thoroughly mix the manure with the soil. Carefully avoid tramping on the ground during the winter. Cultivate or thoroughly stir the soil with a deep working cultivator or harrow *as early in the spring* as it can be worked, and then in the opposite direction with a light one, after which the entire surface should be made fine and level with a smoothing harrow or hand rakes. It is impossible to cultivate the crop economically unless the rows are perfectly straight; to secure this, stretch a line along one side, fourteen feet from the edge, and make a distinct mark along it; then, having made a wooden marker, something like a giant rake with five teeth about a foot long and standing fourteen inches apart, make four more marks by *carefully* drawing it with the outside tooth in, and the *head at right angles* to the perfectly straight mark made by the line. Continue to work around

this line until on the third passage of the marker you reach the side of the field where you began; measure fifteen feet two inches from the last row, stretch the line again and mark around in the same way. This is better than to stretch a line along one side as it is impossible to prevent the rows gradually becoming crooked, and by this plan we straighten them after every third passage of the marker.

SOWING THE SEED. This should be done as soon as the ground can be gotten ready, and can be done best by a hand seed drill. This should be carefully adjusted to sow the desired quantity of seed about one-half inch deep. The quantity needed will vary with the soil, the seed used, and the kind of onions desired. Thin seeding gives much larger onions than thick seeding. Four or five pounds per acre is the usual quantity needed to grow large onions. We use a drill with a roller, attached, but if the drill has none, the ground should be well rolled with a light *hand roller* immediately after the seed is planted.

CULTIVATION. Give the onions the first hoeing just skimming the ground between the rows, as soon as they can be seen in the row. Hoe again in a few days, this time close up to the plants, after which weeding must be begun. This operation requires to be carefully and thoroughly done. The weeder must work on his knees astride the row, stirring the earth around the plants, in order to destroy any weeds that have just started. At this weeding or the next, according to size of the plants, the rows should be thinned, leaving from eight to twelve plants to the foot. In ten days or two weeks they will require another hoeing and weeding similar to the last, and two weeks later give them still another hoeing, and if necessary, another weeding. If the work has been *thoroughly done at the proper time*, the crop will not require further care until ready to gather.

GATHERING. As soon as the tops die and fall, the bulbs should be gathered into windrows. If the weather is fine they will need no attention while curing, but if it is not they will need to be stirred by simply moving them slightly along the row. Cut off the tops when perfectly dry, about half an inch from the bulb, and then after a few days of bright weather the onions will be fit to store for the winter.

It will not do to store onions in large piles or masses, particularly in warm weather, or if they are the least moist, but if perfectly dry when gathered and they are spread not to exceed two feet in depth, they can be kept in fine condition till spring. Any arrangement will answer that will keep them dry and at a uniform temperature of about 32° Fr., or they may be kept frozen, care being taken not to disturb them. They should be thawed gradually. Repeated freezing and thawing will spoil them.

Extra Early Red

The first to ripen, and one of the handsomest of the red sorts. A small or medium sized, flat variety; an abundant producer and very uniform in shape and size; moderately strong flavored, and comes into use nearly two weeks earlier than the Large Red Wethersfield. Very desirable for early market use.

Pkt. 5c; Oz. 10c; 2 Oz. 15c; ¼ Lb. 25c; Lb. 90c.

EXTRA EARLY RED ONION.

LARGE RED WETHERSFIELD ONION.

Large Red Wethersfield This is the standard red variety and a favorite onion in the east, where immense crops are grown for shipment. Bulb large, somewhat flattened, oval shaped; skin deep purple-red; flesh purplish-white, moderately fine grained and rather strong flavored. Very productive, the best keeper and one of the most popular for general cultivation. It is more inclined to form large necks if planted on unsuitable soils than the Danvers, but is the best variety on poor or dry soils.
Pkt. 5c; Oz. 10c; 2 Oz. 15c; ¼ Lb. 25c; Lb. 90c.

ONION–Continued

SOUTHPORT RED GLOBE The onions from Southport, Conn., generally command an extra price in New York markets because of their beautiful shape and color, due partly to the variety grown and partly to the favorable soil and the extra care taken in handling the crop. The Southport Red Globe is of medium size, spherical, with small neck, very deep, rich red color, and of superior quality. We offer a strain of especially good quality and much superior to that usually sold. Pkt. 5c; Oz. 10c; 2 Oz. 20c; ¼ Lb. 30c; Lb. $1.00

Large Yellow Dutch, One of the oldest sorts. Flat; flesh **or Strasburg** white, fine grained, mild and well flavored. Pkt. 5c; Oz. 10c; 2 Oz. 15c; ¼ Lb. 25c; Lb. 80c.

Yellow Danvers A fine, productive variety of medium size; skin coppery-yellow; flesh white, comparatively mild and well flavored. Pkt. 5c; Oz. 10c; 2 Oz. 15c; ¼ Lb. 25c; Lb. 80c.

SOUTHPORT RED GLOBE ONION.

YELLOW GLOBE DANVERS ONION.

YELLOW GLOBE DANVERS The Danvers onion was originally oval or nearly flat, and it has been thought by many that its small neck and splendid ripening habit could only be obtained in onions of that shape, but we have by careful selection and breeding developed a strain which has to a remarkable degree the ripening habit and small neck of the original Danvers, and yet is decidedly more globular in form, thus giving larger yields and handsomer bulbs without sacrificing any of the good qualities of the most popular of yellow onions. Pkt. 5c; Oz. 10c; 2 Oz. 15c; ¼ Lb. 25c; Lb. 90c.

Southport Yellow Globe Of the same general character and quality as the Red Globe, but the color is a rich yellow. Pkt. 5c; Oz. 10c; 2 Oz. 20c; ¼ Lb. 30c; Lb. $1.00

Australian Brown A variety which has become very popular in California because of its good keeping qualities which are, however, more marked in that climate than in the eastern states. The bulb is medium sized, nearly spherical, being slightly flattened; reddish-brown in color and very hard; rather strong flavored. Pkt. 5c; Oz. 10c; 2 Oz. 15c; ¼ Lb. 25c; Lb. 80c.

MICHIGAN YELLOW GLOBE Finest shape, best color and yields largest crop of any yellow onion. The heaviest yield of onions is always obtained from rich, black lands. On such soils it is found that a globe shaped onion with a somewhat flattened base gives the largest returns, and to meet the demands of the professional onion growers located on such lands, we have developed this variety. The bulbs are large and uniformly spherical, with very small necks, the largest diameter below the center of the bulb; of a rich orange-yellow color; enormous yielders and splendid keepers. No onion grower can afford to plant inferior seed when such as this can be procured. Pkt. 5c; Oz. 10c; 2 Oz. 20c; ¼ Lb. 30c; Lb. $1.00

Extra Early Pearl A variety used for pickling, similar in many characteristics to the Queen, but the bulbs are somewhat thicker and with a little larger neck. Pkt. 5c; Oz. 15c; 2 Oz. 25c; ¼ Lb. 40c; Lb. $1.50

MICHIGAN YELLOW GLOBE ONION.

ONION—Continued

MAMMOTH YELLOW SPANISH, OR PRIZETAKER A very handsome onion of the largest size and nearly globular in form. Skin is yellowish-brown; flesh white, mild and tender. It is one of the best of the large, European sorts. If started very early in hotbeds it will produce a mammoth onion the first season. **Pkt. 5c; Oz. 10c; 2 Oz. 20c; ¼ Lb. 30c; Lb. $1.00**

White Portugal Onion.

MAMMOTH YELLOW SPANISH, OR PRIZETAKER ONION.

White Portugal, or American Silverskin A medium sized onion of mild flavor and with beautiful clear white skin. A favorite with many for use when young as a salad or bunching onion and for pickles; it is also a good keeper and fine for fall and early winter use. An excellent sort for gardeners who do not care to plant more than one variety. **Pkt. 5c; Oz. 15c; 2 Oz. 25c; ¼ Lb. 40c; Lb. $1.50**

WHITE GLOBE Yields abundantly, producing handsome and uniformly globe shaped bulbs. The flesh is firm, fine grained and of mild flavor. Sometimes called Southport White Globe. To produce the beautifully white onions so much sought in every market, one must first of all have good seed. Second, grow them well on rich lands. Third, exercise great care in harvesting and curing the crop. In Southport they "cord" up the onions in long rows, the bulbs on the inside and cover with boards so that the bulbs in the open air are well protected from rain or dew which would be sure to discolor them. We have by years of careful selection and breeding developed a strain which has no equal in uniformity and beauty of shape and color. **Pkt. 5c; Oz. 15c; 2 Oz. 25c; ¼ Lb. 40c; Lb. $1.50**

IMPORTED ONIONS

The flavor of the Italian varieties is mild, and they are in every way well adapted to culinary purposes. The following varieties have been tested in this country and have given perfect satisfaction.

Round White Silverskin This is a uniformly early, small, round, crisp, tender and very handsome variety with an opaque white skin, which does not turn green upon exposure to the sun as quickly as other sorts. An excellent sort for use in bunching, for pickles or when fully mature. **Pkt. 5c; Oz. 15c; 2 Oz. 25c; ¼ Lb. 40c; Lb. $1.50**

EARLY NEAPOLITAN MARZAJOLA. A beautiful, flat, white skinned variety, one of the *earliest* and a good keeper. It can be sown in February or March and will mature a crop very early in the season. In the south the seed can be sown in autumn and large onions produced in March. Known also as Early May. **Pkt. 5c; Oz. 15c; 2 Oz. 25c; ¼ Lb. 40c; Lb. $1.25**

MAMMOTH SILVER KING. An enormous onion, resembling the White Italian Tripoli, but is larger, slightly later and a better keeper, making it more desirable for fall and early winter market. Skin silvery white; flesh very tender and mild flavored. **Pkt. 5c; Oz. 15c; 2 Oz. 25c; ¼ Lb. 40c; Lb. $1.50**

GIANT WHITE ITALIAN TRIPOLI. A large, beautiful, pure white, flat onion of mild and excellent flavor. Will produce a somewhat larger bulb from seed than our White Portugal but to attain full size the seed should be started very early in a hotbed and the plants set out in rich soil. **Pkt. 5c; Oz. 15c; 2 Oz. 25c; ¼ Lb. 40c; Lb. $1.25**

Queen A very white skinned variety of especial value for pickling. If seed is sown out of doors in spring it will produce bulbs about an inch in diameter, maturing very early. If these bulbs are set out the following spring or if plants are grown under glass in winter and set out in the spring they will produce large onions. **Pkt. 5c; Oz. 15c; 2 Oz. 25c; ¼ Lb. 40c; Lb. $1.50**

ONION SETS

To raise onion sets from seed, use good ground prepared as for large onions and sow the seed very thick in broad drills, using forty to sixty pounds per acre. If the seed is sown thin, the bulbs will not only be too large for sets but will not be of the right shape and if sown thick on poor land, they will be necky or bottle-shaped. When onion seed is sown for sets, the seed may be planted somewhat later than for large bulbs, but fine crops are more likely to come from comparatively early sowing.

RED BOTTOM SETS. Treated precisely as top onions are, setting them out in the spring, instead of sowing seed. **Per Lb. 30c; postpaid; 100 Lbs. $8.00**

YELLOW BOTTOM SETS. Like the preceding, except in color, and used in the same manner. **Per Lb. 30c; postpaid; 100 Lbs. $7.50**

WHITE BOTTOM SETS. These do not keep as well as the red or yellow, but produce beautiful white onions early in the season. **Per Lb. 35c, postpaid; 100 Lbs. $9.00**

Prices by the 100 lbs. of all onion sets are subject to fluctuations of the market. The *price per single pound* will hold good throughout the season, or as long as our stock lasts.

The 100 pound prices of Onion Sets are by freight or express at purchaser's expense for transportation.

Parsley

Very useful for flavoring soups and stews and for garnishing. The green leaves are used for flavoring or they may be dried crisp, rubbed to a powder, and kept in bottles until needed.

CULTURE—Parsley requires rich, mellow soil. The seed is even slower than parsnip in germinating and should be sown as early as possible in the spring, in drills one to two feet apart, and when the plants are well up thin to one foot in the row. When the plants are about three inches high cut off all the leaves; the plant will start a new growth of leaves which will be brighter and better curled, and if these turn dull or brown they can be cut in the same way; every cutting will result in improvement. The moss curled variety makes beautiful border plants.

PLAIN. Leaves flat, deeply cut but not curled. It is often preferred on account of its very dark color and because of its hardiness but especially because of its superiority for flavoring, while the curled sorts are more extensively used for garnishing. Pkt. 5c; Oz. 10c; 2 Oz. 15c; ¼ Lb. 20c; Lb. 50c.

CHAMPION MOSS CURLED PARSLEY.

CHAMPION MOSS CURLED. A compact growing, finely cut and densely curled variety, of a deep green color. Owing to its fine color and handsome foliage, it is one of the most popular sorts. Pkt. 5c; Oz. 10c; 2 Oz. 15c; ¼ Lb. 25c; Lb. 75c.

PLAIN PARSLEY.

FINE TRIPLE CURLED OR MYATT'S GARNISHING. A fine, free growing but not large variety. The leaves are bright pale green and exceedingly handsome. Greatly prized for garnishing and table decoration. One of the best for market or private gardens. Pkt. 5c; Oz. 10c; 2 Oz. 15c; ¼ Lb. 20c; Lb. 60c.

TURNIP-ROOTED OR HAMBURG PARSLEY.

TURNIP-ROOTED, OR HAMBURG. The root is the edible portion of this variety and resembles a small parsnip both in color and shape. Flesh white, a little dry, and having a flavor similar to kohl rabi. Foliage same as plain parsley. Very hardy and should be cultivated like parsnip. Extensively grown and used for flavoring soups, etc. Pkt. 5c; Oz. 10c; 2 Oz. 15c; ¼ Lb. 20c; Lb. 50c.

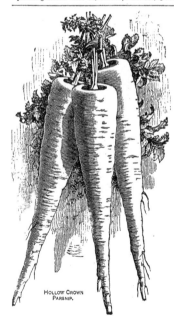

HOLLOW CROWN PARSNIP.

Parsnip

The value of the Parsnip as a culinary vegetable is well known, but is not generally appreciated at its full value for stock feeding. On favorable soil it yields an immense crop of roots, which are more nutritious than carrots or turnips and particularly valuable for dairy stock.

CULTURE—Parsnips do best on a deep, rich, sandy soil, but will make good roots on any soil which is deep, mellow and moderately rich. Fresh manure is apt to make the roots coarse and ill shaped. As the seed is sometimes slow to germinate, it should be sown as early as possible in drills two feet and one-half feet apart; cover one-half inch deep and press the soil firmly over the seed. Give frequent cultivation and thin the plants to five or six to the foot.

LONG WHITE DUTCH, OR SUGAR. Roots very long, white, smooth, tender and of most excellent flavor. Very hardy and will keep through winter without protection. Pkt. 5c; Oz. 10c; 2 Oz. 15c; ¼ Lb. 20c; Lb. 50c.

HOLLOW CROWN, OR GUERNSEY. Root white, very tender, with a smooth, clean skin. The variety is easily distinguished by the leaves growing from a depression on the top or crown of the root. Pkt. 5c; Oz. 10c; 2 Oz. 15c; ¼ Lb. 20c; Lb. 50c.

PEAS

CULTURE—For early peas the soil should be light and warm, but for general crop a moderately heavy soil is better. Fresh manure and very rich or wet mucky soil should be avoided, as they cause a rank growth of vine at the cost of the quality of the peas; such soil is often the cause of early sorts maturing unevenly. Sow *as early as possible* a few of some early variety on warm, quick soil, prepared the fall before. The general crop can be delayed until later, but we have met with better success from sowing all the varieties comparatively early, depending for succession upon selecting sorts that follow each other in maturity. The peas will give quicker returns if covered only one inch deep and where earliness is most important they may be treated in that way; but larger pods and more of them will be produced if the seed be planted in trenches three to six inches deep, *and covered with only one or two inches of soil.* When the plants are five or six inches high, fill the trench level with the surface; this will secure deep rooting, prevent mildew and prolong the bearing season. If the peas be covered to the full depth at first, or if water be allowed to stand in the trenches, they will not germinate or grow well.

The crop should be gathered as fast as it is fit for use. If even a few pods begin to ripen, not only will new pods cease to form, but those partly advanced will stop growing.

ALL WRINKLED PEAS *remain longer in season, are more delicate in flavor and are sweeter than the smooth sorts, for as in sugar corn, the wrinkled appearance indicates a greater amount of saccharine matter.*

EXTRA EARLY VARIETIES

Ferry's First and Best
The earliest and most even strain of white extra early peas in existence, maturing so well together that sometimes a single picking will secure the entire crop. Vines vigorous and hardy, two and one-half to three feet high. bearing three to seven straight pods, each containing five to seven medium sized, smooth peas of fair quality. The seed is small sized, smooth, yellowish-white. Pkt. 10c; Pt. 15c; Qt. 25c; 4 Qts. 75c; Bu. $4.50

D. M. Ferry & Co's Extra Early, Rural New Yorker, and Improved Early Daniel O'Rourke These three varieties are strains of first early white peas, similar to Ferry's First and Best. We offer carefully grown and selected stocks which are fully equal, if not superior to any obtainable elsewhere.

Pkt. 10c; Pt. 15c; Qt. 25c; 4 Qts. 75c; Bu. $4.50

Earliest of All, or
Alaska
By careful selection and growing we have developed stock of this smooth, blue pea of unequaled evenness in growth of vine and early maturity of pods. Vines two and one-half to three feet high, bearing four to seven pods which are filled with medium sized, bright-green peas of good flavor. Seed small, smooth and bluish-green in color. Matures all the crop at once and is an invaluable variety for market gardeners and canners. The stock we offer is much superior to most on the market. Pkt. 10c; Pt. 15c; Qt. 25c; 4 Qts. 75c; Bushel $4.00

Gregory's Surprise
This new, extra early, wrinkled pea is certain to become very popular. The vine is like that of the First and Best and is nearly as early, the pods continuing longer in condition for use and the peas are of better quality. Pkt. 10c; Pt. 25c; Qt. 35c; 4 Qts. $1.25; Bu. $6.50

American Wonder
The earliest of the dwarf wrinkled varieties. Vine stout, branching, about nine inches high and covered with well filled pods containing five to eight large, exceedingly sweet, tender and well flavored peas. Seed medium sized, wrinkled and pale green. We have taken great pains in growing our stock and know it to be much better than that usually offered. Pkt. 10c; Pt. 25c; Qt. 40c; 4 Qts. $1.50; Bu. $7.50

Nott's Excelsior
The best early, dwarf pea. It combines the good qualities of the American Wonder and Premium Gem peas. The vines are larger and more productive than American Wonder and earlier than Premium Gem. The peas, in sweetness and quality, are unsurpassed. Seed wrinkled and green in color. A most desirable sort for the market gardener and unsurpassed for the home garden. Pkt. 10c; Pt. 25c; Qt. 40c; 4 Qts. $1.50; Bushel $7.50

If Peas are wanted by mail or express, prepaid, add 10 cents per pint, 15 cents per quart, for charges.

PEA, EARLIEST OF ALL, OR ALASKA.

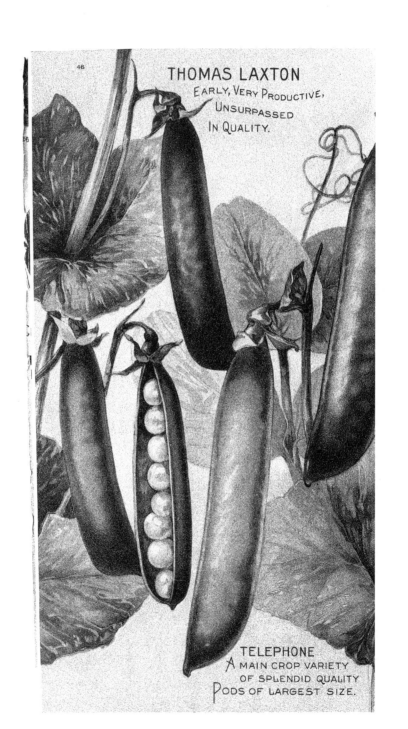

THOMAS LAXTON
Early, Very Productive,
Unsurpassed
In Quality.

TELEPHONE
A main crop variety
of splendid quality
Pods of largest size.

PEAS EXTRA EARLY VARIETIES

Gradus
An extra early, wrinkled pea. Vine of this most distinct sort is similar in appearance to Telephone, but only three to three and one-half feet high. The immense pods are as large as those of the Telephone, uniformly well shaped, handsome and more attractive than those of the first earlies. The peas are very large, of splendid quality and beautiful color which they retain after cooking. This variety is practically the same as that sold as Prosperity. We have taken great pains to secure true stock and have it well grown, so we are sure that every one who purchases our seed will be pleased with the variety. Pkt. 10c; Pt. 30c; Qt. 50c; 4 Qts. $1.75; Bu. $10.00

Improved Alpha
A tall growing, wrinkled pea, almost as early as American Wonder. Vines three to four feet high, slender, mostly unbranched and bearing four to six medium sized, slightly curved pods, each containing four to eight green, medium sized peas which are exceedingly sweet and tender. We offer a very superior strain of this variety and recommend Improved Alpha as the sweetest extra early sort. Pkt. 10c; Pt. 15c; Qt. 25c; 4 Qts. 75c; Bushel $4.50

Premium Gem
This variety is nearly as early as the American Wonder and the very productive vine is decidedly larger, growing to a height of from fifteen to eighteen inches. The pods are large and crowded with six to eight very large peas of fine quality. The seed is green, large, wrinkled, often flattened. Market gardeners use more of this sort than any other wrinkled pea. Pkt. 10c; Pt. 25c; Qt. 35c; 4 Qts. $1.25; Bu. $6.50

McLean's Little Gem
An early, dwarf, green, wrinkled variety, growing about eighteen inches high. When green it is very large, sweet and of delicious flavor. Pkt. 10c; Pt. 25c; Qt. 35c; 4 Qts. $1.25; Bu. $6.50

Thomas Laxton
A new, early, wrinkled variety of great merit. Vine three to three and one-half feet high, similar to that of Gradus, but darker in color, hardier and more productive. Pods large, long, with square ends, similar to but larger, longer and darker than those of the Champion of England and as uniformly well filled. The green peas are very large, fine colored and unsurpassed in quality. We are certain that this pea needs only to be known to become one of the most popular sorts for the market and home garden, as it certainly is one of the very best varieties yet produced. See opposite page. Pkt. 10c; Pt. 30c; Qt. 50c; 4 Qts. $1.75; Bushel $10.00

PREMIUM GEM PEA.

PEAS, SECOND EARLY

Bliss' Everbearing
Vine stout, about two and one-half feet high, bearing at the top six to ten broad pods. If these are picked as they mature and the season and soil are favorable, the plant will throw out branches bearing pods which will mature in succession, thus prolonging the season. The peas are very large and wrinkled, cook very quickly, are tender, of superior flavor and preferred by many to any other sort. Pkt. 10c; Pt. 15c; Qt. 25c; 4 Qts. 75c; Bu. $5.00

McLean's Advancer
A green, wrinkled variety about two and a half to three feet high, with broad, long pods which are abundantly produced and well filled to the ends. Considered by some the best of the second early sorts. This pea is used very extensively by market gardeners because of its productiveness, the fine appearance of its pods, and is popular with consumers on account of its quality. It is also largely used by canners. Careful comparison shows that our stock is unsurpassed. Pkt. 10c; Pt. 15c; Qt. 25c; 4 Qts. 75c; Bu. $4.00

The Admiral
Vines vigorous, about four feet high, comparatively slender, little branched. Pods usually borne in pairs and in great abundance; they are about two and one-half inches long, curved, bright green, crowded with six to nine peas of the very best quality and color. We know of no pea which remains palatable longer after it becomes large enough to use. Seed much wrinkled, of medium size, cream color. This variety ripens about with Telephone. Owing to its great vigor, productiveness, fine color, quality and suitable size of the green peas, it is admirably adapted for canners' use. Pkt. 10c; Pt. 15c; Qt. 25c; 4 Qts. 75c; Bushel $4.00

Telephone
The Telephone has become the leading pea with market gardeners whose trade appreciates fine appearance and high quality. Vines vigorous, growing about four feet high, with large, coarse, light colored leaves and producing an abundance of very large pods filled with immense peas which are tender, sweet and of excellent flavor. It comes into use soon after the Premium Gem and is one of the best sorts for either home or market. Notwithstanding the large amount of inferior and spurious stock which has been sold, no pea has attained greater popularity than this, thus showing that it has sterling merit. The stock we offer is prolific, and has been carefully selected. See opposite page. Pkt. 10c; Pt. 25c; Qt. 35c; 4 Qts. $1.25; Bu. $6.50

Telegraph
Stronger growing and hardier vine with darker foliage and pods than the Telephone; peas very large and of dark green color, seed almost smooth. A splendid sort for the market garden; will give good returns even under conditions that would cause most varieties to fail. Pkt. 10c; Pt. 20c; Qt. 30c; 4 Qts. $1.00; Bushel $5.50

Yorkshire Hero
Vines stout, about two and one-half feet high, bearing at the top a number of broad pods filled with large peas that remain a long time in condition for use, and which never become as hard as most sorts. The peas are of fine quality, and will be preferred to any other by those who like a rich, marrow-like pea. Seed large, wrinkled and flattened. Pkt. 10c; Pt. 15c; Qt. 25c; 4 Qts. 75c; Bushel $5.00

If Peas are wanted by mail or express, prepaid, add 10 cents per pint, 15 cents per quart, for charges.

PEAS, LATE

Horsford's Market Garden The vine of this variety is of medium height, giving the greatest number of pods of any on our list. Pods contain five to seven medium sized, sweet, dark green peas which retain their color and sweetness well after canning. Seed rather small and wrinkled. A very desirable variety for canners' use. Pkt. 10c; Pt. 15c; Qt. 25c; 4 Qts. 75c; Bu. $4.00

IMPROVED STRATAGEM Most stocks of the large podded, semi-dwarf English varieties of peas have been so wanting in uniformity and evenness of type as to disgust American planters, but by constant effort we have developed a stock of this, the best variety of that class, which comes true and we do not hesitate to pronounce it one of the best of the large podded sorts. The pods are of largest size and uniformly filled with very large, dark green pe s of the finest quality. One of the very best wrinkled varieties for market gardeners. Pkt. 10c; Pt. 25c; Qt. 35c; 4 Qts. $1.25; Bushel $7.00

PRIDE OF THE MARKET Vines of medium height, stiff, with large, dark green leaves and bearing at the top, generally in pairs, a good crop of large, dark green pods well filled with large peas of good flavor. We have given this variety special attention, and the stock we offer is so much superior to that commonly sold as to seem a different sort. We recommend it as one of the best of the large podded varieties. Pkt. 10c; Pt. 20c; Qt. 30c; 4 Qts. $1.00; Bushel $6.00

Shropshire Hero Vines about two and one-half feet high, wonderfully productive of large pods which are uniformly well filled with large, fine colored peas of good quality. Seed blue, wrinkled. Pkt. 10c; Pt. 15c; Qt. 25c; 4 Qts. 75c; Bu. $4.50

CHAMPION OF ENGLAND Very productive and universally admitted to be one of the richest and best flavored peas. Height four to five feet; seed light green and much shriveled. Very inferior and mixed stocks of this sort are frequently sold but when the seed is as well grown and selected as that we offer, we consider the variety equal in quality to any in cultivation, and one of the best of its season, either for the amateur or market gardener. Our stock is unequaled. Pkt. 10c; Pt. 15c; Qt. 25c; 4 Qts. 75c; Bu. $4.00

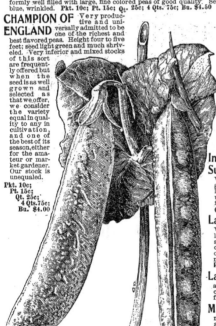

PRIDE OF THE MARKET PEA.

CHAMPION OF ENGLAND PEA.

Improved Sugar Marrow An improved strain of Large White Marrow, maturing nearly two weeks earlier. Vine and foliage light green in color growing about five feet high. Pods large, straight and borne in pairs, uniformly well filled with peas of fine marrow flavor. Pkt. 10c; Pt. 15c; Qt. 20c; 4 Qts. 60c; Bu. $3.50

Large White Marrowfat Cultivated quite extensively for canning. Vines about five feet high and of strong growth. Pods large, cylindrical, rough, light colored and well filled; seed large, smooth, round and light yellow. It is excellent for summer use, but inferior in quality to most of the newer sorts, although undoubtedly one of the most productive of the garden varieties. Pkt. 10c; Pt. 15c; Qt. 20c; 4 Qts. 50c; Bu. $2.75

Large Black Eye Marrowfat An excellent variety, growing about five feet high; a very prolific bearer of large pods; can be recommended as one of the very best Marrowfat sorts. Pkt.10c; Pt.15c; Qt.20c; 4 Qts.50c; Bu.$2.75

MELTING SUGAR There is a class of peas little known in this country, but much used abroad, in which the large, sweet, brittle and succulent pods have none of the tough, inner lining found in the ordinary varieties of garden peas; they are used in the same way as snap or string beans. The best of these edible podded sorts is the Melting Sugar, and our strain is exceptionally fine. The pods are very large, extremely tender, fine flavored, and are borne in great abundance on vines four to five feet high. *Crop failed.*

FIELD PEAS Field Peas deserve more general attention for fodder than they now receive. In the north, for dairy cows and for hogs, they are fully equal to corn, and about six weeks earlier. For cows, the crop should be cut and fed green. For hogs alone it can be used as pasturage.

Field peas can be sown either alone or with oats as early as the condition of the soil will permit. If the stubble from green winter rye or other crops cut in June be turned under and sown to mixed peas and oats, it will furnish a large amount of forage in August when grass pasture is usually short.

As fertilizer, field peas should be plowed under when in blossom. They will grow on land that will not produce clover. No. 1 White and Common White, market price; write for quotation.

If Peas are wanted by mail or express prepaid, add 10 cents per pint, 15 cents per quart, for charges.

Pepper

Peppers are used very extensively as a condiment. In Mexico, the hot varieties are eaten raw as we would eat radishes, but the greatest use is for seasoning other dishes. The large, thick fleshed, sweet varieties are eaten more extensively farther north, and are served in various ways, green or ripe, with vinegar and salt, like tomato salad, or made into mangoes by cutting one side, removing seeds and filling with chow chow pickles. The fruit is often used in stuffing pitted olives. The seed of pepper plant is used as bird food.

The culture of peppers is the same as for egg plant; the plants need quite as much heat to perfect them, though they mature sooner and may be sown a little later. Guano, hen dung, or any other bird manure, hoed into the surface soil when the plants are about six inches high, will wonderfully increase the product, and also improve the quality of the fruit.

RED CHERRY. A second early sort. Plant tall, bearing a profusion of round, bright red fruit which is very pungent when ripe. The plant, when in fruit, is very handsome and an ornament to the garden. **Pkt. 5c; Oz. 25c; 2 Oz. 40c; ¼ Lb. 75c; Lb. $2.50**

RED CHILI. A late variety, used in the manufacture of pepper sauce. The bright, rich red pods are about two inches long, one-third to one-half inch in diameter at the base, tapering to a sharp point and exceedingly pungent when ripe. Requires a long, warm season. The plants should be started quite early in hotbeds. **Pkt. 5c; Oz. 25c; 2 Oz. 40c; ¼ Lb. 75c; Lb. $2.50**

YELLOW CHILI. Similar in form to the Red Chili, but a little shorter and thicker, more pungent and of a very beautiful yellow color. **Pkt. 5c; Oz. 25c; 2 Oz. 40c; ¼ Lb. 75c; Lb. $2.50**

Long Red Cayenne
A favorite variety having a slim, pointed pod about four inches long and when ripe, of a bright red color. Extremely strong and pungent flesh. **Pkt. 5c; Oz. 25c; 2 Oz. 40c; ¼ Lb. 75c; Lb. $2.25**

LARGE BELL, OR BULL NOSE PEPPER.

GOLDEN DAWN. Plants quite dwarf but very prolific. Fruit medium to large in size, of inverted bell shape, rich, golden yellow color, with very thick, sweet, mild flavored flesh. **Pkt. 5c; Oz. 25c; 2 Oz. 40c; ¼ Lb. 75c; Lb. $2.25**

LARGE SQUASH. Fruit large, flat, tomato shaped, more or less ribbed; skin smooth and glossy; flesh mild, thick meated, pleasant to the taste, although possessing more pungency than the other large sorts; very productive and a fine variety for pickling. One of the earliest and most certain to mature. **Pkt. 5c; Oz. 25c; 2 Oz. 40c; ¼ Lb. 75c; Lb. $2.25**

Large Bell, or Bull Nose
Our stock of this well known variety, which is sometimes called Sweet Mountain, is a great improvement on the best stock obtainable only a few years ago. Plant vigorous, compact, very productive, ripening its crop uniformly and early. It is one of the most popular and desirable sorts. Fruit large, cylindrical, with thick, mild flesh; of excellent quality for use in salads and pickles; color, bright red when ripe. **Pkt. 5c; Oz. 25c; 2 Oz. 40c; ¼ Lb. 75c; Lb. $2.25**

Ruby King
An improved American variety reaching the largest size, often four to six inches in length, yet retaining the symmetrical shape of the smaller sorts. It is very bright colored, and the flesh is beautiful, sweet and mild flavored. One of the best for stuffed pickles. **Pkt. 5c; Oz. 25c; 2 Oz. 40c; ¼ Lb. 75c; Lb. $2.25**

Sweet Mountain, or Spanish Mammoth
Plants very vigorous, upright growing with moderately large leaves. The fruit does not ripen until very late. It is very large and long, often eight inches or more in length, by two in diameter, very smooth and handsome, being, when nearly mature, of a bright, deep green color, entirely free from any purple tinge and when fully mature, of a rich red. Flesh very thick, sweet and mild flavored. Well suited to use as a stuffed pickle and especially when green in making pepper salad. **Pkt. 5c; Oz. 25c; 2 Oz. 40c; ¼ Lb. 75c; Lb. $2.25**

SWEET MOUNTAIN, OR SPANISH MAMMOTH PEPPER.

Pumpkin

Pumpkins are not so particular in regard to soil as melons or cucumbers, but in other respects are cultivated the same, though on a larger scale. They are generally raised between hills of corn, but may be planted with success in fields by themselves. The pumpkin more properly belongs to the farm than the garden, especially as it readily mixes with and injures the quality of the finer squash.

LARGE YELLLOW. Grows to a large size and is adapted for cooking purposes and for feeding stock. The shape is irregular, some being round and others elongated or flattened. It is of deep, rich yellow color, fine grain and excellent quality. **Pkt. 5c; Oz. 10c; 2 Oz. 10c; ¼ Lb. 15c; Lb. 40c.** *By freight or express, at purchaser's expense, $20.00 per 100 lbs.*

SWEET CHEESE, OR KENTUCKY FIELD. A most popular variety in the south. Fruit flattened, the diameter being two or three times more than the length; skin mottled light green and yellow, changing to rich cream color as it matures; flesh yellow, tender and of excellent quality. **Pkt. 5c; Oz. 10c; 2 Oz. 15c; ¼ Lb. 20c; Lb. 50c,** *postpaid. By freight or express, at purchaser's expense, $20.00 per 100 lbs.*

Pie Pumpkin
We consider this a true pumpkin rather than a squash as it is sometimes called. The nearly round, comparatively small fruit is covered with a fine, gray netting over a smooth, yellow skin. Flesh very thick, sweet and fine flavored, *Crop failed.*

SUGAR OR NEW ENGLAND PIE. This handsome variety is small but very sweet, fine grained, and of the very best quality. Skin deep orange, flesh rich yellow. Excellent boiled or for pies. **Pkt. 5c; Oz. 10c; 2 Oz. 15c; ¼ Lb. 20c; Lb. 60c.**

SUGAR, OR NEW ENGLAND PIE PUMPKIN.

RADISH

For forcing, sow in hotbeds or under glass in rich, sandy soil, made perfectly level. Scatter evenly over the surface from sixty to one hundred and fifty seeds to the square foot and cover with one-half inch of soil sifted on, and attend carefully to the watering and airing. If the bed is a good one the whole crop can be marketed in twenty-one to forty days after planting. For open ground culture, sow on rich, sandy soil as soon in the spring as it is fit to work, in drills twelve inches apart and thin out the plants if necessary, to prevent crowding. A good dressing of nitrate of soda will greatly stimulate growth and insure tender, brittle roots. Successional sowings from one week to ten days apart will keep up a supply. After the hot weather of summer begins, it is better to sow the summer and winter varieties, as they do not become tough and stringy nor pithy so quickly as the early sorts. Radishes are subject to root maggots which make them useless for culinary purposes. We know of no certain remedy for this pest. We have found that the best preventive measures are to avoid the use of rank manure and not to sow on ground where radishes, turnips or cabbages were grown the year previous. We have been very careful to secure the very best seed possible, and there is none sold under other names which is better than that of the varieties we offer.

TRIUMPH SCARLET STRIPED, FORCING RADISH.

NON PLUS ULTRA, OR EARLY DEEP SCARLET TURNIP, FORCING A handsome, extra early forcing radish. Root small, nearly round; color bright scarlet. Tops very small; flesh white, crisp and well flavored. In shape and color one of the most handsome of the forcing sorts. Pkt. 5c; Oz. 10c; 2 Oz. 15c; ¼ Lb. 20c; Lb. 65c.

PRUSSIAN GLOBE This is the smallest forcing radish offered. Top distinctly small; root round or slightly flattened, very deep red in color and of the best quality. Remains in condition for use the longest of any of the first early forcing sorts and is a favorite where a very small, deep red radish is desired. Pkt. 5c; Oz. 10c; 2 Oz. 15c; ¼ Lb. 20c; Lb. 65c.

TRIUMPH SCARLET STRIPED, FORCING The roots are about the size and shape of Scarlet Turnip, White Tipped, Forcing, but are creamy white, beautifully marked with spots and dashes of carmine. The tops are white and the roots mature as early as any variety in cultivation. Desirable on account of its distinct beauty, earliness and good quality. Pkt. 5c; Oz. 10c; 2 Oz. 20c; ¼ Lb. 30c; Lb. $1.00

EARLY SCARLET TURNIP ROOTED. A small, round, red, turnip-shaped radish with a small top and of very quick growth. A very early variety, deserving general cultivation on account of its rich color and crisp, tender flesh. Desirable for forcing or early outdoor planting. Pkt. 5c; Oz. 10c; 2 Oz. 15c; ¼ Lb. 20c; Lb. 50c.

EARLY SCARLET TURNIP, WHITE TIPPED, FORCING
A beautiful variety, deep scarlet with white tip. As early as Non Plus Ultra, has as small a top, and may be planted as closely. It is more attractive in appearance and cannot fail to give satisfaction as a forcing radish; very popular as a market sort. Sold also as Rosy Gem, Rapid Forcing, etc. Pkt. 5c; Oz. 10c; 2 Oz. 15c; ¼ Lb. 20c; Lb. 65c.

EARLY SCARLET TURNIP, WHITE TIPPED One of the handsomest of the turnip radishes and a great favorite in many large markets for early planting outdoors. It is but little later than the White Tipped, Forcing, and will give entire satisfaction where extreme earliness and small top are not the chief considerations. Roots slightly flattened on the under side; color very deep scarlet with a distinct white tip; flesh white and of the best quality. Pkt. 5c; Oz. 10c; 2 Oz. 15c; ¼ Lb. 20c; Lb. 55c.

EARLY SCARLET TURNIP, WHITE TIPPED RADISH.

EARLY SCARLET GLOBE The roots of this variety are slightly olive shaped, a rich, bright scarlet in color; flesh white and tender; fit to pull as early as Non Plus Ultra but much larger when matured. We specially recommend this to gardeners whose markets demand a large, first early forcing radish. Pkt. 5c; Oz. 10c; 2 Oz. 15c; ¼ Lb. 20c; Lb. 60c.

Early White, Turnip Rooted An early, pure white radish, a little more flattened than Early Scarlet Turnip Rooted and a trifle later in maturing. While generally used for early outdoor planting, its very small top makes it suitable for forcing. Flesh white, semi-transparent, crisp and tender. Pkt. 5c; Oz. 10c; 2 Oz. 15c; ¼ Lb. 20c; Lb. 50c.

EARLY SCARLET GLOBE RADISH.

EARLY DEEP SCARLET, OLIVE SHAPED, SHORT LEAF This differs from the Early Scarlet Olive Shaped, in being earlier, having a smaller top and terminating more abruptly at the tip, all of which qualities make it very desirable for forcing; an excellent sort. Pkt. 5c; Oz. 10c; 2 Oz. 15c; ¼ Lb. 20c; Lb. 65c.

CRIMSON GIANT TURNIP A variety extraordinary in that, while growing to an unusually large size, it is always tender, crisp and of mild flavor. It remains in perfect condition a remarkably long time, and unlike other forcing varieties, does not become pithy even when twice their size in diameter. Root turnip shaped; color a beautiful crimson-carmine; flesh firm, crisp and tender. While very desirable as a second early forcing variety, we specially recommend it for outdoor planting. Pkt. 5c; Oz. 10c; 2 Oz. 15c; ¼ Lb. 25c; Lb. 75c.

☞ *The above varieties of radish are especially developed and selected for forcing. They should be grown quickly and used when small and tender, as they become pithy and tasteless when overgrown. Most of them are at their best when less than an inch in diameter.*

RADISH—Continued,

rly Scarlet, Root olive sha ed or a little longer. p Skin
lve Shaped scarlet; neck small; flesh white, tender
nd excellent. Early and best adapted or general crop, although may be sed for forcing. Pkt. 5c; Oz. 10c; Oz. 15c; ¼ Lb. 20c; Lb. 50c.

'ench Breakfast A quick-growing, medium
ized radish, rather oblong in shape; color beautiful scarlet, except near the tip, vhere it is pure white. A splendid variety or the table on account of its excellent juality and attractive color. Pkt. 5c;)z. 10c; 2 Oz. 15c; ¼ Lb. 20c; Lb. 50c.

lf Long Deep Scarlet The roots of t h i s
iardy and desirable variety are of a very orilliant, deep, rich red color and half long vith a somewhat tapering point; the flesh s very white, crisp and tender, and holds ts juiciness well, not becoming pithy till juite overgrown. Pkt. 5c; Oz. 10c; Oz. 15c; ¼ Lb. 20c; Lb. 55c.

)ng Brightest Scarlet, This is one of the
/hite Tipped brightest and handsomest colored scarlet rad-
ishes known and a decided improvement in earliness and color over other varieties of this class. Roots mature in about twenty-five days from time of planting and continue in good condition until full grown when they are as large in diameter but a little shorter than Early Long Scarlet Short Top. It has a small top and can be used for forcing. Pkt. 5c; Oz. 10c; 2 Oz. 15c; ¼ Lb. 20c; Lb. 55c.

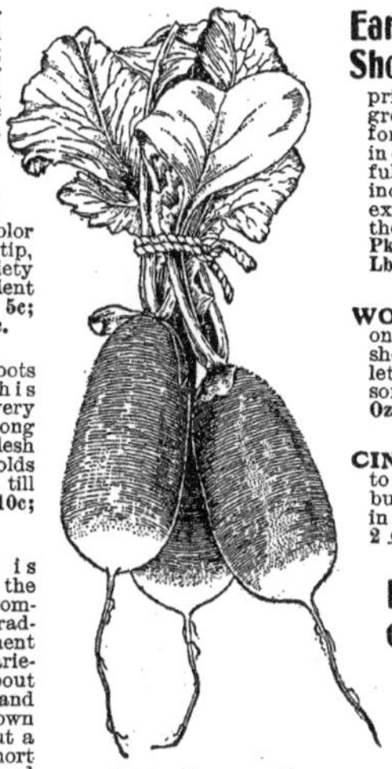

FRENCH BREAKFAST RADISH.

Early Long Scarlet, This variety is a standard and ex
Short Top, Improved cellent sort either for
private gardens or the market. The roots grow half out of the ground, are very uniform in shape, smooth and very bright red in color, and continue crisp and tender until fully matured when they are about six inches long. This is the variety grown so extensively in Petite Cote, Ontario, where the finest radishes in America are produced. Pkt. 5c; Oz. 10c; 2 Oz. 15c; ¼ Lb. 20c; Lb. 50c.

WOOD'S EARLY FRAME: This is not only a good variety for forcing, being shorter and thicker than the old Long Scarlet Short Top, but is one of the very best sorts for first crop out of doors. Pkt. 5c; Oz. 10c; 2 Oz. 15c; ¼ Lb. 20c; Lb. 50c.

CINCINNATI MARKET. Very similar to Early Long Scarlet, Short Top, Improved, but deeper red in color and remains longer in condition for use. Pkt. 5c; Oz. 10c; 2 Oz. 15c; ¼ Lb. 20c; Lb. 60c.

Long White Vienna, A very excellent variety
or Lady Finger with long, very smooth, white
roots which are crisp and tender. It matures shortly after Wood's Frame and is one of the most desirable of the white, summer sorts. Pkt. 5c; Oz. 10c; 2 Oz. 15c; ¼ Lb. 20c; Lb. 50c.

Improved Chartier, Although this American variety is too large for forcing, it is one of the very
or Shepherd best for sowing outdoors. The roots are in good condition for the table very early and continue hard and crisp until they reach a diameter of about an inch and a quarter, thus affording good roots for a much longer time than any of the preceding varieties. The long, cylindrical roots are scarlet-rose in color and gradually taper and shade into white at the tip. Pkt. 5c; Oz. 10c; 2 Oz. 15c; ¼ Lb. 20c; Lb. 50c.

Early Golden Yellow Oval A comparatively new sort, very popular in
the New York market. It matures very quickly, has a small top and neck, and resists the summer heat better than the scarlet or white kinds. Root oval, very smooth and handsome; bright, light yellow in color, and of fine quality. Our stock is grown from selected roots and is very fine. Pkt. 5c; Oz. 10c; 2 Oz. 15c; ¼ Lb. 20c; Lb. 60c.

Early White Giant Stuttgart Root large, often four inches in di-
ameter. top-shaped; skin white; flesh white and crisp, and not becoming pithy until very late, so that those not used as a summer radish can be stored for winter use. Pkt. 5c; Oz. 10c; 2 Oz. 15c; ¼ Lb. 20c; Lb.

White Strasburg When comparatively small, this variety is in good condition for use
and continues crisp and tender until matured, when the roots are four to five inches long and about two inches in diameter. This is considered one of the best large summer sorts. Pkt. 5c; Oz. 10c; 2 Oz. 15c; ¼ Lb. 20c; Lb. 55c.

LARGE WHITE SUMMER, TURNIP ROOTED. One of the earliest of the summer varieties. Root round, smooth, very white and handsome; flesh crisp, tender and rather pungent in flavor. Pkt. 5c; Oz. 10c; 2 Oz. 15c; ¼ Lb. 20c; Lb. 50c.

Golden Globe This variety is of quick growth, affording crisp and tender radishes even in
the hottest climate and is extensively grown in the south. Root uniformly globe shape, with skin golden yellow in color. Pkt. 5c; Oz. 10c; 2 Oz. 15c; ¼ Lb. 20c; Lb. 50c.

YELLOW SUMMER, TURNIP ROOTED. Very symmetrical, nearly round, with grayish-white skin, covered with a bright yellow russeting, thus making it very attractive. The flesh is firm, white and rather pungent. Pkt. 5c; Oz. 10c; 2 Oz. 15c; ¼ Lb. 20c; Lb. 50c.

GRAY SUMMER, TURNIP ROOTED, Turnip shaped, though often irregular in form. The skin of the upper part is mottled with greenish-brown, and often marked with transverse, white lines. Flesh mild, of greenish-white color and moderately solid. Medium early and a good variety for summer use. Pkt. 5c; Oz. 10c; 2 Oz. 15c; ¼ Lb. 20c; Lb. 60c.

IMPROVED CHARTIER, OR SHEPHERD RADISH.

RADISH, EARLY LONG SCARLET, SHORT TOP, IMPROVED.

Winter Radishes

Winter Radishes are not appreciated and grown by Americans as much as their merit warrants. They are easily grown, have few insect enemies and can be easily preserved through the winter, and there is no vegetable which furnishes a more acceptable relish. While quick growth is not so essential for these as for the earlier sorts, they do best on a rich soil which has been made as fine and friable as possible. Sow late in spring or during the summer in rows two feet apart and thin the plants about four to the foot. They may be pulled as wanted through the fall and on the approach of severe freezing weather should be harvested, part packed in damp sand and stored in a cool cellar or other easily accessible, cool place for winter use and the balance buried in the ground as one would bury potatoes for spring use.

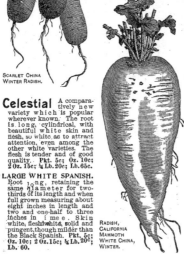

SCARLET CHINA
WINTER RADISH.

Scarlet China Roots cylindrical, or largest at the bottom, tapering abruptly to a small tap. Skin very smooth and of a bright rose color; flesh firm, crisp, tender and quite pungent. Pkt 5c; Oz. 10c; 2 Oz. 15c; ¼ Lb. 20c; Lb. 60c.

CALIFORNIA MAMMOTH WHITE CHINA. First introduced into this country by the Chinese in California. It is pure white, about one foot long and two or three inches through, tapering regularly to the tip. The flesh is tender and crisp, keeping well through the winter. Pkt. 5c; Oz. 10c; 2 Oz. 15c; ¼ Lb. 20c; Lb. 65c.

RADISH, LONG BLACK SPANISH, WINTER.

RADISH, CALIFORNIA MAMMOTH WHITE CHINA, WINTER.

Celestial A comparatively new variety which is popular wherever known. The root is long, cylindrical, with beautiful white skin and flesh, so white, as to attract attention, even among the other white varieties. The flesh is tender and of good quality. Pkt. 5c; Oz. 10c; 2 Oz. 15c; ¼ Lb. 20c; Lb. 65c.

LARGE WHITE SPANISH. Root long, retaining the same diameter for two-thirds of its length and when full grown measuring eight inches in length and two and one-half to three inches in diameter. Skin white, flesh white, solid and pungent, though milder than the Black Spanish. Pkt. 5c; Oz. 10c; 2 Oz. 15c; ¼ Lb. 20c; Lb. 60.

ROUND BLACK SPANISH. Roots round, sometimes top shaped, three or four inches in diameter; skin black, flesh white, very compact and highly flavored. An excellent sort for winter, as the roots keep a long time. Pkt. 5c; Oz. 10c; 2 Oz. 15c; ¼ Lb. 20c; Lb. 60c.

Half Long Black Winter An American sort of the same general character as the Long Black Spanish, but by many considered superior to either the Round or the Long Black Spanish. It is intermediate in shape between the two, and seems to combine the good qualities of each. Crop failed.

LONG BLACK SPANISH. One of the latest as well as the hardiest of radishes; an excellent sort for winter use. Roots of medium size, oblong, black and flesh of firm texture. Pkt. 5c; Oz. 10c; 2 Oz. 15c; ¼ Lb. 20c; Lb. 60c.

... Rhubarb, or Pie Plant ...

Rhubarb, familiarly known as Pie Plant, or Wine Plant, is cultivated in gardens for its leaf stalks, which are used for pies and tarts. Immense quantities are now annually sold in all the large markets. No private garden should be without it.

CULTURE—Rhubarb succeeds best in deep, somewhat retentive soil, and the richer this is and the deeper it is stirred, the better. Sow in drills an inch deep, and thin out the plants to six inches apart. In the fall, transplant into very highly manured and deeply stirred soil, setting them four to six feet apart each way, and give a dressing of coarse manure every spring. The stalks should not be plucked until the second year, and the plant never allowed to exhaust itself by running to seed. Our seed is saved from selected plants of the Linnæus, Victoria, Giant and other improved sorts, but like the seeds of fruit trees, rhubarb seed cannot be relied upon to reproduce the same varieties. Pkt. 5c; Oz. 15c; 2 Oz. 25c; ¼ Lb. 40c; Lb. $1.50, postpaid.

Rhubarb Roots, by express, not prepaid, 10c each; $1.00 per dozen; by mail, prepaid, 15c each, $1.50 per dozen.

RHUBARB, OR PIE PLANT.

Roquette A hardy annual. The long, smooth, glossy leaves when young are used like mustard for salads. It grows to a height of from nine to fifteen inches. Sow in shallow drills one foot apart, in early spring, and for succession every three or four weeks thereafter. The young leaves will be ready for cutting in about six weeks from time of planting. Water freely. Pkt. 5c; Oz. 10c; 2 Oz. 20c; ¼ Lb. 30c; Lb. $1.00

Salsify, or Vegetable Oyster

The long, white, tapering root of Salsify when cooked forms a good substitute for oysters, having a very similar flavor.

CULTURE—It succeeds best in a light, well enriched soil, which should be stirred to a good depth. Coarse and fresh manure should be avoided, as it will surely cause the roots to grow uneven and ill-shaped. Sow early and quite deep, giving the general culture recommended for parsnip. The roots are perfectly hardy, and may remain out all winter, but should be dug early in spring, as they deteriorate rapidly after growth commences. Store a quantity for winter use in a pit, or in a cellar, packed in damp earth or sand.

LARGE WHITE. The common variety; roots medium sized, smooth; flesh white. **Pkt. 5c; Oz. 10c; 2 Oz. 20c; ¼ Lb. 30c; Lb. $1.00**

MAMMOTH SANDWICH ISLAND. This is larger, stronger growing and less liable to branch than the Large White. It is an invaluable sort for market gardeners' use. **Pkt. 5c; Oz. 15c; 2 Oz. 25c; ¼ Lb. 40c; Lb. $1.25**

SALSIFY.

LARGE LEAVED FRENCH SORREL.

... Sorrel ...

The improved varieties of Sorrel when well grown and cooked like spinage make a very palatable dish. Sow in drills early in spring and thin the seedlings to six or eight inches apart in the row. One may commence cutting in about two months, and the plants will continue in full bearing from three to four years.

LARGE LEAVED FRENCH. The best garden variety, having large, pale green leaves of fine quality. **Pkt. 5c; Oz. 10c; 2 Oz. 20c; ¼ Lb. 30c; Lb. $1.00**

... Spinage ...

Should be planted in very rich ground, the richer the better. Sow in drills twelve to eighteen inches apart and begin thinning out the plants when the leaves are an inch wide. All should be cut before hot weather, or they will be tough and stringy. For early spring use, sow early in autumn and protect the plants with a light covering of leaves or straw. South of Cincinnati spinage can be grown through the winter with very little, or no covering.

Savoy Leaved The earliest variety and one of the best to plant in autumn for early spring use. Plant of upright growth, with pointed leaves which are crimped like those of Savoy cabbage. It grows rapidly to a suitable size for use and is quite hardy, but runs to seed quickly in warm weather. **Pkt. 5c; Oz. 10c; 2 Oz. 15c; ¼ Lb. 20c; Lb. 50c.**

ROUND SUMMER BROAD LEAVED. This variety is generally preferred in the north for early spring sowing and is the most popular with our market gardeners. The leaves are large, thick and fleshy. Though not quite as hardy as the Prickly Winter, it stands exposure very well. **Pkt. 5c; Oz. 10c; 2 Oz. 10c; ¼ Lb. 15c; Lb. 35c.**

BROAD FLANDERS. One of the most vigorous and strong growing varieties. The leaves are nearly round, uniformly deep green, quite thick and slightly crimped in the center. A very desirable sort. **Pkt. 5c; Oz. 10c; 2 Oz. 10c; ¼ Lb. 15c; Lb. 40c.**

Early Giant Thick Leaved An early maturing sort, with large leaves of fine, deep color. **Pkt. 5c; Oz. 10c; 2 Oz. 10c; ¼ Lb. 15c; 45c.**

Improved Thick Leaved A variety which grows very rapidly, forming a cluster of large, very thick, slightly wrinkled leaves of fine color and quality when cooked. Especially recommended for market gardeners. **Pkt. 5c; Oz. 10c; 2 Oz. 10c; ¼ Lb. 15c; Lb. 40c.**

SAVOY LEAVED SPINAGE.

Victoria An excellent sort which forms a very large, exceedingly thick, very dark green leaf somewhat curled in the center. It becomes fit for use nearly as early as any, remaining so much longer than most kinds and cannot fail to please, whether grown for the market or in the private garden. **Pkt. 5c; Oz. 10c; 2 Oz. 10c; ¼ Lb. 15c; Lb. 40c.**

Long Standing An improved, round seeded strain of excellent quality, coming quickly to maturity and remaining in condition for use much longer than most sorts. The leaves are smooth and very dark, rich green. Very popular with market gardeners. **Pkt. 5c; Oz. 10c; 2 Oz. 10c; ¼ Lb. 15c; Lb. 40c.**

Long Standing Prickly The plants mature a little later than the round leaved sorts but yield a large quantity of very thick and finely colored leaves. Has prickly seed. **Pkt. 5c; Oz. 10c; 2 Oz. 10c; ¼ Lb. 15c; Lb. 40c.**

PRICKLY WINTER. A very hardy variety and will withstand severe weather with only a slight protection of leaves or straw. The seed is prickly; leaves oblong or arrow shaped. It is used for fall sowing which in this latitude is made about the first of September. **Pkt. 5c; Oz. 10c; 2 Oz. 10c; ¼ Lb. 15c; Lb. 35c.**

VICTORIA SPINAGE.

SQUASH

The Squash is one of the most nutritious and valuable of all our garden vegetables. The summer varieties come to the table early in the season, while the winter sorts can be had in perfection from August until the summer varieties are again in condition. Few farmers appreciate the value of winter squash as food for stock. We think an acre of squash, costing no more to cultivate and much less to secure, will usually give as much food available for feeding stock as an acre of corn and we strongly urge our readers to try a "patch" for this purpose.

CULTURE—Squash plants are very tender and sensitive to cold, and planting must be delayed until settled warm weather. The general methods of culture are the same as those given for cucumbers and melons, but squash is less particular as to soil. The summer varieties should be planted four to six feet apart each way and the winter sorts eight to ten. Three plants are sufficient for a hill. In gathering the winter sorts care should be taken not to bruise or break the stem from the squash, as the slightest injury will increase the liability to decay.

SUMMER SQUASHES

Mammoth White Bush Scallop

Many seedsmen have listed Mammoth White Bush Scallop Squash but until we sent out our stock in 1895, there was no uniformly large, clear white, scalloped squash in trade. The fruit is a beautiful, clear waxy-white instead of the yellowish-white so often seen in the old Early White Bush Scallop and is superior to that variety in size and beauty. The handsomest of the scalloped squashes. Pkt. 5c; Oz. 10c; 2 Oz. 15c; ¼ Lb. 25c; Lb. 90c.

EARLY WHITE BUSH SCALLOP. A well known variety of dwarf habit and upright growth. Color creamy white; excellent for table use while young and tender. Pkt. 5c; Oz. 10c; 2 Oz. 15c; ¼ Lb. 25c; Lb. 75c.

LONG ISLAND WHITE BUSH. A variety that has become quite popular in the east. Vine very productive; fruit rather small and often nearly spherical, thick, with only a slight indication of a scallop; skin white, flesh tender and of good quality. Pkt. 5c; Oz. 10c; 2 Oz. 20c; ¼ Lb. 30c; Lb. $1.00

EARLY YELLOW BUSH SCALLOP. A very early, flat, scalloped variety of largest size; color yellow; flesh pale yellow and well flavored. We have developed a strain of the old Yellow Bush Scallop which is fully as productive but uniformly larger and flatter than the old stock and has a very small seed cavity. Its superiority is so great that we should be justified by prevailing custom in renaming it. Pkt. 5c; Oz. 10c; 2 Oz. 15c; ¼ Lb. 25c; Lb. 90c.

White Summer Crookneck
Introduced by us in 1895.

This excellent variety of our own introduction is the result of years of careful breeding and selection and it is now one of the most fixed and distinct of our summer squashes. The fruit is similar in size and shape to the Summer Crookneck, but of a beautiful ivory white color and unsurpassed in quality. We recommend this sort as the most beautiful and one of the very best of the summer varieties. Pkt. 5c; Oz. 10c; 2 Oz. 20c; ¼ Lb. 30c; Lb. $1.00

Mammoth Summer Crookneck

Vine larger and stronger growing than the Summer Crookneck and producing fruit fully twice as large, deeper colored and with rough surface. Its large size and attractive color make it a favorite with market gardeners. Pkt. 5c; Oz. 10c; 2 Oz. 15c; ¼ Lb. 25c; Lb. 90c.

SUMMER CROOKNECK. The old, standard sort; very early and productive. Fruits when mature about one foot long, with crooked neck, and covered with warty excrescences; color bright yellow; shell very hard when ripe. Pkt. 5c; Oz. 10c; 2 Oz. 15c; ¼ Lb. 75c.

ITALIAN VEGETABLE MARROW. (*Cocozella di Napoli*). A variety producing large, oblong fruits, dark green at first, but becoming marbled with yellow and lighter green in stripes as they mature. The very young and tender fruits when sliced and fried in oil, constitute a vegetable delicacy very popular especially in Naples. Pkt. 5c; Oz. 10c; 2 Oz. 20c; ¼ Lb. 30c; Lb. $1.00

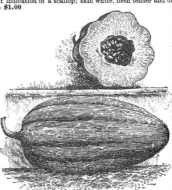

FORDHOOK SQUASH.

AUTUMN AND WINTER SQUASHES

Fordhook

A fall or early winter variety of excellent flavor and superior keeping qualities. Fruit of medium size slightly ridged; a creamy yellow outside; when cooked the flesh has a very pleasing flavor. Pkt. 5c; Oz. 10c; 2 Oz. 20c; ¼ Lb. 30c; Lb. $1.00

The Delicious

We are convinced that this Squash is particularly excellent in quality and in that respect is by some preferred even to the Hubbard. It is a very early winter variety of medium size; shell moderately hard but very thin; flesh thick, fine grained and bright yellow in color. Even when immature this squash is in condition for use and is of very fine flavor. Pkt. 5c; Oz. 15c; 2 Oz. 25c; ¼ Lb. 40c; Lb. $1.50

Hard Shelled Marrow

The best sort for canning or drying. We have been at work on this variety for several years and now have it so well fixed that it comes uniformly true to type. The fruit is very large, oval, of deep orange-red color and though quite smooth, has as hard a shell as the Hubbard. The flesh is very thick, of rich orange-red color without a tinge of green even close to the shell, and unequaled for making pies, having a flavor and quality similar to, but much finer than that of the choicest pumpkin. Pkt. 5c; Oz. 10c; 2 Oz. 20c; ¼ Lb. 30c; Lb. $1.00

THE DELICIOUS SQUASH.

The Two Best SUMMER SQUASHES

Golden Hubbard

This is a true Hubbard Squash, except in color, which is bright red. The vine is a vigorous but not rampant grower and wonderfully productive, expending the energy derived from liberal fertilizing in the production of an increased number rather than of overgrown and coarse fruits as some varieties are apt to do. The fruits are very uniform in size, weighing from six to eight pounds and in shape are like the Hubbard; although in condition for use much earlier, they are wonderfully long keepers and can be held over in good condition for spring use. The shell is warty, hard and strong and of a very beautiful, orange-red color, except for a bit of olive-green on the blossom end. The flesh is a deep orange and uniformly so to the shell, never having the green tinge so objectionable in the older sort. It cooks very dry, fine grained and good flavored. We believe this to be a very superior table variety; certainly it has become very popular. Pkt. 5c; Oz. 10c; 2 Oz. 20c; ¼ Lb. 30c; Lb. $1.00

GOLDEN HUBBARD SQUASH.

BOSTON MARROW SQUASH.

Boston Marrow

A fall and winter variety; large oval form, skin thin; when ripe, bright with a netting of light cream colo rich salmon-yellow; fine grained excellent flavor, but not as dry Hubbard. We have an unusual stock of this sort. Pkt. 5c; Oz 2 Oz. 15c; ¼ Lb. 25c; Lb. 75c.

Hubbard

This is a superior ety, and one of th of winter squashes; flesh bright o yellow, fine grained, very dry, and rich flavored; keeps well through the v boils or bakes exceedingly dry, and is esteem many to be as good baked as the sweet] Our stock is most carefully selected with re

quality of the flesh, and color and wartiness of the shell, but the latter peculiarities are largely determined by th in which the squashes are raised. We have compared our stock with that sold as Chicago, or Warty Hubbar have found it much superior. Pkt. 5c; Oz. 10c; 2 Oz. 20c; ¼ Lb. 30c; Lb. $1.00

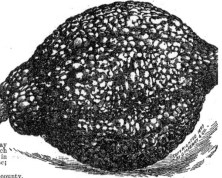

HUBBARD SQUASH.

Tobacco

CULTURE—The seed should be sown as early as possible after danger of frost is over. A good plan is to burn a quantity of brush and rubbish in the spring on the ground intended for the seed bed; then dig and thoroughly pulverize the earth and mix with the ashes, after which the seed may be sown and covered very lightly. When the plants are about six inches high, transplant into rows four or five feet apart each way; cultivate thoroughly with plow and hoe.

STERLING. The brightest of the yellow type, and being the earliest to ripen is *surest* in localities liable to early frosts. Pkt. 5c; Oz. 20c; 2 Oz. 35c; ¼ Lb. 60c; Lb. $2.00

LACKS. Broad leaf, tough, fine fibre. On gray soils cures bright and elastic; on dark soils rich and gummy. Known as Jessup or Beat All in some localities. Good and reliable. Pkt. 5c; Oz. 25c; 2 Oz. 40c; ¼ Lb. 75c; Lb. $2.50

HESTER. A variety originated in Granville county, N. C., which seems to have greater adaptability, doing better over a wider range of soils and latitude than most of the yellow varieties, and may, on this account, be considered the surest cropper. It has size, shape, texture and color and ripens early. Pkt. 5c; Oz. 20c; 2 Oz. 35c; ¼ Lb. 60c; Lb. $2.00

SWEET ORONOCO. Used for first-class plug fillers, and makes, when sun cured, the best Natural Chewing Leaf, A favorite for the "Homespun" wherever known. Known as Little Oronoco in some localities. Makes an Eastern Filler unsurpassed. Pkt. 5c; Oz. 20c; 2 Oz. 35c; ¼ Lb. 60c; Lb. $2.00

BRADLEY BROAD LEAF. A popular variety for export, manufacturing and cigars. Pkt. 5c; Oz. 20c; 2 Oz. 35c; ¼ Lb. 60c; Lb. $2.00

PERSIAN ROSE. Finer than the Muscatel, and may be relied upon to make the finest cigar stock. Pkt. 5c; Oz. 30c; 2 Oz. 55c; ¼ Lb. $1.00; Lb. $3.00

White Burley

This variety is especially valuable to manufacturers either for cut or plug tobacco. It is sometimes used for wrappers. Pkt. 5c; Oz. 30c; 2 Oz. 55c; ¼ Lb. $1.00; Lb. $3.00

BIG HAVANA. A hybrid Havana or Cuban seed le heavy cropper, of fine texture, delightful flavor a earliest cigar variety to mature and ripen. Will two crops from one planting in the south, while it ness makes it most desirable for high latitudes. P Oz. 25c; 2 Oz. 40c; ¼ Lb. 75c; Lb. $2.50

Sumatra

A very vigorous variety of Spanish producing cigar wrappers of the b quality and especially popular with Florida gr Pkt. 5c; Oz. 50c; 2 Oz. 85c; ¼ Lb. $1.50; Lb. $5.

CONNECTICUT SEED LEAF. Best adapted to the c of the middle and northern states, as it is more har endures the cold better than the tender varieties south. In many of the northern states and in Canad variety is grown almost exclusively and is the stapl Pkt. 5c; Oz. 20c; 2 Oz. 35c; ¼ Lb. 60c; Lb. $2.00

Havana

The leaf of this variety is very thin a textured. It possesses a very delicate and is extensively used for cigar wrappers. P Oz. 40c; 2 Oz. 75c; ¼ Lb. $1.25; Lb. $4.00

TOMATO

All our Tomato Seeds are from seed stocks carefully selected and saved by ourselves. We challenge comparison of our stocks with any offered.

CULTURE—Tomatoes do best on light, warm, not over rich soil, and success depends upon securing a rapid, vigorous and unchecked growth during the early part of the season. Sow in hotbeds from six to eight weeks before the plants can be set out of doors, which is when danger from frost is past; when the plants have four leaves transplant into shallow boxes or cold frames, setting them four or five inches apart; give plenty of air and endeavor to secure a vigorous but steady and healthy growth, so that at the time of setting in the open ground they will be strong and stocky. Even a slight check while the plants are small will materially diminish their productiveness. Set out of doors as soon as danger from frost is over, but before doing so harden off the plants by gradually exposing them to the night air and by the withdrawal of water until the wood becomes hard and the leaves thick and of a dark green color. Transplant carefully and cultivate well as long as the vines will permit.

To insure best results in respect to early ripening as well as the amount and perfection of fruit, it is advisable to train up and trim the vines, especially if the patch is rather small. When the plants have been properly started and are six to ten inches high they will begin to throw out branches. Select one of the largest and most vigorous of these and pinch off all others except this one and the main stem. Care must be exercised not to pinch off the fruiting branches, which, as they appear, can be distinguished by the buds that are formed very early. In a short time these two remaining branches will become equally vigorous and as ordinary varieties will grow four to six feet high during the season, they should be securely tied at intervals of about ten inches to a long stake, preferably two inches square, which has been securely set in near the root of the vine. Fruit will set to almost any height desired if all side branches are kept trimmed off.

By such a method of training and trimming the fruits are kept clear from the ground and with free access of sunlight they ripen much earlier; the vitality, otherwise exhausted in superfluous branches and leaves, is utilized in forming fruits of largest size, greatest perfection of shape and best quality.

EARLIANA Sometime ago we were able to secure a strain considerably improved and much superior to that usually sold as Spark's Earliana, and we now offer carefully selected seed of this most valuable first early sort. Vine similar in growth, maturing bulk of crop only a little later than Atlantic Prize, but the fruit is larger, distinctly smoother, solid and of very good quality. Early, smooth and of large size it is a particularly profitable tomato for market gardeners. Pkt. 5c; Oz. 30c; 2 Oz. 55c; ¼ Lb. $1.00; Lb. $3.00

EARLIANA TOMATO.

NOLTE'S EARLIEST This very early sort is more prolific than Atlantic Prize and continues in profitable production much longer. Vine the most hardy of any of the first early sorts, insuring a good yield even when growth conditions are not the most favorable. Fruit large, bright red in color and of excellent quality. Pkt.5c; Oz.30c; 2 Oz.40c; ¼ Lb.75c; Lb.$2.50

Atlantic Prize We have in this variety a sort which, because of its small, compact vine, can be set much closer than the later sorts, and which will, under similar conditions ripen up the greater portion of its crop before the fruit of the later sorts begins to color. The fruit is of good size, form and color; though a little soft it commands a ready sale, as it comes to market at a time when it meets with competition from but a few early sorts; in respect to earliness this being as yet unequaled by any. Excellent for market gardeners and desirable, because of its earliness, for home use. Pkt.5c; Oz. 25c; 2 Oz. 40c; ¼ Lb. 75c; Lb. $2.25

EARLY MICHIGAN One of the best second early sorts. Its first fruits are very early but the vines continue to bear for a long time. Vines large, with large, dark green leaves, vigorous and wonderfully productive, being, under high culture, one of the heaviest croppers; fruit medium sized to large, and unlike most varieties it produces larger fruits as the season advances; perfectly smooth, solid, but without a hard core; deep, rich red color and of excellent flavor. This kind is admirably adapted to canners' use. Pkt. 5c; Oz. 25c; 2 Oz. 40c; ¼ Lb. 75c; Lb. $2.25

D. M. FERRY & CO'S OPTIMUS A variety introduced by us and we believe the best table tomato, as far as quality is concerned. Vine medium sized, but vigorous, healthy and productive. Fruit medium sized, oval, very smooth and of exceedingly bright crimson-scarlet color; very free from cracks and rotting but little. The flesh is a distinct crimson-scarlet color. It is also one of the best in flavor and entirely free from the hard spots found in so many others. The Optimus is not only one of the best for home use and for market, but one of the best canning tomatoes. Pkt.5c; Oz.25c; 2 Oz.40c; ¼ Lb.75c; Lb.$2.25

FAVORITE. Vine medium sized, having clusters of three to seven large tomatoes which are of rich, dark red color, oval outline and smooth; flesh very firm, without green spots. Pkt. 5c; Oz. 25c; 2 Oz. 40c; ¼ Lb. 75c; Lb. $2.25

ROYAL RED. Vines stronger and more vigorous than the Favorite. The fruit is larger, brighter, deeper red and fully as good in quality. This is certainly a fine tomato for those who prize large size and bright color. Pkt. 5c; Oz. 25c; 2 Oz. 40c; ¼ Lb. 75c; Lb. $2.25

STONE This is the heaviest and most solid fruited of the large tomatoes of good quality. Our stock is distinctly superior to most of that offered under this name, being more uniform, better colored and larger. Vines vigorous and productive. Fruit round, apple-shaped, very large, very deep red in color and astonishingly heavy. Pkt. 5c; Oz. 25c; 2 Oz. 40c; ¼ Lb. 75c; Lb. $2.25

QUARTER CENTURY. Vine dwarf and compact, like the well known Dwarf Champion. Fruit scarlet-red, medium sized, very smooth and of excellent quality, either for the table or for canning. Earlier than Dwarf Stone. Pkt. 5c; Oz. 30c; 2 Oz. 55c; ¼ Lb. $1.00; Lb. $3.00

Dwarf Stone Vine dwarf but very vigorous and productive. While maturing with the later sorts the fruit is of good color, exceedingly smooth, very solid, and the largest in size of any of the dwarf varieties. Pkt. 5c; Oz. 40c; 2 Oz. 75c; ¼ Lb. $1.25; Lb. $4.00

STONE TOMATO.

TOMATO—Continued

Improved Trophy
The Trophy was the first of the modern improved sorts, and it had qualities of color, size and solidity which entitled it to hold a place against the much lauded new kinds; though all admitted it lacked in smoothness and regularity. By most careful breeding and selection, there has been produced a strain in which all the original good qualities are retained and even more highly developed, yet it compares favorably with any in smoothness, regularity and symmetry of the fruit. We offer our Improved Trophy as a sort whose large, strong growing, vigorous and productive vine, very large, very solid, smooth, fine flavored and beautiful, deep, rich red fruit will satisfy the most exacting. **Pkt. 5c; Oz. 25c; 2 Oz. 40c; ¼ Lb. 75c; Lb. $2.50**

Matchless
A large, bright red tomato which has become very popular in the east. The fruit is large, very smooth and symmetrical, ripening well to stem. The flesh is a rich, bright red color and of fine quality though softer than that of either Improved Trophy or Stone. **Pkt. 5c; Oz. 25c; 2 Oz. 40c; ¼ Lb. 75c; Lb. $2.50**

Perfection
This is one of the handsomest tomatoes grown, and all who have tried its invariably large, round, smooth, handsome, red fruit pronounce it of the highest quality. It has been used very satisfactorily for forcing under glass. **Pkt. 5c; Oz. 25c; 2 Oz. 40c; ¼ Lb. 75c; Lb. $2.25**

Buckeye State
A late, purple fruited variety, and we think one of the best late sorts. The vine is exceptionally strong growing and vigorous. It should be given more room than most. Fruit very large, round, smooth and of good quality. **Pkt. 5c; Oz. 25c; 2 Oz. 40c; ¼ Lb. 75c; Lb. $2.50**

Acme
We have given a good deal of attention to the improvement of this variety and think we have succeeded in making it one of the smoothest and most uniform, medium sized, early, purple fruited sorts. Vine large, hardy and productive, ripening its first fruit almost as early as any, and continuing to bear abundantly until cut off by frost. Fruit in clusters of four or five, invariably round, smooth and of good size, free from cracks and stands shipment remarkably well; flesh solid and of excellent flavor. For market gardeners who want an early, purple fruited tomato, either for home market or to ship, also for private gardens or for canners, it is one of the best. This variety is used for planting under glass. **Pkt. 5c; Oz. 25c; 2 Oz. 40c; ¼ Lb. 75c; Lb. $2.25**

Essex Early Hybrid
Very similar to the Acme, fruit dark purple, always smooth and handsome; in quality it is classed with the best. Will certainly give satisfaction. **Pkt. 5c; Oz. 25c; 2 Oz. 40c; ¼ Lb. 75c; Lb. $2.25**

Beauty
We have been selecting this to a larger, smoother fruit than the original stock, and think we have made it one of the smoothest and best of the large, purple sorts. Vines large, vigorous and heavy bearers; fruit large, uniform in size, very smooth; color of skin purplish-pink; flesh light pink and of excellent flavor. While we think the color weak for canning, it is used considerably for this purpose. **Pkt. 5c; Oz. 25c; 2 Oz. 40c; ¼ Lb. 75c; Lb. $2.25**

Dwarf Champion
This is a purple fruited variety which forms very stout, strong plants about two feet high. The branches are short, making a bushy plant that stands quite erect. This sort is often sold as Tree Tomato. Fruit smooth, medium sized, color purplish-pink, fairly solid, but has no hard core, and is of good flavor. About as early as any purple fruited tomato, and is quite popular in some localities, particularly for home use. The dwarf habit of the vines makes it very desirable for forcing as it can be planted closer to the glass, and more closely on the bench than the tall growing kinds. Our stock is a very superior strain with larger, smoother fruit than the original. **Pkt. 5c; Oz. 30c; 2 Oz. 55c; ¼ Lb. $1.00; Lb. $3.00**

DWARF CHAMPION TOMATO.

Purple Dwarf
This variety is very similar to Dwarf Champion both in vine and color of fruit. While the fruits mature a little later they are distinctly larger and for this reason more desirable for market. **Pkt. 5c; Oz. 40c; 2 Oz. 75c; ¼ Lb. $1.25; Lb. $4.00**

Magnus
A variety of recent introduction, producing purple fruit of the largest size; much smoother than most of the large fruited sorts and matures earlier. **Pkt. 5c; Oz. 25c; 2 Oz. 40c; ¼ Lb. 75c; Lb. $2.50**

Honor Bright
The best sort for distant markets and a late crop. No variety of recent introduction has more real and distinctive merit than this. Unfortunately the yellowish-green foliage, and the slow ripening of the fruit, tend to prejudice people against the sort, but in spite of its appearance the vine can be depended upon to give a big crop of uniformly good, large fruit. This, when allowed to ripen on the vine, is of excellent quality, and when ripened off the vine, while in transit to some distant market or on shelves in the house after frost has killed the vines, is of better quality than that of most varieties so handled. We know of no kind so well suited to growing in the south for shipment north. The proper method is to pick when just passing out of the white stage, wrap in paper and pack in boxes. It should be set out earlier than most sorts because of its slow maturing. In the north the vines may be pulled at the approach of frost and hung in a moist place, safe from freezing. They will then give for a month firm, ripe, marketable fruit of brilliant red color. **Pkt. 5c; Oz. 25c; 2 Oz. 40c; ¼ Lb. 75c; Lb. $2.50**

PEACH. A distinct and very attractive appearing tomato, highly desirable for preserving, eating from the hand or for table decoration. Fruit resembles a peach in shape and size, and the color, a light purplish pink with a delicate bloom, makes the resemblance still more striking; flesh tender and of good flavor. **Pkt. 5c; Oz. 25c; 2 Oz. 40c; ¼ Lb. 75c; Lb. $2.50**

GOLDEN QUEEN. The superior flavor of the yellow varieties is bringing them into favor as table fruit, and those who think of a yellow tomato as the rough fruit of the old yellow sorts will be surprised at this smooth, beautiful fruit which, though large, is as smooth and well shaped as the best of the red varieties, and of a fine and distinct flavor. **Pkt. 5c; Oz. 25c; 2 Oz. 40c; ¼ Lb. 75c; Lb. $2.50**

BEAUTY TOMATO.

TOMATO—Continued

WHITE APPLE. This old sort is often presented as a novelty under a new name. While no one should plant largely of it for market or home use, it is a good variety for eating from the hand. The fruit is about one and one-half inches in diameter, round, perfectly smooth and of a yellowish-white color. Flesh very mild flavored, delicate and is valued by some for making preserves. **Pkt. 5c; Oz. 25c; 2 Oz. 40c; ¼ Lb. 75c; Lb. $2.50**

RED PEAR SHAPED. Used for preserves and to make "tomato figs." Fruit bright red, distinctly pear shaped and of excellent flavor. Our stock is the true pear shaped and not the larger red plum tomato which is often sold under this name. **Pkt. 5c; Oz. 25c; 2 Oz. 40c; ¼ Lb. 75c; Lb. $2.50**

YELLOW PEAR SHAPED. Similar to the Red Pear Shaped but of rich, clear yellow color and on this account sometimes considered preferable; quite distinct from the variety which is sometimes sold under this name. **Pkt. 5c; Oz. 25c; 2 Oz. 40c; ¼ Lb. 75c; Lb. $2.50**

YELLOW PLUM. Fruit plum shaped, of clear, deep yellow color; flesh yellow and fine flavored. Much esteemed for preserves. **Pkt. 5c; Oz. 25c; 2 Oz. 40c; ¼ Lb. 75c; Lb. $2.50**

RED CHERRY. Fruit small, about five-eighths of an inch in diameter; perfectly round and smooth. Fine for pickles and preserves. **Pkt. 5c; Oz. 25c; 2 Oz. 40c; ¼ Lb. 75c; $2.50**

YELLOW CHERRY. Differs from the preceding in color only. **Pkt. 5c; Oz. 25c; 2 Oz. 40c; ¼ Lb. 75c; Lb. $2.50**

HUSK TOMATO, OR GROUND CHERRY. This is liked by many for preserves and eating from the hand. The seed we offer is that of the *true* Yellow Ground Cherry, not the purple fruited sort which is scarcely edible. **Pkt. 5c; Oz. 30c; 2 Oz. 55c; ¼ Lb. $1.00; Lb. $3.00**

YELLOW PEAR SHAPED TOMATO.

TURNIP

The value of Turnips and Ruta Bagas for feeding stock in fall and winter is not fully appreciated, as they are much liked by all kinds of stock and serve to keep them in good condition. We earnestly recommend that farmers increase their sowings largely, for we are sure the crop will prove remunerative.

This wholesome and agreeable vegetable is most easily affected in its form and flavor by soil, climate and mode of culture. There are a great many varieties, but our list comprises the best for the garden or farm.

Sow in drills about two feet apart and half an inch deep, or sow broadcast, but in either case be sure to have the ground rich and freshly stirred. Thin early and keep free from weeds so that the young plants will not be checked in growth. Any over-crowding will result in rough and poorly flavored roots. It is important to get the spring and summer crop started very early so that the turnips may have time to grow to sufficient size before hot weather causes them to become tough and bitter.

In middle and western states sow for fall and main crop from middle of July to last of August and in the manner given for spring sowing. In the field, turnips are often sown broadcast, though in most cases better results are obtained by drill culture.

For winter keeping, store the turnips in a cool cellar and cover with sand or turf to keep them fresh. Another method is to put them in a pit dug in dry soil where there will be no danger of water standing and to cover with straw overlaid with earth sufficiently deep to keep out frost. Thus protected, turnips will keep well till spring.

Extra Early White Milan

This variety is remarkably early. The top is very small, upright and compact, so that the rows can be planted close together. The clear white roots are very smooth, flat, symmetrical and beautiful. The flesh is white, tender and sweet. **Pkt. 5c; Oz. 10c; 2 Oz. 15c; ¼ Lb. 25c; Lb. 90c.**

Extra Early Purple Top Milan

Similar to the White Milan, except that the roots are a little flatter and a beautiful purple-red on the upper portion. All in all, these Milan turnips leave nothing more to be desired in the way of an extra early garden turnip. **Pkt. 5c; Oz. 10c; 2 Oz. 15c; ¼ Lb. 20c; Lb. 65c.**

White Egg

A quick growing, egg-shaped, perfectly smooth, pure white variety with small top and rough leaves. It grows half out of the ground. The flesh is very sweet, firm and mild, never having the rank, strong taste of some varieties. **Pkt. 5c; Oz. 10c; 2 Oz. 15c; ¼ Lb. 20c; Lb. 60c.**

Early White Flat Dutch Strap Leaved

A most excellent early, garden variety and largely used in the southern states. Root medium sized, flat; color white; very early, sweet and tender. It is desirable for table use, but like other early sorts is spongy and inferior when overgrown. **Pkt. 5c; Oz. 10c; 2 Oz. 15c; ¼ Lb. 20c; Lb. 50c.**

EXTRA EARLY WHITE MILAN TURNIP.

WHITE EGG TURNIP.

:: *TURNIP*— Continued

Early Purple Top, Strap Leaved

This is an early variety and a great favorite for table use; form flat, but thicker than Purple Top Milan and of medium size; color purple or dark red above ground, white below; flesh white, fine grained and tender; leaves few, entire, upright in growth. Pkt. 5c; Oz. 10c; 2 Oz. 15c; ¼ Lb. 20c; Lb. 50c.

Purple Top White Globe

A variety that is globular and nearly as large as the Pomeranean White Globe, of beautiful appearance and the white flesh is of most excellent quality, equally desirable for table or stock. It keeps well and is a fine market sort. Pkt. 5c; Oz. 10c; 2 Oz.15c; ¼ Lb. 20c; Lb. 50c.

COW HORN, OR LONG WHITE. This variety is pure white, except a little shade of green at the top and is carrot-like in form, growing nearly half out of the ground and slightly crooked. It is delicate and well flavored, of very rapid growth and has obtained considerable favor as a market sort for fall and early winter use. Pkt. 5c; Oz. 10c; 2 Oz.15c; ¼ Lb. 20c; Lb. 50c.

EARLY PURPLE TOP STRAP LEAVED TURNIP.

COW HORN, OR LONG WHITE TURNIP.

LARGE WHITE NORFOLK. A standard sort, usually grown for feeding stock, but though a little coarse in texture it is of very good quality for the table. The roots are large, spherical, or slightly flattened and very white. It is allowed to stand out during the winter in the south and southwest, where the tops are used for greens. Pkt. 5c; Oz. 10c; 2 Oz. 10c; ¼ Lb. 15c; Lb. 45c.

POMERANEAN WHITE GLOBE. This is one of the most productive kinds and in good, rich soil roots will frequently grow to twelve pounds in weight. It is globe shaped, skin white and smooth; leaves large and dark green. Used largely for stock feeding, but is also excellent for table use. Pkt. 5c; Oz. 10c; 2 Oz. 10c; ¼ Lb. 15c; Lb. 45c.

Sweet German

This variety is very popular in many sections, notably so in the New England states; grows to a large size and is considered one of the best for table use or for feeding stock. It partakes largely of the nature of the Ruta Baga and should be sown a month earlier than the flat turnips. The flesh is white, hard, firm and sweet; keeps nearly as well as the Ruta Baga. Highly recommended for winter and spring use. Pkt 5c; Oz. 10c; 2 Oz.15c; ¼ Lb. 20c; Lb. 50c.

SEVEN TOP. Cultivated extensively in the south for the tops which are used for greens. It is very hardy and will grow all winter, but does not produce a good root, and is only recommended for the tops. *Crop failed.*

YELLOW FLESHED TURNIPS

Large Amber Globe

One of the best yellow fleshed varieties for a field crop for stock. Flesh yellow, fine grained and sweet; color of skin yellow; top green. Grows to a large size, is hardy, keeps well and is a good cropper. Very popular in the south. Pkt. 5c; Oz. 10c; 2 Oz. 15c; ¼ Lb. 20c; Lb. 50c.

Yellow Stone

A very beautiful and desirable sort. The roots are of medium size, uniformly globular and perfect in shape; skin smooth and of beautiful pale yellow color. The flesh is crisp, tender and of fine quality. Pkt. 5c; Oz. 10c; 2 Oz. 15c; ¼ Lb. 20c; Lb. 60c.

YELLOW GLOBE. A round, smooth, medium sized, light yellow turnip, with crisp, firm flesh of fine quality, and a very attractive and beautiful sort. Pkt. 5c; Oz. 10c; 2 Oz. 15c; ¼ Lb. 20c; Lb. 60c.

Orange Jelly, or Robertson's Golden Ball

One of the most delicate and sweetest yellow fleshed turnips yet introduced. Not of large size, but firm, hard, and of most excellent flavor. Keeps well and is superior as a table variety. Pkt. 5c; Oz. 10c; 2 Oz.15c; ¼ Lb. 20c; Lb. 50c.

PURPLE TOP YELLOW ABERDEEN. Roots medium sized, round; flesh pale yellow, tender and sugary; the plant is hardy, productive and keeps well. It is an old esteemed variety, considered as approaching very nearly to the Ruta Baga in hardiness and firmness of texture. Is valuable for feeding cattle for which use it is extensively grown. Pkt. 5c; Oz. 10c; 2 Oz. 15c; ¼ Lb. 20c; Lb. 50c.

PURPLE TOP WHITE GLOBE TURNIP.

ORANGE JELLY, OR ROBERTSON'S GOLDEN BALL TURNIP.

RUTA BAGAS, OR SWEDES

CULTURE OF RUTA BAGAS—Sow the seed from about the middle of June to the middle of July. Ruta Bagas require ground enriched with well rotted manure and should be sown in drills about two and one-half feet apart and the young plants thinned eight to twelve inches apart in the row. Keep free from weeds by frequent cultivation and when the roots are full grown and before hard freezing weather, pull them, cut off the tops and store in a root cellar or pit. Ruta Bagas are sometimes sown broadcast and left to take their chances with the weeds and bugs. So treated the crop is seldom a success, though occasionally on new clearings free from weed seed, fair results are obtained.

Monarch or Tankard This is a yellow fleshed sort, having very large, tankard shaped roots, with relatively small necks and tops. Color· purplish-crimson above ground, yellow below; flesh very solid, fine grained and of the best flavor, Pkt. 5c; Oz. 10c; 2 Oz. 15c; ¼ Lb. 20c; Lb. 50c.

American Purple Top, or Improved Long Island This is a strain of Purple Top Yellow Ruta Baga of American origin, selected to a smaller top and much shorter neck than is usually found, while the roots grow to a large size and are of the finest quality and excellent for table use and stock feeding. We consider this one of the most desirable kinds on our list. Pkt. 5c; Oz. 10c; 2 Oz. 15c; ¼ Lb. 20c; Lb. 50c.

YELLOW SWEDE. Shape oblong; dull reddish color above ground but yellow underneath; is hardier than the common turnip and will keep solid until spring. Pkt. 5c; Oz. 10c; 2 Oz. 10c; ¼ Lb. 15c; Lb. 45c.

CARTER'S IMPERIAL PURPLE TOP. A most excellent sort either for table use or feeding stock. Flesh yellow, solid, firm, sweet and rich. It is a hardy sort and yields heavily. Pkt. 5c; Oz. 10c; 2 Oz. 10c; ¼ Lb. 15c; Lb. 45c.

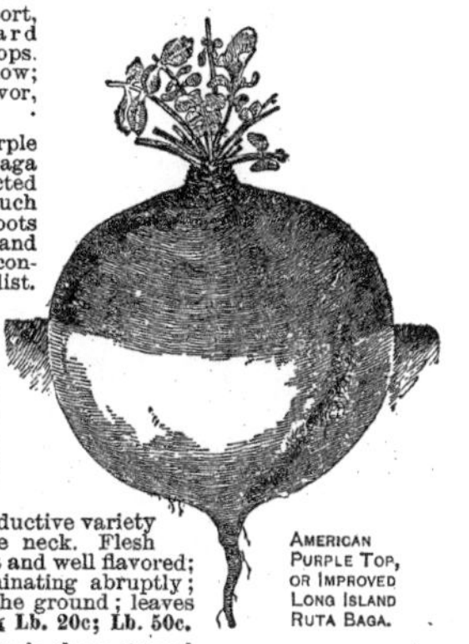

D. M. Ferry & Co's Improved Purple Top Yellow A hardy and productive variety having but little neck. Flesh yellow, of solid texture, sweet and well flavored; shape slightly oblong, terminating abruptly; color deep purple above and bright yellow under the ground ; leaves small, light green. Pkt. 5c; Oz. 10c; 2 Oz. 15c; ¼ Lb. 20c; Lb. 50c.

WEST NORFOLK. Shape oblong; color reddish-purple above ground but yellow underneath. Hardier than the common turnip and will keep solid until spring. Pkt. 5c; Oz. 10c; 2 Oz. 15c; ¼ Lb. 20c; Lb. 60c.

MONARCH OR TANKARD RUTA BAGA.

AMERICAN PURPLE TOP, OR IMPROVED LONG ISLAND RUTA BAGA.

Laing's Purple Top A large, early sort of fine quality. Roots globe shaped; skin purplish-red above ground and yellow below; flesh yellow; necks small; tops peculiar in that their leaves are strap or entire. An excellent variety in every way. Pkt. 5c; Oz. 10c; 2 Oz. 15c; ¼ Lb. 20c; Lb. 60c.

DRUMMOND'S. An improved strain of Purple Top Swede, excelling in uniformity of shape, color and quality. This variety is considered by many an excellent table sort. Pkt. 5c; Oz. 10c; 2 Oz. 10c; ¼ Lb. 15c; Lb. 45c.

Shepherd's Golden Globe A choice English strain in which the tops of the large, round roots are bronze green; the flesh is deep orange color; very uniform and true. Pkt. 5c; Oz. 10c; 2 Oz. 15c; ¼ Lb. 20c; Lb. 50c.

BANGHOLM. A very superior variety both in form and quality. Of large size, small neck, few or no side roots and yields well. Flesh yellow, sweet and solid; skin yellow, with purple top. Pkt. 5c; Oz. 10c; 2 Oz. 10c; ¼ Lb. 15c; Lb. 45c.

GREEN TOP. Bulb very large, spherical, with green top. Pkt. 5c; Oz. 10c; 2 Oz. 15c; ¼ Lb. 20c; Lb. 50c.

SUTTON'S CHAMPION. Roots large, spherical, purple on top; flesh yellow, tender and sweet; an excellent keeper and enormous yielder. Pkt. 5c; Oz. 10c; 2 Oz. 10c; ¼ Lb. 15c; Lb. 45c.

EAST LOTHIAN. A very hardy and desirable sort. Purple top. Pkt. 5c; Oz. 10c; 2 Oz. 15c; ¼ Lb. 20c; Lb. 50c.

SKIRVING'S KING OF SWEDES. Though this sort reaches a large size the yellow flesh is of m.st excellent quality. Pkt. 5c; Oz. 10c; 2 Oz. 10c; ¼ Lb. 15c; Lb. 45c.

HALL'S WESTBURY. A very popular variety which, it is claimed, will endure dry weather better than most sorts. Pkt. 5c; Oz. 10c; 2 Oz. 15c; ¼ Lb. 20c; Lb. 50c.

Budlong's White Rock Though sometimes called a turnip this is more like a ruta baga. The root is large, both skin and flesh very white and is one of the best varieties we have for table use. An excellent keeper and a desirable sort for market gardeners. Pkt. 5c; Oz. 10c; 2 Oz. 15c; ¼ Lb. 20c; Lb. 50c.

WHITE SWEDE, OR SWEET RUSSIAN TURNIP. This variety is an excellent keeper and very desirable either for the table or for stock. It grows to a very large size; flesh white, solid, of firm texture, sweet and rich. Pkt. 5c; Oz. 10c; 2 Oz. 15c; ¼ Lb. 15c; Lb. 45c.

D. M. FERRY & CO'S IMPROVED PURPLE TOP YELLOW RUTA BAGA.

Perfection White A Ruta Baga that is absolutely neckless; top strap leaved, flesh white and unusually fine grained; growth vigorous and with us even under adverse conditions it has given a better yield than the yellow fleshed sorts. While in common with all ruta bagas it is valuable for stock feeding, the white flesh is so very fine grained and excellent in quality that it is particularly desirable for table use and for this we strongly recommend it. Pkt. 5c; Oz. 10c; 2 Oz. 15c; ¼ Lb. 20c; Lb. 60c.

PERFECTION WHITE RUTA BAGA.

Aromatic, Medicinal ᴬⁿᵈ Pot Herbs

GENERAL CULTURAL DIRECTIONS

Most of the varieties thrive best on sandy soil, and some are stronger and better flavored when grown on that which is rather poor, but in all cases the soil should be carefully prepared and well cultivated, as the young plants are for the most part delicate and easily choked out by weeds. Sow as early as the ground can be made ready, in drills sixteen to eighteen inches apart, taking pains that the soil is fine and pressed firmly over the seed, or they may be planted as a second crop—the seeds sown in beds in April, and the plants set out in June. Most of them should be cut when in bloom, wilted in the sun and thoroughly dried in the shade.

ANISE (*Pimpinella anisum*). A well known annual herb whose seeds, which have an agreeable, aromatic odor and taste, are used for dyspepsia and colic and as a corrective of griping and unpleasant medicines. **Pkt. 5c; Oz. 10c; 2 Oz. 20c; ¼ Lb. 30c; Lb. $1.00**

BALM (*Melissa officinalis*). A perennial herb, easily propagated by division of the root or from seed. The leaves have a fragrant odor, similar to lemons, and are used for making balm tea for use in fevers, and a pleasant beverage called balm wine. **Pkt. 5c; Oz. 25c; 2 Oz. 40c; ¼ Lb. 75c; Lb. $2.50**

BASIL, SWEET (*Ocimum basilicum*). A hardy annual from the East Indies. The seeds and stems have a flavor somewhat similar to that of cloves and are used for flavoring soups and sauces. **Pkt. 5c; Oz. 15c; 2 Oz. 25c; ¼ Lb. 40c; Lb. $1.50**

BORAGE (*Borago officinalis*). A hardy annual used as a pot herb and for bee pasturage. The bruised leaves immersed in water give it an agreeable flavor. **Pkt. 5c; Oz. 15c; 2 Oz. 25c; ¼ Lb. 40c; Lb. $1.25**

CARAWAY (*Carum carui*). Cultivated for its seed which is used in confectionery, cakes, etc. The leaves are sometimes used in soups. If sown early in August the plants will give a fair crop of seed the next season, but when sown in the spring will not generally seed until the next year. **Pkt. 5c; Oz. 10c; 2 Oz. 15c; ¼ Lb. 25c; Lb. 75c.**

CARAWAY, for Flavoring. Oz. 10c; 2 Oz. 15c; ¼ Lb. 25c; Lb. 50c.

CATNIP, or CAT-MINT (*Nepeta cataria*). A hardy perennial, well known as a valuable mild nervine for infants. Sow in fall or early spring, in drills twenty inches apart. **Pkt. 5c; Oz. 30c; 2 Oz. 55c; ¼ Lb. $1.00; Lb. $3.00**

CORIANDER (*Coriandrum sativum*). A hardy annual, cultivated for its seed which has an agreeable taste and is used in confectionery and to disguise the taste of medicine. Gather on a dry day, bruising the stems and leaves as little as possible, for when injured they have a disagreeable odor which they impart to the seed. **Pkt. 5c; Oz. 10c; 2 Oz. 15c; ¼ Lb. 25c; Lb. 75c.**

CORIANDER for Flavoring. Oz. 10c; 2 Oz. 15c; ¼ Lb. 20c; Lb. 50c.

DILL (*Anethum graveolens*). An annual, cultivated for its seed which has an aromatic odor and a warm, pungent taste. It is good for flatulence and colic in infants. It is sometimes added to pickled cucumbers to heighten the flavor. **Pkt. 5c; Oz. 10c; 2 Oz. 15c; ¼ Lb. 20c; Lb. 60c.**

FENNEL, SWEET (*Fœniculum officinale*). A hardy perennial. The leaves are largely used in soups, fish sauces, garnishes and salads. The seed is sometimes used in confectionery. **Pkt. 5c; Oz. 10c; 2 Oz. 20c; ¼ Lb. 30c; Lb. $1.00**

HOREHOUND (*Marrubium vulgare*). A perennial herb with a strong, aromatic smell and a bitter, pungent taste. It is a tonic and enters largely into the composition of cough syrups and lozenges. Will thrive in any soil but is stronger if grown on light, poor land. **Pkt. 5c; Oz. 20c; 2 Oz. 35c; ¼ Lb. 60c; Lb. $2.00**

HYSSOP (*Hyssopus officinalis*). A hardy perennial with an aromatic flavor and a warm, pungent taste. It is a stimulant and expectorant and is used in asthma and chronic catarrh. The flowering summits and leaves are the parts used. **Pkt. 5c; Oz. 20c; 2 Oz. 35c; ¼ Lb. 60c; Lb. $2.00**

SWEET MARJORAM.

LAVENDER (*Lavendula spica*). A hardy perennial, growing about two feet high. It is used for the distillation of lavender water or dried and used to perfume linen. It should be picked before it becomes dry and hard and dried quickly. **Pkt. 5c; Oz. 15c; 2 Oz. 25c; ¼ Lb. 40c; Lb. $1.25**

MARJORAM, SWEET (*Origanum marjorana*). A perennial plant but not hardy enough to endure the winter of the north. The young, tender tops are used green for flavoring, or they may be dried for winter use. **Pkt. 5c; Oz. 15c; 2 Oz. 25c; ¼ Lb. 40c; Lb. $1.25**

ROSEMARY (*Rosmarinus officinalis*). A hardy perennial with fragrant odor and a warm, aromatic, bitter taste. May be easily raised from seed but does not reach a size fit for use until the second season. The dried leaves deteriorate rapidly with age. **Pkt. 5c; Oz. 35c; 2 Oz. 60c; ¼ Lb. $1.00; Lb. $3.50**

RUE (*Ruta graveolens*). A hardy perennial with a peculiar smell. The leaves are bitter and so acrid as to blister the skin. It is a stimulant and anti-spasmodic but must be used with great caution, as its use sometimes results in serious injury. It must not be suffered to run to seed and does best on poor soil. **Pkt. 5c; Oz. 15c; 2 Oz. 25c; ¼ Lb. 40c; Lb. $1.50**

SAFFRON (*Carthamus tinctorius*). A hardy annual from Egypt, that has become naturalized in many parts of the country. Cultivated for its flowers, which are used in dyeing and to make the cosmetic powder called *rouge*. **Pkt. 5c; Oz. 10c; 2 Oz. 20c; ¼ Lb. 30c; Lb. $1.00**

SAGE (*Salvia officinalis*). A hardy perennial possessing some medicinal properties, but cultivated principally for use as a condiment; it being used more extensively than any other herb for flavoring and dressing. Cut the leaves and tender shoots just as the plant is coming into flower and dry quickly in the shade. The plants will survive the winter and may be divided. If this is done they will give a second crop superior in quality. **Pkt. 5c; Oz. 25c; 2 Oz. 40c; ¼ Lb. 75c; Lb. $2.25**

SAVORY, SUMMER (*Satureia hortensis*). A hardy annual, the dried stems, leaves and flowers of which are extensively used for flavoring, particularly in dressings and soups. **Pkt. 5c; Oz. 10c; 2 Oz. 20c; ¼ Lb. 30c; Lb. $1.00**

TANSY (*Tanacetum vulgare*). A hardy perennial plant from Europe, but grows wild in many parts of this country. The leaves, when green, have a peculiar, aromatic odor, which they lose in drying. Cultivated for its medicinal properties, which are those common to bitter herbs. **Pkt. 5c; Oz. 30c; 2 Oz. 55c; ¼ Lb. $1.00; Lb. $3.00**

THYME (*Thymus vulgaris*). This herb is perennial, and is both a medicinal and culinary plant. The young leaves and tops are used for soups, dressing and sauce; a tea is made from the leaves which in some cases will relieve nervous headache. Sow as early as the ground will permit. **Pkt. 5c; Oz. 25c; 2 Oz. 40c; ¼ Lb. 75c; Lb. $2.50**

WORMWOOD (*Artemisia absinthium*). A perennial plant of strong and fragrant odor and aromatic, but intensely bitter taste. The leaves are used as a tonic and vermifuge and as a dressing for fresh bruises. It may be raised from seed, propagating by cuttings or dividing the roots. A dry, poor soil is best adapted to bring out the peculiar virtues of this plant. **Pkt. 5c; Oz. 20c; 2 Oz. 35c; ¼ Lb. 60c; Lb. $1.75**

SUMMER SAVORY.

... GRASS SEEDS ...

Prices on Grass Seeds subject to change. The pound prices include postage; 100 pound prices are by freight or express, at purchaser's expense.

RHODE ISLAND BENT GRASS (*Agrostis canina*). A valuable perennial for lawns and pasturage. Much, like Red Top, though smaller. Thrives on light, dry soils as well as on rich, moist ones. For lawn purposes, if used alone, it should be sown at the rate of about forty pounds per acre; for pasture, if used alone, twenty-four pounds per acre. **Lb.** 40c; $25.00 per 100 Lbs.

CREEPING BENT GRASS (*Agrostis Stolonifera*). Particularly valuable for lawns that are to be used as croquet and tennis grounds, because it is benefited more than hurt by tramping and by its bright color adds to the beauty of the lawn. **Lb.** 40c; $25.00 per 100 Lbs.

Red Top
(*Agrostis vulgaris*). In Pennsylvania and states further south, this is known as *Herd's Grass*, a name applied in New England and New York to Timothy. It is a good, permanent grass, standing our climate well and makes good pasture when fed close. Is valuable for low, wet meadows, producing a large return in good hay. When sown alone, use about twenty-eight pounds of the chaff seed per acre. Sow in spring or fall.

RED TOP Unhulled Fancy (*free from light chaff*). **Lb.** 20c; 100 Lbs. $6.50

RED TOP, FANCY (*cleaned from chaff*). Sow eight to ten pounds per acre. **Lb.** 30c; $12.50 per 100 Lbs.

TALL MEADOW OAT GRASS (*Avena elatior*). A hardy perennial much used in the south and west. Its roots penetrate deep, and it thrives on any good soil. It yields a heavy crop, and is valuable both for meadow and pasture. If used alone, sow from thirty to forty pounds per acre. **Lb.** 40c; $24.00 per 100 Lbs.

AWNLESS BROME GRASS (*Bromus inermis*). A perennial grass valuable for binding the soil of embankments and on account of its ability to resist both drought and cold. On light, dry soils it is used for both hay and pasturage, but is not recommended for locations where better grasses will succeed. Should be used at the rate of forty pounds per acre. **Lb.** 30c; $15.00 per 100 Lbs.

MEADOW FESCUE, OR ENGLISH BLUE GRASS.

Orchard Grass
(*Dactylis glomerata*). One of the most valuable grasses on account of its quick growth and valuable aftermath. It is ready for grazing in spring two weeks sooner than most grasses and when fed off is again ready for grazing in a week and will continue green when other grasses are withered by dry weather. It is palatable and nutritious and stock eat it greedily when green. It has a tendency to grow in tufts and does better if sown with clover and as it ripens at the same time as clover, the mixed hay is of the best quality. When sown alone, about twenty-eight pounds are required per acre; if sown with clover, half that quantity. It is perennial and will last for years, but its habit of growth unfits it for lawns. **Lb.** 35c; $18.00 per 100 Lbs.

HARD FESCUE (*Festuca duriuscula*). Similar to Sheep's Fescue, but not so dense and growing somewhat taller; this often will cover sandy soil under the shade of large trees where no other grass will grow; is a desirable addition to lawn grass. Sow thirty pounds per acre.
Lb. 25c; $15.00 per 100 Lbs.

TALL FESCUE (*Festuca elatior*). A valuable perennial grass, very productive and nutritious. It is native to moist, heavy soil, where it probably does best, but it succeeds well on any good soil, wet or dry. If used alone, sow forty pounds per acre. **Lb.** 50c; $30.00 per 100 Lbs.

SHEEP'S FESCUE (*Festuca ovina*). A small tufted, hardy grass, forming a cluster of narrow, cylindrical leaves. It is of value in mixture for lawns, on dry soils and in shady locations. Sow about thirty-five pounds per acre.
Lb. 25c; $15.00 per 100 Lbs.

MEADOW FESCUE, OR ENGLISH BLUE GRASS (*Festuca pratensis*). A perennial grass from two to four feet high, with flat, broad leaves. This is one of the standard European grasses. It needs rich ground and succeeds well on prairie soil. This is an excellent pasture grass to take the place of the wild grasses, as it yields a large amount of early and late feed. Sow about twenty-five pounds per acre. **Lb.** 25c; $12.00 per 100 Lbs.

PERENNIAL RYE GRASS (*Lolium perenne*). A very valuable variety for permanent pasture. Succeeds well on almost any soil, but is particularly adapted to moderately moist or irrigated lands. Sow thirty to forty pounds per acre, in spring. **Lb.** 20c; $8.00 per 100 Lbs.

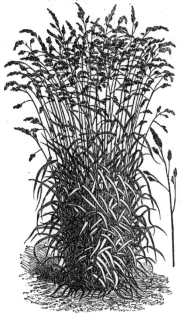

ORCHARD GRASS.

GRASS SEEDS—Continued

Prices on Grass Seeds subject to change. The pound prices include postage; 100 pound prices are by freight or express, at purchaser's expense.

Timothy (*Phleum pratense*). This is the most valuable of all the grasses for hay, especially in the north. Thrives best on moist, loamy soils of medium tenacity. It should be cut just when the blossom falls. Sow early in the spring or fall, at the rate of twelve pounds per acre, if alone, but less if mixed with other grasses. Lb. 20c; 100 Lbs. at market price.

Wood Meadow Grass (*Poa nemoralis*). Grows from one and a half to two feet high; has a perennial creeping root and an erect, slender, smooth stem. One of the best varieties to sow in shaded situations, such as orchards and parks, for either hay or pasturage. Sow about thirty pounds per acre. Lb. 60c; $40.00 per 100 Lbs.

KENTUCKY BLUE GRASS (*Poa pratensis*). Sometimes called June Grass, but the true June or (Fancy) Wire Grass is much inferior. (Clean) Kentucky Blue Grass is the most nutritious, hardy and valuable of all northern grasses. In conjunction with White Clover it forms a splendid lawn; for this purpose use not less than fifty-four pounds of Blue Grass and six pounds of White Clover per acre. If sown by itself for meadow or pasturage about twenty-eight pounds per acre will be required. Sow early in the spring, or in October or November. Lb. 30c; 100 Lbs. $13.00

FOWL MEADOW, OR FALSE RED TOP (*Poa serotina*). This variety succeeds best on low, moist land and is valuable for locations too wet for the successful cultivation of other commercial grasses. It stands longer in good condition for cutting than most species and can be mowed almost any time from July to October. When three feet high it falls down, or lodges, and after a little time every joint puts forth new branches. The stalk is always sweet and tender and cattle and sheep are fond of it. Requires about twenty-five pounds of seed per acre. Sow in spring or fall. Lb. 50c; 100 Lbs. $35.00

ROUGH STALKED MEADOW (*Poa trivialis*). A strong growing, hardy grass, well suited to deep, moist soils but of little value on soil which is poor or dry. Sow about twenty pounds per acre. Lb. 50c; 100 Lbs. $35.00

Extra Fine Mixed Lawn Grass (*Central Park Mixture*). The essentials for a fine lawn are: First, a rich, well drained soil; second, careful preparation of the ground, making it as fine and smooth and mellow as possible; third, a wise selection of seeds; fourth, sowing at such a time as to give the young plants a chance to become well established before being subjected to very dry or cold weather or to the direct rays of the hot summer sun. However much care is bestowed on the soil and seed, no lawn will be beautiful without frequent mowing and rolling. Too much care cannot be bestowed upon the selection of grasses, as some varieties are the most luxuriant in spring, others in summer, others again in autumn and a combination of the proper sorts is required for a perfect, carpet-like lawn. We have given much thought and, made many experiments to secure the best selection and think our Central Park Mixture is the best possible for permanent lawns. It may be planted early in spring or fall and should be sown at the rate of sixty to one hundred pounds per acre; much more is required than for hay or pasturage. If sown in the spring, sow as early as possible, making the surface very fine and smooth, then raking it over and sowing the seed just before a rain, which, if the surface has just been raked, will cover the seed sufficiently. If the expected rain does not come, cover by rolling with a light roller. For fall seeding sow before the autumn rains and early enough to enable the young grass to become well established before very cold weather, when a light dressing of manure should be given. One pound of this mixture is sufficient to sow 600 square feet. Lb. 45c; 100 Lbs. $25.00

FINE MIXED LAWN GRASS A thoroughly good, inexpensive mixture. Lb. 30c; 100 Lbs. $15.00

MIXTURES FOR GOLF LINKS While there are on the market numerous ready prepared golf mixtures of more or less value, we have found that the best results are obtained by giving individual attention to each customer and making a special mixture to suit his needs. We have thus overcome the difficulties presented by the great dissimilarity of local conditions of various links and are willing to give you the benefit not only of our experience on some of the best greens in this country but of expert knowledge of grass seeds as well. Write us a description of your links, telling what the nature of the soil is, how drained, how much it has the sun, whether the winters are long or open, and whether the summers are wet or dry, and we will offer you two or more mixtures especially adapted to the various parts of *your grounds.*

CLOVER SEEDS

There are no plants so valuable for fertilizers as the Clovers. They have the faculty of absorbing nitrogen from the air and also of rendering available much of the inert plant food of the soil. Their long, powerful tap roots penetrate to a great depth, loosen the soil, admit air and by their decay add immensely to the fertility of the soil.

Prices of Clover subject to change. The pound prices include postage; 100 pound prices are by freight or express, at purchaser's expense.

ALFALFA, OR LUCERNE (*Medicago sativa*). It is useless to sow this clover on land having a stiff clay or hard-pan sub-soil, as the roots naturally penetrate to a great depth and *must* do so if the plants live any time. Sow on rich, moist loam or sandy soil having a deep, porous sub-soil. Prepare the land thoroughly and sow seed at the rate of fifteen to twenty-five pounds per acre with a broadcaster or grass seeder. Cover with a brush or light harrow. The young plants are quite tender and the land must be free from weeds until they become established. ¼ Lb. 15c; Lb. 35c; 100 Lbs. at market price.

BOKHARA (*Melilotus alba*) *Sweet Clover.* This is exceedingly valuable as pasturage for bees. It is occasionally found growing wild by the roadside in company with the more common sweet clover (*Melilotus officinalis*), and may be distinguished from it by its white flowers and less coarse and more leafy stems. ¼ Lb. 15c; Lb. 40c.

ALSIKE, OR SWEDISH (*Trifolium hybridum*). The most hardy of all clovers; perennial. On rich, moist soils it yields an enormous quantity of hay or pasturage, but its greatest value is for sowing with other clovers and grasses, as it forms a thick bottom and greatly increases the yield of hay; cattle prefer it to any other forage. The heads are globular, fragrant and much liked by bees, which obtain a large amount of honey from them. Sow in spring or fall, at the rate of six pounds per acre, when used alone. ¼ Lb. 15c; Lb. 35c; 100 Lbs. at market price.

CRIMSON TREFOIL, OR SCARLET ITALIAN (*Trifolium incarnatum*). An annual variety, in common use in the south for feeding green and for hay and also found very profitable on the sandy soils of New Jersey. The yield in fodder is immense and after cutting, it at once commences growing again, continuing until severe, cold, freezing weather. It grows about one foot high; the roots are nearly black; leaves long; blossoms long, pointed and of very deep red or carmine color. Makes good hay. It is sown in August or September in the south, but should not be planted in the north until spring. Sow ten to fifteen pounds per acre. ¼ Lb. 10c; Lb. 25c; 100 Lbs. at market price.

MAMMOTH, OR LARGE RED (*Trifolium pratense*). Grows nearly twice the size of the common Red Clover, often making a stand when the other clovers fail. Sow about eight to twelve pounds per acre. Lb. 35c; 100 Lbs. at market price.

MEDIUM RED, OR JUNE (*Trifolium pratense*). This is by far the most important of all the varieties for practical purposes. Sow in spring or fall, and if no other grasses are used, at the rate of eight to twelve pounds per acre; more is required on old, stiff soils than on new and lighter ones. Lb. 30c; 100 Lbs. at market price.

WHITE DUTCH (*Trifolium repens*). A small, creeping perennial variety, valuable for pasturage and for lawns. It accommodates itself to a variety of soils, but prefers moist ground. Sow in spring, at the rate of six pounds per acre, or when used with other grasses, half that amount. ¼ Lb. 15c; Lb. 40c; 100 Lbs. at market price.

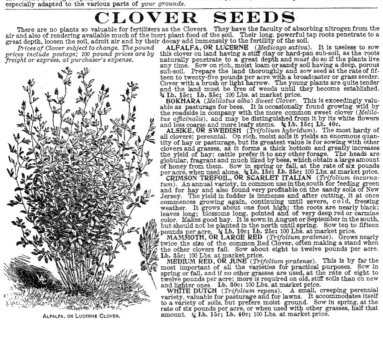

ALFALFA, OR LUCERNE CLOVER.

MISCELLANEOUS FARM SEEDS

Prices of all articles quoted on this page, except Rape, Sugar Cane and Sunflower, subject to change. The pound prices include postage; bushel and 100 pound prices are by freight or express at purchaser's expense.

BARLEY, COMMON Barley succeeds best on rich lands more sandy and lighter than those adapted to wheat. It is sown in the spring and can be grown farther north than any other grain. Use about two and one-half bushels per acre.
3 Lbs. by mail 50c; 100 Lbs. $2.40

BUCKWHEAT, COMMON Buckwheat should be sown about the 20th of June, broadcast, at the rate of about one-half bushel per acre; the average yield being from twenty-five to thirty bushels. It should be threshed as soon as dry, for if allowed to stand in mass, it is apt to spoil.
3 Lbs. by mail 50c; 100 Lbs. $2.75

BUCKWHEAT, JAPANESE The plants are large and vigorous, maturing seed early and resisting drought and blight remarkably well; the grain is much larger and has a thinner hull than the Common or the Silver Hull. We recommend this especially for well drained or sandy land and the dry climate of the western plains.
3 Lbs. by mail 50c; 100 Lbs. $3.00

BUCKWHEAT, SILVER HULL This improved variety is much better than the old sort. It is in bloom longer, matures sooner and yields double the quantity per acre. The husk is thinner, the corners less prominent and the grain of a beautiful light gray color. 3 Lbs. by mail 50c; 100 Lbs. $3.25

FLAX (*Linum usitatissimum*). Sow late enough in the spring to avoid frost and early enough to secure a good stand and enable the crop to ripen before the fall rains. A fair average quantity of seed to be sown on an acre is one-half bushel, when cultivated for seed; if for the fibre a larger quantity should be sown. Cut before quite ripe and if the weather be dry, let it lie in the swath a few hours, when it should be raked and secured from the weather; thresh early in the fall and in dry weather.
Lb. 20c; 100 Lbs. $4.50

HEMP (*Cannabis sativa*). If raised for manufacturing, must be sown broadcast, at the rate of one-half bushel to the acre; if for seed, it should be planted in hills four feet apart and the plants thinned out to three or four most vigorous stems in each hill. Lb. 25c; 100 Lbs. $7.50

HUNGARIAN (*Panicum Germanicum*). This is a species of annual millet, growing less rank, with smaller stalks often yielding two or three tons of hay per acre. It is very valuable and popular with those who are clearing timber lands. Sow and cultivate like millet. Lb. 20c; 100 Lbs. at market price.

MILLET, COMMON (*Panicum miliaceum*). Requires a dry, light, rich soil and grows two and a half to four feet high, with a fine bulk of stalks and leaves and is excellent for forage. For hay, sow broadcast, about twenty-five pounds per acre, from May 1st to August 1st. For grain, sow in drills, about twelve pounds per acre and not later than June 20th. Lb. 20c; 100 Lbs. at market price.

MILLET, GERMAN, OR GOLDEN An improved variety, medium early, growing five to five feet high. The heads, though numerous, are very large and compact. The seeds are contained in rough, bristly sheaths and are round, golden, yellow and beautiful in appearance. Lb. 25c; 100 Lbs. at market price.

Rape

DWARF ESSEX FOR SOWING There is but one variety of Rape that has proven profitable to sow in America and that is the Dwarf Essex. Do not be deluded into buying inferior grades offered by unscrupulous dealers through exaggerated advertisements. Such seed is often more or less mixed with the annual variety which is not only worthless as forage, but once planted is likely to become a pernicious weed. **There is no plant that will give as heavy a yield of forage at such a small cost as this** and its general cultivation would add largely to the profits of American farms. Especially valuable for green manuring and pasture. When fed off by sheep, it will probably do more to restore and make profitable exhausted soils than any other plant. Biennial.

CULTURE—Prepare the ground as for turnips and sow in June or July, with a turnip drill, in rows two and one-half feet apart, at the rate of two and one-half pounds of seed per acre. It may be sown broadcast, either with other fall forage crops or by itself, using from one to five pounds of seed per acre. ¼ Lb. 10c; Lb. 25c, postpaid. By freight or express, at purchaser's expense. 10 Lbs. 90c; 100 Lbs. $5.00

RYE, SPRING Although this grain is often planted especially for paper makers, who prefer it to any other, its principal value is as a "catch" crop, to sow where winter grain has failed. The straw is shorter and stiffer than the winter variety and is always easily secured, while the grain, although smaller, is of equal value. 3 Lbs. by mail 50c; 100 Lbs. $2.85

RYE, FALL OR WINTER The time for sowing is from the middle of August to the last of September. Prepare the ground as for wheat and sow broadcast or with a drill at the rate of one and one-half bushels per acre. This has no equal as a crop to be used for late fall and early spring pasture and is one of the best to turn under for green manure. 3 Lbs. by mail 50c; 100 Lbs. $3.00

Sugar Cane (Sorghum)

ALBAUGH EARLY The best early variety and the one which we especially recommend for the north, where the season is short. It is practically as early as the old Early Amber and yields much more per acre either of syrup or seed. The plant is large, of strong, vigorous and erect habit and stands up much better than Early Amber. It may be planted as late as the 15th of June and will be in condition to harvest for syrup in September. Cane seed should not be planted before the weather is warm in the spring. Three to four pounds of seed are required per acre. ¼ Lb. 10c; Lb. 20c, postpaid. $5.00 per 100 lbs., by freight or express, at purchaser's expense.

EARLY ORANGE An exceedingly valuable variety; very large, of strong and vigorous habit and does not fall down. It is early and often yields as much as 240 gallons of very beautifully colored and highly flavored syrup to the acre. We recommend it highly to all desiring a superior cane. ¼ Lb. 10c; Lb. 20c, postpaid. $5.00 per 100 pounds, by freight or express, at purchaser's expense.

Sunflower

LARGE RUSSIAN This variety has large heads, borne at the top of a single unbranched stem and having much more and larger seed than the common sort. It is used extensively for feeding poultry. Sow the seed as soon as the ground is fit for planting corn, in rows five feet apart and ten inches apart in the row. Cultivate same as corn. When the seed is ripe and hard, cut off the heads and pile loosely in a rail pen having a solid floor or in a corn crib. After curing sufficiently so that they will thresh easily, flail out or run through a threshing machine and clean with an ordinary fanning mill. This variety will yield 1,000 pounds or more of seed per acre. Some species of Sunflowers are planted largely in the flower garden for ornament. (*See Sunflower, page 91*). Pkt. 5c; ¼ Lb. 10c; Lb. 20c, postpaid. $6.00 per 100 lbs., by freight or express, at purchaser's expense.

VETCHES, OR TARES, SPRING (*Vicia sativa*). A pea-like plant grown extensively in England and to a considerable extent in Canada for stock feeding, but not as much used in the United States as it should be. Culture same as field peas. Sow two bushels per acre. *Market price.*

VETCHES, SAND, WINTER OR HAIRY (*Vicia villosa*). A very hardy forage plant growing well on soils so poor and sandy that they will produce but little clover. The plants, when mature, are about forty inches high and if cut for forage as soon as full grown and before setting seed, they will start up again and furnish even a larger crop than the first. The seed is round and black and should be sown at the rate of one and one-half bushels to the acre. *Market price.*

WILD RICE (*Zizania aquatica*). An annual which sows itself about the middle of September, lies dormant all winter, in spring commences to sprout as soon as water gets warm, reaching the surface in the first half of June. It grows very rapidly in one to three feet of water, ripens late in August or early in September. It should be sown broadcast from a boat, in one or two feet of water and where there is a mud bottom. It succeeds best when planted in the fall before the ice forms but it has been successfully planted in spring and also through the ice in winter. As an attraction for wild fowl it cannot be equaled. In large ponds and lakes it purifies the water, affords a refuge for the small fry from the large fish, as well as furnishing them plenty of food from the animalculæ upon its stalks; for planting in fish ponds it is especially desirable. It also does well along the shores of marshes and makes a good hay. Lb. 30c; $15.00 per 100 Lbs.

BIRD SEEDS

A DESCRIPTIVE LIST OF
Choice Flower Seeds

MOST flowering plants will live in almost any soil, but to give them a fair chance to develop, some care should be taken to make the ground suited to their needs. Many flowers are better if produced on plants of vigorous growth, hence a portion of the garden should be prepared by deep digging, thorough pulverization and liberal enriching with large quantities of WELL ROTTED manure. Since some other varieties produce the largest and finest colored flowers when grown on rather light, poor soil, a portion of the garden should NOT be enriched.

Cultural directions are given on the packets, and we urge purchasers to study them carefully. While some seeds need special treatment, the following general rules will apply to all. Make the surface of the soil as fine, smooth and level as possible; do not plant when the ground is wet; cover each lot of seeds to a uniform depth, which should not be more than four or six times the diameter of the seed; press the soil firmly over the seed; plant in rows, so that the starting plants can be seen easily; be careful not to allow the young plants to be crowded or to be smothered by weeds.

ALL FLOWER SEEDS SENT POSTPAID ON RECEIPT OF PRICE

Send us $1.00 and select PACKETS to the value of..$1.15	Send us $4.00 and select PACKETS to the value of..$4.85
" 2.00 " " " " 2.35	" 5.00 " " " " 6.15
" 3.00 " " " " 3.60	" 10.00 " " " " 12.50

These Rates apply only to Seeds in Packets, but not to Seeds by Weight or Measure.
No discount can be allowed on Flower Seeds by Weight.

Abobra Viridiflora
A rapid growing, climbing, half hardy, tuberous rooted perennial gourd. The scarlet fruit is not larger than a cherry and is strikingly in contrast with the dark green, finely cut foliage. The plant needs a warm, sunny situation. Height fifteen feet..................Pkt. 10cts

Abutilon
(*Flowering-Maple*). An attractive perennial, greenhouse shrub, producing a profusion of bell-shaped, drooping flowers, which vary in color in different plants from white or yellow to deep orange and crimson, veined with yellow. Well adapted for house culture and for bedding outdoors. Will bloom the first season if seeds are sown under glass in March. *Finest mixed*...........................Pkt. 25cts

Acroclinium
(*Everlasting*). Very pretty, half hardy annual, producing white and rose colored, daisy-like flowers. These are the "Immortelles" so desirable for wreaths and winter bouquets. Height one foot. Roseum, light rose....Pkt. 5cts
Mixed........Pkt. 5cts Album, pure white.... " 5cts

Adlumia Cirrhosa
(*Mountain Fringe, Wood Fringe, Alleghany Vine*). A beautiful, graceful climber and profuse bloomer. Hardy biennial. Height fifteen feet. White and pink.......................................Pkt. 10cts

Adonis Autumnalis
(*Adonis Flower, Pheasant's Eye*). A handsome, hardy, herbaceous annual, one foot high. The finely cut, dark green foliage, in which are set the intense blood red flowers, gives the plant a very striking appearance. It grows readily in a place shaded by a house or fence, and requires but little care...........Pkt. 5cts

Ageratum ::
A beautiful, hardy annual. The flowers, borne in dense clusters, are very useful for bouquets, and the plants are very attractive in the garden. The different varieties are from six inches to two feet in height and covered with bloom nearly all summer.

Mexicanum, light blue, about fifteen inches high......................Pkt. 5cts
Imperial Dwarf White, height about six inches..........................Pkt. 5cts
Tom Thumb Dwarf Blue, desirable for edging, six inches high.......Pkt. 5cts
Lasseauxl, rose colored, about eighteen inches high....................Pkt. 5cts
Conspicuum, valuable for winter; white, eighteen inches high..........Pkt. 5cts
Mixed, seeds of the above varieties mixed.............▼.........Pkt. 5cts

Agrostemma
Very useful for cutting for bouquets, and pretty in masses in beds. The annual variety is known as Rose of Heaven, the perennial as Rose Campion. One and a half feet high. Hardy.
Coronaria, crimson; perennial..Pkt. 5cts
Cœli-rosa, rose, white center; annual .... " 5cts

Agrostis Nebulosa
(*Ornamental Grass*). An ornamental grass in which the small seeds are so gracefully poised in large, open clusters as to have the effect of a cloud, and when dried can be effectively used in dried bouquets. Grows easily in any common garden soil. Hardy annual; about one and a half feet high..........................Pkt. 5cts

AGERATUM.

Alyssum

Sweet (Maritimum). This very hardy annual comes into bloom very early in the spring, covering itself with innumerable clusters of small, pure white flowers; they have a peculiar, delicate fragrance, and are useful in all kinds of small bouquets. Grows one foot high. **Pkt. 5cts**

Alyssum, Little Gem. A beautiful white variety of Sweet Alyssum, especially adapted to edgings, borders and rock work. The plants grow about six inches high and produce hundreds of flowers, which form a compact mass of bloom about fifteen to eighteen inches in diameter. Hardy annual..**Pkt. 10cts**

Alyssum, Golden (*Saxatile*). Flowers golden yellow; desirable for rock work; showy in masses. Hardy perennial; height one foot........... **Pkt. 5cts**

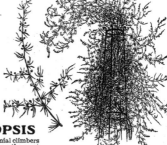

ASPARAGUS VERTICILLATUS.

AMPELOPSIS

These hardy, perennial climbers are deservedly among the most popular vines for covering walls, arbors, etc. They are easily grown from seed which should be soaked in warm water before planting.

Quinquefolia (*Virginia Creeper, or American Woodbine*). Though a common native climber, this is one of the very best plants for covering unsightly objects, or it may be easily trained into festoons of exceeding grace and beauty...............................**Pkt. 5cts**

Veitchii (*Japan, or Boston Ivy*). This plant will cling and creep along the smoothest wall, covering it with a mantle of ivy-like green leaves whose colors change to brilliant hues in the fall. It makes but feeble growth the first year from seed, but when once established grows very vigorously and rapidly. Hardy perennial......................**Pkt. 10cts**

ANEMONE

Coronaria (*Wind Flower*). Among the earliest and brightest of spring flowers. The colors run through several shades. Hardy perennial; about six inches high...................**Pkt. 5cts**

ANTIRRHINUM—(*See Snapdragon*).

AQUILEGIA—(*See Columbine*).

ARABIS

Among the earliest blooming plants, and very useful for rock work, edgings, etc. Hardy perennial; nine inches high.

Alpina, pure white.................................**Pkt. 5cts**

Aristolochia Sipho

(*Dutchman's Pipe*). A vigorous growing climber with curiously shaped purple-brown flowers and very large, heart-shaped leaves which have a tropical appearance; very effective for verandas. Hardy perennial; grows from fifteen to thirty feet high ....**Pkt. 10cts**

ARMERIA

Maritima (*Thrift, or Sea Pink*). These handsome plants are well adapted for ornamenting rock work and edging walks. Hardy perennial; six inches high..**Pkt. 5cts**

ASPARAGUS

Sprengeri. One of the most graceful and beautiful of house plants; particularly valuable for hanging baskets. The sprays are from three to four feet long and are of a light green color. Soak the seed in warm water before planting. A greenhouse perennial...........**Pkt. 15cts**

Verticillatus. A beautiful climber having feathery foliage and scarlet berries which are quite ornamental. Hardy perennial; about ten to fifteen feet high.......**Pkt. 10cts**

ASPERULA

Azurea setosa. A profuse blooming, dwarf, hardy annual with sweet-scented, lavender-blue flowers. Height less than one foot....................**Pkt. 5cts**

ALYSSUM, SWEET.

AMARANTHUS

These plants afford brilliant contrasts of color, being useful for tall borders and groups; also, where foliage effects are desired. The leaves and stems are of different shades of red blended with green.

Melancholicus ruber, blood red foliage. Hardy annual; two and a half feet high ....**Pkt. 5cts**

Tricolor, a hardy annual with leaves of red, yellow and green; well known as "Joseph's Coat." Two to three feet high.........**Pkt. 5cts**

Salicifolius, two and a half to three feet high. Leaves beautifully undulated, varying from green to bronze, and later to a bright orange-red. Tender annual.......................................**Pkt. 10cts**

Henderi, drooping foliage, richly colored in shades of red and green. Tender annual..**Pkt. 10cts**

AMMOBIUM

Alatum grandiflorum, (*Everlasting*). Valuable for winter bouquets in connection with grasses and other everlastings. The flowers are pure white. Hardy annual; two feet high......................**Pkt. 5cts**

ASPERULA AZUREA SETOSA.

Aster:

THE CHINA ASTER, in its many varieties, is not only one of the most profitable annuals for the professional florist, but one of the best for the home garden. The plants are of vigorous growth and quite hardy, even enduring a slight frost without serious injury. By planting the different strains and at different times, one may have in the latitude of Detroit a constant succession of bloom from the last of July till the middle of October without the aid of a greenhouse, or even a hot-bed. They do best in moderately light soil, but will thrive in almost any used for a garden, provided it is well enriched and made friable.

The seed may be planted out of doors as soon as the ground is warm and dry, and at intervals till the first of July. The more costly seed may be sown in boxes kept in the house or a hot-bed, but given plenty of air and light, and the young plants set in the open ground as soon as the weather is favorable.

Insects may be kept at bay by syringing with clear water for the red spider, or with that containing about one-fourth teaspoonful of Paris green to ten gallons water, for those that eat the foliage, or sprinkling with tobacco water or dust to keep off the plant louse. We offer choice seed of the best types that have been grown for us by the most skilful cultivators in America and Europe, and which is more certain to give good results than most of that on the market.

EARLIER AND SOME DWARF SORTS

Extra Early Hohenzollern

Our high opinion of last season concerning the desirability of this new class of asters has been confirmed. Plants of medium size, as early as the earliest, but producing abundantly blooms of the largest size, measuring fully four inches in diameter. The petals are of open Comet type, and unusually graceful in their seemingly careless arrangement. Heretofore we have been able to offer no aster having the desirable combination of extreme earliness, large size and splendid cutting qualities.

Rose. The earliest of all asters.............**Pkt. 25cts**
White. Pure white; a few days later than Rose................................. "   25cts
Silver Lilac. A charming delicate shade; a little later than White..................... "   25cts

Queen of the Earliest. A compact growing plant, but of branching habit and medium height; one of the earliest to produce flowers, which are white and borne on long stems...........................**Pkt. 10cts**
Queen of the Market. Plants about one foot high, bearing from ten to fifteen finely formed flowers on long and graceful stems, and coming into bloom very early. Many colors mixed ....**Pkt. 10cts**

Victoria

A strain in which the petals curve outward, overlapping like those of the double dahlia. Plants about eighteen inches high and very free flowering; flowers very brilliant in color. Good for pot culture.

Bright Red........................**Pkt. 10cts**
Peach Blossom.................... "   10cts
Violet .... "   10cts
White, pure...................... "   10cts
White, turning blue.............. "   10cts
Mixed colors .... "   10cts

Truffaut's Perfection Pæony Flowered

The plants are about eighteen inches high and produce very large, perfectly formed and brilliantly colored flowers with petals curving upward and inward forming blooms of great beauty. The different colors come quite true to name.

Snow White ....**Pkt. 10cts**
Light Blue...................................... "   10cts
Rose .... "   10cts
Crimson... "   10cts
Scarlet, white edge............................ "   10cts
Mixed, a carefully proportioned mixture of all colors .... "   10cts

Imbricated Pompon. Plant about eighteen inches high. Flowers of fine form, with the petals arranged in perfect symmetry; very beautiful. Many colors mixed....................................**Pkt. 5cts**
Jewel, or Ball Shaped. Plant about eighteen inches high, producing abundantly, on long stems, ball-shaped flowers composed of very broad, comparatively short petals. Mixed colors..........**Pkt. 10cts**
Charlotte Roumanille. A large flower of the Comet class, of clear rose color with white center, and remains fresh for a long time......................**Pkt. 15cts**
Diamond, Plant about eighteen inches high, with very large and double flowers of great brilliancy of color. Mixed colors............................**Pkt. 15cts**
Princess (Pure White, or Snowball). Plant wonderfully floriferous, often producing as many as thirty fine flowers made up of broad, imbricated petals, and of fine color. One of the best for cut flowers..........................**Pkt. 10cts**
Cocardeau, or Crown. Plant about two feet high. Flowers quite flat, made up of short, broad petals, white-centered, with borders of various shades; very distinct and beautiful. Mixed colors....................................**Pkt. 10cts**
Lilliput. Plant about eighteen inches high, bearing a great many small but perfectly formed flowers which are among the most brilliantly colored of all asters. Mixed colors..**Pkt. 10cts**

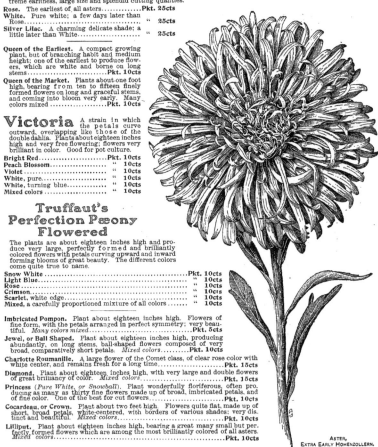

ASTER,
EXTRA EARLY HOHENZOLLERN.

ASTER Continued

DWARF SORTS

Christmas Tree Of dwarf, branching habit, but the flowers are borne on comparatively long stems. Very desirable for early cutting.
Rose, with white center.........................Pkt. 25cts
Light Blue, with white center.................... " 25cts

Very Dwarf, or Pygmæa. The plant is made up of a cluster of leaves close to the ground, surmounted by a bunch of large, bright colored flowers. *Mixed colors....*Pkt. 10cts
Triumph. One of the finest of the dwarf sorts; plants about nine inches high, c o v e r e d with deep scarlet flowers...Pkt. 15cts
Shakespeare. Plants about six inches high and as much in diameter, made up of finely formed and colored flowers. *Mixed colors.*.............................Pkt, 10cts
Dwarf Victoria. Flowers like those of the Tall Victoria, but borne on plants about a foot high. A fine sort for borders. *Mixed colors.*.........................Pkt. 10cts
Pyramidal Bouquet. The plant is a perfect bouquet of fifteen to twenty large flowers which quite conceal the foliage. About ten inches high. *Mixed colors.*Pkt. 10cts
Dwarf Chrysanthemum. Plant about twelve inches high, bearing flowers which are often three inches in diameter and very bright in color. *Mixed colors*..........Pkt. 5cts

ASTER, TRUFFAUT'S (SEE PAGE 68).

TALLER AND LATER SORTS

Comet In this class the petals are very long and recurved, having much the effect of the finest chrysanthemums. They are of varied and beautiful colors, and one of the most popular sorts, continuing in bloom till quite late in the season. *Finest mixture*..Pkt. 15cts
Comet, Giant White. The plant is more vigorous and taller growing than the ordinary Comet, and the flowers are larger and equal in form.........................Pkt. 15cts
Comet, Giant Mixed. A carefully proportioned mixture of various colors..................................Pkt. 15cts

Japanese. A very vigorous growing sort, producing large flowers made up of very long, semi-tubular and twisted petals, and having the effect of a large Japan chrysanthemum. *Mixed colors*.........................Pkt. 10cts
Washington. Plants two feet tall, flowers very large, often fully four inches in diameter. *Mixed colors.*..Pkt. 15cts
Giant Emperor. Produces flowers of the largest size, fine form and clear white color.....................Pkt. 10cts
Goliath, Mont Rose. Very large, well formed flowers of delicate pink color.................................Pkt. 15cts
Goliath, Mont Blanc. Like Mont Rose, but white in color.. Pkt. 15cts

ASTER, COMET.

Semple's Branching

A class of very strong growing asters not coming into bloom until very late, but producing flowers so large, double, perfect in form, and borne on such long stems, that florists often sell them for chrysanthemums.

Deep Carmine.............Pkt. 10cts		Dark Purple................Pkt. 10cts
Lavender................... " 10cts		Rose Pink................... " 10cts
Light Blue.................. " 10cts		White....................... " 10cts
Pink......................... " 10cts		Semple's Mixed............. " 10cts

Aster, Finest Mixed, a mixture of the finest strains and colors.......... " 5cts

Auricula Called also Primula Auricula and French Cowslip. This is an old and well known favorite. It thrives best in a moist soil and cool atmosphere. Tender perennial; height six inches.
Alpine, the most hardy variety; a good mixture.........................Pkt. 15cts
Finest Prize, mixture of all the choicest varieties....................... " 20cts

BACHELOR'S BUTTON—(*See Centaurea*).

Balloon Vine (*Cardiospermum halicacabum*). Remarkable for its inflated membranous capsules containing the seed. It is sometimes called "Love-in-a-Puff." A rapid and graceful climber. Flowers white. Tender annual; six feet high.................Pkt. 5cts

BALSAM

Known as Lady Slipper and Touch-Me-Not. Balsams have been so much improved by cultivation that with good seed and proper care a *single flower* is the exception, each blossom being fully as double as a rose. The colors range from white to dark purple, and are either self colored or spotted and striped. Balsams are tender and should be started in boxes indoors or in the open ground when danger of frost is past. The seeds are large and germinate quickly. The plants prefer a rich, moist or even wet sandy loam, and must not suffer for moisture. Better results are obtained when only a few main branches are allowed to grow, all the secondary and weak ones being pinched out. Well grown plants should stand two feet apart each way. Hardy annual; one to two feet high.
Double Solferino, satiny white, streaked and spotted with crimson and lilac. *Very choice.*Pkt. 5cts
Double Camellia, extra fine mixed, as double as a camellia, which it resembles; white, blotched with various colors...................................... " 5cts

Double Pure White, well adapted for florists, for bouquets; very double·····················Pkt. 10cts
Double Dark Red (*Atrosanguinea plenissima*), a very double, dark red variety·················· " 10cts

Mixed Double Rose, has perfectly double, rose-like blossoms of almost every shade and color... " 5cts
Mixed Double Dwarf, about one foot high........ " 5cts
Mixed Double Tall, about two feet high.......... " 5cts

Bartonia Aurea A pretty flowering plant of the gentian family, producing a profusion of fine, bright metallic yellow blossoms about two inches across, and fragrant in the evening. Tender annual; one foot high. Pkt. 5c

Begonia

Some of the newer forms of begonias are among the most brilliantly beautiful of flowering plants. With care they can be grown from seed. Sow in February or March, in pots, on a smooth surface of fine soil, without any covering of earth but cover the pot with glass and keep in a warm but shaded place, taking great care not to wash out the very small seeds or young plants in watering. The plants will give an abundance of bloom the first year and at the end of the season they may be dried off by withholding water, the tubers kept in a dry place, free from frost, and planted the following spring, when they will bloom more freely than before.

TUBEROUS-ROOTED BEGONIAS

Single Mixed..............................Pkt. 25cts
Double Mixed.............................. " 35cts
Robusta Perfecta, of robust, compact habit, dark green foliage and brilliant, double, cinnabar scarlet flowers........ " 25cts

FIBROUS-ROOTED BEGONIAS

Of the kinds offered under this head, *Begonia Rex* is grown for its ornamental foliage, while the others are among the very best for flowering in the house, or in partly shaded locations outdoors.

Vernon (*Semperflorens atropurpurea*). Flowers brilliant, rich red, and are set off perfectly by the abundant, glossy green leaves which are broadly margined with bronze and purple. Extremely hardy and floriferous; the best of the semperflorens class ..Pkt. 15cts

Semperflorens alba. A very useful variety, well adapted for house or outdoor culture. Plants of compact, dwarf habit, and under proper treatment, almost continuous bloomers. Easily grown; flowers pure white....................................Pkt. 15cts

Semperflorens rosea. Like Semperflorens alba except flowers are rose colored................................Pkt. 15cts

Rex, ornamental leaved varieties; finest mixed.......... " 25cts

For Begonia Bulbs, see Bulbs and Roots.

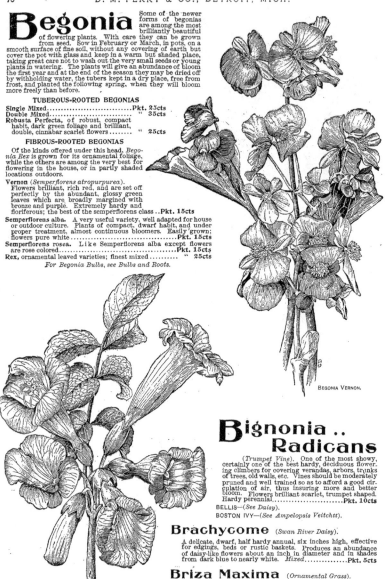

BEGONIA VERNON.

BIGNONIA RADICANS.

Bignonia .. Radicans

(*Trumpet Vine*). One of the most showy, certainly one of the best hardy, deciduous flowering climbers for covering verandas, arbors, trunks of trees, old walls, etc. Vines should be moderately pruned and well trained so as to afford a good circulation of air, thus insuring more and better bloom. Flowers brilliant scarlet, trumpet shaped. Hardy perennial.........................Pkt. 10cts

BELLIS—(*See Daisy*).

BOSTON IVY—(*See Ampelopsis Veitchtt*).

Brachycome (*Swan River Daisy*).

A delicate, dwarf, half hardy annual, six inches high, effective for edgings, beds or rustic baskets. Produces an abundance of daisy-like flowers about an inch in diameter and in shades from dark blue to nearly white. *Mixed*..............Pkt. 5cts

Briza Maxima (*Ornamental Grass*).

Grows about one foot high, and is valuable for winter bouquets and wreaths. The seed clusters are heart shaped and gracefully poised on such slender stems that they are almost constantly in motion. The plant is known to many as Quaking Grass. Hardy annual..............................Pkt. 5cts

Browallia These handsome, profuse bloomers are used freely both for indoor and outdoor planting, on account of the ease with which they may be grown and their usefulness for cut flowers. Half hardy annual.
Roezli, eight to twelve inches high; produces white and blue flowers..........**Pkt. 15cts**
Elata, height eighteen inches; mixed....................................., " 5cts

Bryonopsis An ornamental climber of the gourd family, bearing green fruit which changes in color as the season advances to bright scarlet striped with white. Tuberous-rooted perennial but may be treated as a tender annual; about ten feet high....................................**Pkt. 5cts**

Calampelis Scabra (*Eccremocarpus*). A beautiful, tender climber from Chili, with graceful, delicate foliage. Late in the season it produces racemes of bright orange flowers, which in turn give place to delicate pendant seed pods. Tender perennial; fifteen feet high....................................**Pkt. 10cts**

Calandrinia Fine dwarf plants for growing in masses; produce an abundance of blossoms; well suited for edgings, rockeries, etc. Tender annual; one-half to one foot high.
Grandiflora, rosy lilac....**Pkt. 5cts** Umbellata, crimson....**Pkt. 5cts**

Calla Aethiopica (*Ethiopian Lily*). An old and very desirable plant, either as an aquatic or as an ornament for the drawing room or conservatory. Will flower in one year from planting of the seed. Half hardy perennial.
Pkt. 10cts

Calliopsis, or Coreopsis

Very showy border plants, producing in great profusion and for a long time flowers which are bright yellow and rich brown, either self colored or with these colors and red contrasted.

Coreopsis tinctoria. Although a native plant this is one of the most desirable of our garden flowers. It produces an abundance of brilliantly colored flowers, varying from clear yellow to deep, rich brown, often the two colors being beautifully contrasted in the same blossom. They are borne on long, graceful stems and are very desirable for decorative purposes. Very hardy and profuse blooming annual. *Fine mixed*..**Pkt. 5cts**

Lanceolata grandiflora, a hardy perennial, blooming the first year and producing on long stems a constant succession of very rich yellow flowers about three inches in diameter; exceedingly valuable for decorative purposes.......**Pkt. 10cts**

Callirhoe (*Poppy Mallow*). Extremely handsome purple border plants, producing large, rich, purple-red flowers. Hardy annual.
Choicest mixed....................................**Pkt. 5cts**

Camellia Japonica House or greenhouse evergreen, perennial shrubs easily grown from seeds, though they germinate slowly. As varieties do not come true from seed one may have the pleasure of getting something distinct and of great merit. Mixed fine double varieties....................................**Pkt. 25cts**

Canary Bird Flower (*Tropæolum canariense*). A beautiful climber with curiously shaped, little, canary colored blossoms. Will blossom freely from July until killed by frost. Tender annual......**Pkt. 5cts**

Calceolaria A favorite and universally admired genus, remarkable for its large, beautifully spotted blossoms, produced in almost countless variations of marking. Grown in pots in the conservatory, greenhouse or garden. Herbaceous annuals or shrubby evergreen perennials.
Hybrida grandiflora, flowers of immense size. Seed saved from finest specimens....................**Pkt. 25cts**
Hybrida tigrina, flowers of the largest size, beautifully spotted. Seed saved from *choicest collection*.......... " 25cts
Finest hybrids mixed, seed saved only from the *most perfect flowers*, embracing many of recent introduction; all desirable.................................... " 25cts
Rugosa, shrubby; grown in and out of doors. Saved from the *finest shrubby varieties mixed*.................... " 25cts

CALENDULA—(*See Marigold*).
CALIFORNIA POPPY—(*See Eschscholtzia*).

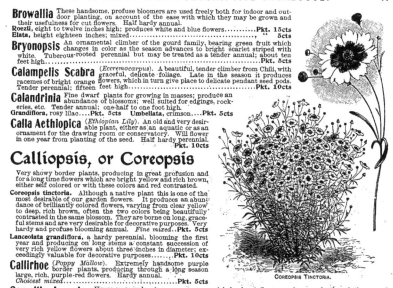

COREOPSIS TINCTORIA.

Candytuft

(*Iberis*). Showy, branching plants six to eighteen inches high. Indispensable for cutting and very effective in beds or masses. If sown in spring will bloom from July to September, or if in the fall will blossom from May to July. Hardy annual.

Lilac, shading to light purple..................**Pkt. 5cts**
White .... " 5cts
Rocket (*Empress*), white, extra large trusses. A great improvement in the size and quality of the flowering trusses over the common white variety.....**Pkt. 5cts**
Fragrant, white.................................... " 5cts
Purple, a rich dark shade.................... " 5cts
Rose Carmine, dwarf, compact habit......... " 10cts
Fine Mixed.................................... " 5cts
Dwarf Mixed Hybrid, about six inches high. " 10cts
Perennial (*Sempervirens*), hardy, evergreen, sub-shrub; height ten inches; flowers white, very pretty.................................... " 10cts

Canterbury Bell

(*Campanula Medium*). Handsome, hardy, biennial of stately growth, rich color and profuse bloom. Succeeds best in light, rich soil and should be transplanted or thinned to eighteen inches or two feet apart. Has large, bell shaped flowers which are strikingly effective. Height one to four feet. One of the wild forms of Campanula is the "Blue Bells of Scotland."

Double White.....**Pkt. 10cts** Double Mixed......**Pkt. 5cts**
Double Blue ......" 10cts Single Mixed...... " 5cts
Calycanthema, Mixed. Flowers large, of fine form, white, lilac, rose and purple. Known also as "Cup and Saucer" plant; the calyx forming a cup around the base of the bell...**Pkt. 10cts**

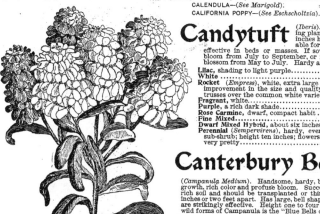

CANDYTUFT.

Carnation ..

(*Dianthus Caryophyllus*).

"Carnation," "Pink," "Clove Pink," "Florists' Pink" are names applied by different people to the same or to different plants of several species as well as to hybrids between them. They are all easily grown from seed and very free blooming, the flowers being bright colored and with a most delicious, clove-like fragrance. Some of the varieties are very desirable for the professional florist and make fine house plants for the amateur. Others do best in the open ground and are among the most desirable of garden plants. Half hardy perennial.

CARNATION
MARGUERITE.

LARGE FLOWERING CARNATIONS BEST SUITED FOR POT CULTURE

These are the sorts most grown by florists who are constantly striving to produce new varieties. It is said that $10,000 was paid for one of superior merit. While these choice varieties are propagated by cutting, planters may get some just as good from the seed we offer and are certain to get a large proportion of double and very beautiful flowers.

Double Perpetual Flowering Mixed. An exceedingly beautiful variety producing very double flowers of various shades and colors. Seed saved from choicest double flowers...........................**Pkt. 25cts**

Fine Double Selves. Seeds from named varieties grown in the open ground and likely to give some flowers fully equal to the best greenhouse sorts...........................**Pkt. 10cts**

Fine Double Striped. Seed from fine named striped varieties... " **15cts**

Choicest White Ground. Seed from choice, large flowered, named varieties, with nearly white flowers, bordered or tinted with red or purple. Sure to give large and beautiful flowers................. " **35cts**

Extra Choice Double Mixed. Seed from an immense collection of choice French, German, Italian and English named sorts. Certain to produce a large proportion of double and finely formed and colored flowers in an almost endless variety of shades and markings.. " **25cts**

Choice Double Mixed. A mixture of all colors and types.. " **10cts**

Picotee, Extra Fine Double Mixed. Extra fine seed from spotted and splashed, named varieties, sure to give flowers of splendid quality................. " **25cts**

VARIETIES OF CARNATIONS ADAPTED TO BOTH POT AND OUTDOOR CULTURE

For outdoor culture a good, rich compost is indispensable to the production of fine carnations; there is scarcely any plant to which a congenial soil is of so much importance.

Double Dwarf Vienna Mixed. Large flowered and comes into bloom early. Produces flowers of many colors and beautiful markings...............................**Pkt. 10cts**

Early Double Snow White. A splendid sort for either pot culture or the garden. The plants are vigorous, erect and bushy in growth. Comes into flower very early and furnishes abundant bloom for a long time. The flowers are large, double, clear white and wonderfully fragrant. One of the most profitable plants for florists, but should also have a place in every private garden............**Pkt. 25cts**

Double Red Grenadin. Plants a little smaller and less erect than the White Grenadin but come into bloom a little earlier and are fully as floriferous. Flowers double, fragrant and of rich, deep red color...........**Pkt. 15cts**

Marguerite Carnation. The plants of this wonderfully fine strain may be made to flower in four months. The flowers are large, double and very fragrant and appear in very attractive shades of color. One of the best "pinks" in cultivation.......................................**Pkt. 5cts**

Double Florists' Pink (*Plumarius Scoticus fl. pl.*) This is the double form of common garden or clove pink, and though so common is one of the best of our hardy, garden perennials...**Pkt. 25cts**

CANNA

Stately, ornamental plants, very desirable for bedding outdoors, producing clusters of large flowers of the most intense and brilliant colors. Plant the seeds in February, first soaking them for a day in hot water. In August the plants come into bloom and continue to flower very freely until cut down by frost. Nothing can exceed the beauty and variety of color of these magnificent bedding or greenhouse plants. Tender perennial. Store roots in cellar in winter.
Finest Large Flowering Mixed. About three feet high....**Pkt. 5cts**

CANNA.

Castor Bean (Ricinus)

Tall, majestic plants for lawns, with leaves of glossy green, brown or bronzed metallic hue and long spikes of scarlet or of green, prickly fruit. Of very quick growth in rich soil. Tender annual, six to fifteen feet high.

Zanzibariensis, a comparatively new species of wonderfully vigorous growth. Plants grow from ten to fifteen feet high. Leaves have a brilliant lustre, measure about thirty inches across, and in different plants range from bright green with green stems to deep bronze with dark red stems. *Mixed varieties.*..**Pkt. 5cts**

Sanguineus (*Tricolor*). Blood red stalks with red venation in leaves; height about six feet.................**Pkt. 5cts**

Mixed..........................." 5cts

Centaurea

The Centaureas are an exceedingly interesting genus of plants, embracing annuals, biennials and perennials, which, though botanically alike, are very different in appearance. Some are very valuable for the beauty of their silvery white, velvet-like foliage, the flowers being unattractive; others are highly prized for the beauty of their flowers. They are all easily grown from seed.

VARIETIES CULTIVATED FOR THEIR FOLIAGE

Candidissima. Ornamental plants of great beauty; foliage deeply cut, silvery white and densely covered with white hairs. Half hardy perennial...................**Pkt. 15cts**

Gymnocarpa. Sometimes called *Dusty Miller.* Valuable because of its silvery gray foliage and graceful, drooping habit of growth. Half hardy perennial; one-half to two feet high....................**Pkt. 10cts**

VARIETIES CULTIVATED FOR THEIR FLOWERS

Cyanus (*Bachelor's Button, Corn Flower*). This is the flower seen in such great abundance in the fields of Europe, and to a less extent in this country; though a weed *there,* in its improved forms it is one of the most attractive of garden flowers. If seed is sown as soon as the ground is fit in the spring and the flowers picked so as to prevent the plant exhausting itself by seeding, it will furnish a profusion of bright blue, white or pink flowers from July till late in autumn. One to two feet high. *Mixed,* all colors.....................**Pkt. 5cts**

Double Mixed (*Bachelor's Button*). Produces larger, more globular flowers than the common variety..........**Pkt. 5cts**

Odorata (*Sweet Sultan*). An old fashioned, hardy annual about eighteen inches high, with long stemmed, sweet scented, light blue or purple flowers. ....**Pkt. 10cts**

Marguerite. A sweet-scented, white Centaurea, about as large as a medium sized carnation. It is a sport from Centaurea Odorata and the plants are about eighteen inches high. The flowers are beautifully laciniated and produced on long stems; their lasting quality after being cut is remarkable. Hardy annual...................**Pkt. 10cts**

Imperialis Mixed. An excellent, sweet-scented variety. The flowers are finely laciniated and are about the size of a carnation. They have long stems and keep well after cutting. The colors range through white, rose, lilac, purple and yellow. Hardy annual; about eighteen inches high..........**Pkt. 10cts**

Celosia

A class of plants having colored foliage, and in which the innumerable small flowers and seed vessels, together with their supports, form a very brilliantly colored mass, sometimes gracefully arranged like plumes and sometimes more dense, being corrugated and frilled at the edge like a cockscomb. They form the gayest possible decoration, retaining their brilliant coloring for a long time after being cut. Very commonly grown out of doors but also adapted for the greenhouse or conservatory. Half hardy annuals. Plant in light, rich soil, and give plenty of moisture.

Pyramidalis plumosa mixed. The plant is about eighteen inches high and is covered with long, brilliantly colored and gracefully formed plumes in red, yellow or violet.........**Pkt. 5cts**

Triumph of the Exposition. Plant of pyramidal form, bearing many exceedingly graceful, feather-like spikes of intensely brilliant crimson color. Height about two feet....**Pkt. 10cts**

Variegated. A strain between the plumosa and cockscomb types in which the plumes are broadened at the top into many small, comb-like forms and are variegated and striped in red and yellow........................**Pkt. 10cts**

Japan. The plant grows to the height of two and a half or three feet, and is covered with spikes on stems which are very finely cut and of great brilliancy of color................**Pkt. 10cts**

DWARF AND TREE COCKSCOMB TYPES

Giant Empress. A very beautiful variety in which the dwarf plant has dark red leaves and forms immense, bright crimson combs.........................**Pkt. 10cts**

Glasgow Prize (*President Thiers*). The whole plant seems to be formed into an immense comb, densely corrugated and of indescribably brilliant color. One of the most striking examples of the possibility of modifying the form of plants by cultivation and selection ....**Pkt. 10cts**

Dwarf Rose. Large, rose colored combs.............." 10cts

Dwarf Yellow. Large, yellow combs................." 10cts

Dwarf Mixed. A mixture of the best dwarf-growing sorts.." 5cts

CENTAUREA MARGUERITE.

Chrysanthemum

Chrysanthemums have deservedly become very popular. They are showy and effective in the garden, and are desirable for cut flowers. Our list affords a fine range for selection.

The Carinatum and Coronarium varieties are hardy annuals one and one-half to two feet high and are most desirable for the garden. The others are the taller and later blooming sorts so largely used by florists.

EARLY BLOOMING GARDEN SORTS

Carinatum Burridgeanum, crimson white center; single.......................**Pkt. 5cts**

Carinatum Eclipse, pure golden yellow, with a bright purplish-scarlet ring or center on the ray florets, the disc being dark brown; very striking ...." 5cts

Coronarium, double white ...." 5cts

Coronarium, double yellow, very attractive, rich golden yellow flowers abundantly produced.. " 5cts

Mixed, *Carinatum and Coronarium varieties.* " 5cts

Later and Taller Fall Blooming and Florists' Sorts

Japonicum, fl. pl., Japanese variety. Flowers of peculiar form and much beauty; combining numerous shades of color. Half hardy perennial.......................**Pkt. 25cts**

Indicum, fl. pl., half hardy perennial; very double; mixed colors..................." 25cts

Frutescens (*Marguerite, or Paris Daisy*). A well known, small, single, white, daisy-like flower, gold centered ...." 10cts

Superb mixed double, seed from finest Chinese and Japanese varieties......................." 25cts

CHEIRANTHUS CHEIRI—(*See Wallflower*).

CHEIRANTHUS MARITIMUS—(*See Virginian Stock*).

CINERARIA

Cinerarias are easily grown from seed, require little heat, are free blooming and give brilliant flowers in a variety of colors. Greenhouse perennials which can be planted out in summer. They thrive best in a mixture of loam and peat. One to two feet high.

Maritima candidissima (*sometimes called Dusty Miller*). Cultivated for its handsome, silvery white foliage; very ornamental as a decorative pot plant or for bedding purposes..........Pkt. 10cts

Hybrida, choicest mixed, from best large flowering varieties.
                                      Pkt. 25cts

Hybrida, flore pleno, the flowers are perfectly and evenly double and in great variety of colors............Pkt. 25cts

Hybrida, very dwarf, large flowered, growing *only eight inches high*. Blooms profusely; many colors; desirable......Pkt. 25cts

Hybrida, single dwarf white. This is perhaps the finest sort among Cinerarias. The plant is about one and one-half feet high and covered with large, beautiful white flowers having purplish centers. An abundant bloomer in early spring and excellent for Easter decoration...............Pkt. 25cts

CLARKIA

Beautiful, hardy annuals from California, with rose colored, white and purple flowers, in delicate but very brilliant shades. The plants are about eighteen inches high and profuse bloomers. *Mixed double*............Pkt. 5cts

CLEMATIS

Well known and universally admired climbers, some of the varieties being remarkable for the size and beauty of their blossoms and others for their gracefulness. Fine for covering arbors, verandas, etc., as they cling readily to almost any object. Most of the kinds are hardy, herbaceous perennials, but some little protection in northern latitudes through winter, is advised.

Virginiana (*Virgin's Bower*). A rapid climber, growing twenty feet in a single season. The blossoms are small, white and in large clusters...............Pkt. 10cts

Flammula, a slender but vigorous climber, from ten to fifteen feet high, with clusters of small, white, fragrant flowers in August and September. Sometimes called Sweet Virgin's Bower...............Pkt. 5cts

Mixed, furnishes varieties having clusters of purple and white flowers...............Pkt. 10cts

Clianthus Dampieri

(*Glory Pea*). A greenhouse plant bearing clusters of very curiously shaped and intensely brilliantly colored flowers, scarlet with black center. Plants do not bear transplanting and should be kept rather dry.
                 Pkt. 20cts

Cobœa Scandens

A fine, rapid growing climber with handsome foliage and large, bell-shaped flowers, green at first, but rapidly changing to a beautiful, deep violet-blue. A well established plant will run about thirty feet in a season, covering a large veranda with handsome foliage and beautiful flowers. Tender perennial...............Pkt. 5cts

COCKSCOMB—(*See Celosia*).

COIX LACHRYMA—(*See Job's Tears*).

CINERARIA HYBRIDA.

COLEUS

Probably the best known and most popular of ornamental foliage plants. Leaves are of many shades of color and have a rich, velvety appearance of extraordinary beauty. No lawn should be without these decorative plants. Tender perennial.

Finest Hybrids mixed, *extra choice*...............Pkt. 25cts

Large Leaved, mixed, *extra choice*, certain to produce plants of exceeding beauty...............Pkt. 25cts

Large Leaved, Copper Colored. This coleus is of great merit and is worthy of a prominent place in greenhouse and garden. Leaves large and plants grow about two feet high. Foliage beautifully variegated in shades of rich red, bronze and copper color and quite distinct....Pkt. 25cts

COLUMBINE

(*Aquilegia*). Every well regulated garden has a space devoted to hardy perennials, and no bed of perennials would be complete without a due proportion of columbines. They are of the easiest culture, and when once established, will furnish for many years a magnificent display of the handsomest flowers each spring and summer. The beds should be kept clear of weeds and given each year a liberal dressing of well rotted manure. Hardy herbaceous perennials; two to three feet high.

Cœrulea hybrida, double, a vigorous growing, very handsome variety with blue and white flowers......Pkt. 10cts

Californica hybrida, one of the handsomest of all the columbines, having orange, red and yellow flowers...Pkt. 10cts

Vervæneana fol. variegatis, plants variegated leaved and producing double rose colored blossoms......Pkt. 10cts

Mixed double, *best and finest colors*.......... " 5cts

CONVOLVULUS MAJOR—(*See Morning Glory*).

CONVOLVULUS MINOR

(*Dwarf Morning Glory*). Dwarf plants of trailing, branching habit, each covering a space about two feet in diameter. At mid-day they are completely covered with a mass of pure white and brilliant, many colored blossoms which remain open in clear weather till evening. Half hardy annual; one foot high.

Mixed...............Pkt. 5cts

COREOPSIS—(*See Calliopsis*).

COSMOS

A very effective, autumn flowering plant. Quite hardy and rapid growing, forming bush-like plants five to eight feet high and covered with large, single, dahlia-like flowers. Should be started in this latitude in March and transplanted to open ground about June 1st.

Hybrida, large white. This variety produces a profusion of large, pure white flowers, which, being gracefully poised on long stems are useful for decorative purposes:...............Pkt. 5cts

Hybrida, Giant mixed..............." 5cts

EARLY FLOWERING COSMOS. We have secured an early flowering strain which is sure to come into bloom before frost, even when started outdoors, and will give a great profusion of bloom until late in the autumn.

Dawn. An early flowering strain in which all the flowers are white.
                                   Pkt. 5cts

Early Flowering, mixed. Comparatively dwarf plants, producing both white and colored flowers, coming into bloom much earlier than the giant forms...............Pkt. 5cts

CUCURBITA—(*See Gourd*).

COSMOS.

Cyclamen
Well known and universally admired tuberous rooted plants producing exceedingly handsome red and white flowers. Tender perennial; one foot high.

Persicum, mixed. Of great beauty and many colors. Pkt. 15c

Persicum, giganteum, mixed. Characterized by beautiful foliage and profuse bloom; each flower is from two to two and a half inches long. Very choice......Pkt. 20cts

CYPRESS VINE
(Ipomœa Quamoclit). A most beautiful climber with delicate, dark green, feathery, foliage and an abundance of bright, star-shaped, rose, scarlet or white blossoms, which contrast most effectively with the graceful foliage. Tender annual; about fifteen feet high.

Scarlet...Pkt. 5cts White...Pkt. 5cts Mixed...Pkt. 5cts

Dahlia
The Dahlia has always been a favorite for autumn flowering.
The flowers are so symmetrical and perfect and the range of colors so large and varied that they will always be popular where display is wanted. Both the single and double strains of this magnificent race of plants may be had in the greatest variety and beauty from seed. If planted early and forced they can be made to flower the first season. Tender herbaceous perennials.

Finest double, mixed. Seed *saved from choicest double flowers*..........Pkt. 15cts

Finest single, mixed. Brilliant flowers running through a wide range of striking colors......................Pkt. 10cts

For Dahlia roots, see page 94.

Daisy
The Daisy has been so far improved by selection and careful cultivation that *good* seed will give at least eighty per cent. of double flowers that are as large as any of the named sorts that are propagated by division of the roots and are sold at a high price. The plants bloom well in the house and are splendid for early spring and summer flowering when planted in a slightly shaded situation.

Double white.....................Pkt. 10cts

Double mixed....................." 5cts

Double red (*Longfellow*) finest strain............." 10cts

Datura
Large, branching plants, producing very large, handsome, double or single trumpet-shaped blossoms of exquisite fragrance. Tender annuals; three feet high.

Wrighti. Pure white at the center, passing into lilac and blue; magnificent single flowers.................Pkt. 5cts

Chlorantha, fl. pl. Large, double yellow blossoms, richly scented...Pkt. 5cts

Mixed. Yellow, white and lilac....................." 5cts

DELPHINIUM—(*See Larkspur*).

    DEW PLANT—(*See Mesembryanthemum*).

    DIANTHUS—(*See Pink*).

        DIANTHUS BARBATUS—(*See Sweet William*).

        DIANTHUS CARYOPHYLLUS—(*See Carnation*).

DIGITALIS—(*See Foxglove*).

    DOLICHOS—(*See Hyacinth Bean*).

        EDELWEISS—(*See Gnaphalium*).

        ELICHRYSUM—(*See Helichrysum*).

        ERAGROSTIS—(*See Love Grass*).

EULALIA JAPONICA
A most magnificent and exceedingly graceful, ornamental grass from Japan, growing five to six feet high..................................Pkt. 10cts

EUPHORBIA VARIEGATA
A beautiful foliage plant sometimes known as "Snow on the Mountain." The leaves are veined and margined with white. Plant in sunny situation. Hardy annual; two feet high..Pkt. 5cts

FERNS
Flowerless plants, too well known to need description. Many of the most beautiful sorts can be propagated from seed (spores) only. Their exceeding grace and beauty will well repay all care bestowed upon them.

Fine mixed.....................................Pkt. 20cts

Finest species, mixed..........................." 25cts

CYCLAMEN GIGANTEUM.

Eschscholtzia
(California Poppy). The state flower of California. A genus of the Poppy family, fully as valuable as the common Poppy for garden ornamentation as it blooms almost continually throughout the season. A bed of these in full bloom is most handsome and beautiful in color. Hardy annuals; height one foot, except Bush.

BUSH. A new and distinct variety of unusual merit. One of the best of the California Poppies. Leaves are coarser and larger than the common kinds. Flowers are about three inches in diameter, and are formed of broad, bright yellow petals with wavy edges. Stems ten inches, high. Height of plant about two feet....................Pkt. 5cts

Californica. Bright yellow.........................." 5cts

Californica, double white. Creamy white........." 5cts

Crocea striata. Orange yellow, delicately striped " 5cts

Mandarin. The outer side of the petal is tinged with scarlet, the inner side rich orange........." 5cts

Mixed.." 5cts

FEATHER GRASS
(Stipa Pennata). An ornamental grass of much beauty, used in the formation of winter bouquets. Hardy perennial; one foot high................Pkt. 5cts

FEVERFEW—(*See Matricaria and Pyrethrum*).

FORGET-ME-NOT
(Myosotis). A favorite old fashioned flower, bearing clusters of blue blossoms. It thrives well in the shade or open border. Hardy perennial.

Alpestris, plant of compact, bushy habit, six to eight inches high; flowers large, blue..........................Pkt. 5cts

Dissitiflora, very deep blue; early blooming, six to eight inches high..............................." 15cts

Four O'Clock
(Marvel of Peru). The plants are large, and each needs three or four feet of space each way for its best development. The flowers are funnel shaped, white, red, yellow or striped with these colors, and open about four o'clock in the afternoon, remain open all night, and generally perish before noon the next day. The abundance of new flowers produced daily affords a constant succession of fine blooms. The French call it *Belle de Nuit*, "Beauty of Night." Will grow in any common garden soil. Sow seed in open ground. Hardy annual; two feet high.

Gold striped.......Pkt. 5cts

White..........Pkt. 5cts

Red............." 5cts

White, red striped.. " 5cts

Mixed............." 5cts

FOXGLOVE
(Digitalis). Grows to the height of three or four feet, affording dense spikes of brilliantly colored flowers which are terminal and half as long as height of plant. Colors white, lavender and rose. A valuable flower in every perennial garden; does not usually blossom until the second year. Hardy biennials or perennials.
Ivery's Spotted, a fine variety of colors; robust and hardy...............**Pkt. 5cts**
Splendid mixed.. " **5cts**

French Honeysuckle
(Hedysarum). Very handsome, free flowering plants, producing racemes of beautiful pea-shaped flowers; well adapted for borders or rock work. Hardy perennial; four feet high. Coronarium, scarlet..................**Pkt. 5cts**
Coronarium, album, white............................... " **5cts**

Fuchsia
There are a great many exceedingly beautiful varieties propagated by cuttings, but the plants are easily grown from seed and one can depend upon getting fine flowers, some of which are as beautiful as the expensive named sorts. Tender perennial.
Double, finest mixed....................**Pkt. 25cts**

GAILLARDIA
Showy plants, flowering the first year and among the gayest ornaments of the garden.
Picta, one foot high; flowers crimson and yellow. Hardy annual; with root protection in winter is a perennial..**Pkt. 5cts**
Picta Lorenziana. For general decorative purposes, as well as for bouquets, this is invaluable. The gay colored flowers are abundantly produced from July even until hard freezing weather. Hardy annual; one foot high; with root protection in winter becomes a perennial. Sulphur, orange, claret and amaranth, mixed...........**Pkt. 5cts**
Grandiflora. The largest flowers of the species; blossoms scarlet and orange; excellent for cutting. Hardy perennial....................**Pkt. 5cts**

GAILLARDIA.

Gamolepis Tagetes
A free flowering plant of great value for beds and borders. The leaves are fern-like and the numerous bright yellow, daisy-like flowers are produced on long stems which rise in a mass well above the foliage. Half hardy annual; about eight inches high. Will flower in June and July from seed sown early in spring.................**Pkt. 5cts**

GERANIUM
(Pelargonium.) The constant succession of bloom till frost comes, the brilliant colors of the flowers and the exquisite markings of the leaves of some of the varieties, render the Geranium very desirable for pot culture and bedding. Half hardy perennial.
Propagation by seed is the only way to obtain new varieties.
Zonale, white leaved varieties......................**Pkt. 25cts**
    "   golden and bronze leaved.................. " **25cts**
    "   green leaved, large flowered sorts, all colors mixed...................... " **25cts**
    "   double flowered sorts, all colors mixed... " **25cts**
Apple Scented, *very fragrant leaves*.............. " **25cts**
Diadematum, splendid variety with dark flowers......................**Pkt. 25cts**
Odier, five blotched....**Pkt. 25cts** Fancy, splendid mixed, all shades " **25cts**
The last three varieties are commonly known as *Lady Washington* geraniums.

Gilia Tricolor
A very graceful plant which will thrive in almost any situation, producing a cloud of gracefully poised blue flowers with yellow and purple centers. Hardy annual; one foot high....**Pkt. 5cts**

Gladiolus
The varieties of this magnificent plant are now numbered almost by hundreds; each year brings forth new and choice selections which have been produced from seed. This is the only method of obtaining new varieties. Half hardy perennial. Seed from the finest named sorts mixed....................**Pkt. 15cts** *For Gladiolus bulbs see page 95.*

Globe Amaranth
(Gomphrena). A desirable everlasting valued for its handsome, globular heads of flowers which if cut when well matured, will retain their beauty through the winter. Tender annual; twelve to eighteen inches high.
Purple..**Pkt. 5cts**   Striped..**Pkt. 5cts**   White..**Pkt. 5cts**   Mixed..**Pkt. 5cts**

Gloxinia
Greenhouse perennial plants, producing rich and beautifully colored flowers. They are delicate and not easily grown, but the flowers are of such superb beauty as to amply repay one for the trouble of a trial.   Hybrida, mixed......**Pkt. 25cts**

Gnaphalium Leontopodium
(Edelweiss). This is the true Edelweiss found on the Alps and highly esteemed by travelers in Switzerland. Flowers star-shaped, pure white and downy in texture. If plucked when on the point of opening and dried in the shade, will retain their beauty for years. Perennial; one foot high..**Pkt. 10c**

Godetia
Beautiful garden plants, having large, delicately shaded blossoms. Easily cultivated in any good garden soil. Hardy annual; about one foot high.
Rubicunda Splendens. A showy variety. Rosy lilac flowers, with purple stain in the center...**Pkt. 5cts**
Rosea Alba *(Tom Thumb).* Delicately blotched blossoms, white at the outer portion, rose at base of petals...**Pkt. 5cts**
Duchess of Albany. A magnificent sort producing a profusion of large, rich, satiny-white flowers, measuring about four inches across.............**Pkt. 5cts**
Lady Albermarle. Carmine crimson; compact habit; very beautiful.. " **5cts**

FOXGLOVE.

Gourd

(*Cucurbita*). A tribe of climbers with curiously shaped and colored fruit. Being of rapid growth, they are fine to cover old fences, trellises, stumps, etc. Tender annual; ten to twenty feet high.

Dish Cloth. A rapid climber, having long, green fruit, the inside is a fibrous mass, which, when the shell and seeds are removed, makes an excellent bath sponge..................................**Pkt. 5cts**
Orange. The well known Mock Orange........................ " 5cts
Japanese Nest Egg. The fruits are white and about the size of hen's eggs; as they do not crack and are not hurt by heat or cold, they make excellent nest eggs............................ " 5cts
Apple Shaped. Yellow, beautifully striped .... " 5cts
Pear Shaped. Striped yellow, green and cream color .... " 5cts
Pear Shaped, ringed. Exceedingly beautiful fruit with rings of various shades of yellow running around it; green ends........ " 5cts
Bottle. Curiously and handsomely shaped fruit..**Pkt. 5cts**
Corsican. Elegant fruit and rapid climber........ " 5cts
Siphon, or Dipper. Useful for dippers.·........ " 5cts
Powder Horn. In the form of a powder horn..... " 5cts
Hercules' Club. The longest of all the varieties.. " 5cts
Mixed .... " 5cts

Grammanthes
Gentianoides

A charming little succulent plant producing an abundance of bright scarlet and orange yellow, star-shaped blossoms. It is especially adapted for rock work, hanging baskets, edging, etc. Tender annual; six inches high.................**Pkt. 10cts**

GYNERIUM—(*See Pampas Grass*).

Gypsophila

Delicate, free flowering, little plants, covered with a profusion of white and pink, small, star-shaped flowers. Well adapted for hanging baskets or edgings, and valuable in conjunction with other flowers for making bouquets. Will thrive anywhere.

Elegans, mixed. White and pink flowers. Hardy annual; one foot high...**Pkt. 5cts**
Muralis. One of the most charming and graceful border plants to be found in any collection. As easily grown as candytuft, but is at its best in limestone soil. Pink flowers. Hardy annual; six inches high.............**Pkt. 5cts**

HEDYSARUM—(*See French Honeysuckle*).

HELIANTHUS—(*See Sunflower*).

Helichrysum

Large, full, double flowers of various colors, from bright yellow to scarlet. Desirable as dried specimens and for use in making winter bouquets. For this purpose the flowers should be gathered when on the point of expanding. Hardy annual; six inches to two feet high.

Bracteatum (*Golden Eternal Flower*). Bright yellow..**Pkt. 5cts**
Nanum Atrosanguineum, fl. pl. Deep crimson,.. " 5cts
Monstrosum, fl. pl., mixed. Varieties of largest double flowers.. " 5cts
Mixed. *The above varieties.*...................... " 5cts

Heliotrope

Highly valued for the fragrance of their flowers and duration of bloom. Half hardy perennial, blooming the first year from seed.

Anna Turrell, violet-blue...............................**Pkt. 10cts**
King of the Blacks, *splendid*........................ " 10cts
Triomphe de Liege, deep blue.................... " 10cts
Dark varieties, mixed, *very choice*............... " 10cts

Helipterum

A desirable, distinct, dwarf everlasting with large, globular clusters of bright yellow or white flowers; retain their color for years. Excellent for forming winter bouquets. Hardy annual; one foot high. *Mixed* ....**Pkt. 5cts**

HESPERIS MATRONALIS—(*See Rocket*).

Heuchera Sanguinea

A hardy perennial plant about eighteen inches high, easily grown from seed and producing long spikes of brilliant crimson flowers. These are very desirable in the garden or as cut flowers for florists' use. If started early indoors will bloom abundantly the first season, but the second season will give more and finer flowers.........**Pkt. 10cts**

Hibiscus Africanus

A very vigorous plant of easiest culture, about two feet high and producing large, handsome, cream colored, single flowers. Hardy annual...........................**Pkt. 5cts**

Honesty

An interesting plant because of the silver-like tissue of the seed pods, which are very fine for skeletonizing and use in winter bouquets. Hardy perennial; two feet high .....**Pkt. 5cts**

HONEYSUCKLE—(*See French Honeysuckle*).

HOLLYHOCK.

Hollyhock

The modern hollyhock is quite different and much more beautiful than the plant of twenty years ago, being much more compact in growth; the flowers are larger, richer colored, and the double varieties are fuller and of better form. For a background to a flower garden there can be nothing better. Hardy perennial; five feet high.

Chater's finest mixed, double varieties of the greatest perfection....................................**Pkt. 15cts**
Double blood red..**Pkt. 10cts** **Double blush pink** " 10cts
" **purple-red.** " 10cts " **pink**........ " 10cts
" **deep rose...** " 10cts " **salmon .....** " 10cts
" **canary yellow** " 10cts " **lemon yellow** " 10cts
" **pure white.** A special strain of our own development in which the plant is more compact and earlier blooming and the flowers larger and of better shape than those of the old white...............**Pkt. 10cts**
" **choice mixed,** a well proportioned mixture of all colors................................. " 10cts
" **mixed**.. " 5cts

Humulus Japonicus

An easily grown, hardy annual climber; frequently growing fifteen to twenty feet and desirable for covering unsightly objects or shading verandas. Self sowing after the first year.**Pkt.5c**

Hyacinth Bean

A fine climber,producing abundantly clusters of purple or white flowers which are followed by ornamental seed pods. Tender annual; ten to twenty feet high.
Purpurea, purple.....**Pkt. 5cts** **Alba,** white.....**Pkt. 5cts**
Mixed, the above mixed........................... " 5cts

IBERIS—(*See Candytuft*).

Ice Plant

(*Mesembryanthemum Crystallinum*) Handsome and curious plant for hanging baskets, rock work, vases and edgings. The leaves and stems are succulent and appear as though covered with ice crystals. Tender annual trailer; six inches high..**Pkt. 5cts**

Impatiens Sultani Compact growing plants producing a constant succession of brilliant rose-scarlet flowers. Very desirable for pot culture or the open ground.........Pkt. 25cts

INDIAN SHOT—(*See Canna*).

Ipomœa
A beautiful climber for the greenhouse or the open air. Blooms earlier and more profusely in rather poor soil but gives more vigorous plants and attractive foliage if soil be rather rich. Tender annual; five to ten feet high.

Setosa. A vigorous, rapid growing vine with large, handsome, three-lobed leaves and stems covered with brown hair. The flowers are delicate blue and are produced in clusters. One of the most distinct and beautiful Ipomœas. .Pkt. 10cts

Coccinea (*Star Ipomœa*). The plant is like that of the Morning Glory but is covered with a profusion of small, brilliant red, star-shaped flowers.......Pkt. 5cts

Bona Nox, violet-blue.. " 5cts

Limbata, mixed, very large and beautiful violet or blue flowers with white margins and throats..Pkt. 5cts

Fine mixed.. " 5cts

IPOMŒA, IMPERIAL JAPANESE—(*See Morning Glory*).
IPOMŒA QUAMOCLIT—(*See Cypress Vine*).
IPOMOPSIS—(*See Tree Cypress*).   JAPAN HOP—(*See Humulus Japonicus*).

Job's Tears (*Coix Lachryma*). Curious ornamental grass with broad, corn-like leaves and seeds of a light slate color. Valuable for the formation of winter bouquets, in connection with everlasting flowers. Strings of handsome beads are made from the seeds. Hardy annual; three feet high...Pkt. 5cts

JOSEPH'S COAT—(*See Amaranthus Tricolor*).

Lantana
These plants form small, hardy shrubs and produce pink, yellow, orange and white flowers in great abundance the first season from seed. *Finest French Hybrids mixed*.Pkt. 5c

LARKSPUR, DOUBLE DWARF ROCKET.

Linaria Cymbalaria
(*Kenilworth Ivy*). A pretty trailing plant for covering rock work, and very useful for hanging baskets. Hardy perennial....................Pkt. 10cts

Linum
(*Scarlet Flax*). **Grandiflorum Rubrum.** A beautiful and effective plant, of slender and delicate growth, having a profusion of bright flowers. If the seed be sown in hotbed and the plants transplanted into good, rich soil, one foot apart, the period of flowering will be much advanced but the seed can be sown in open ground after the weather is warm. Hardy annual; about one and one-half feet high........................Pkt. 5cts

Lobelia
A most elegant and useful genus of plants of easy culture and well adapted for bedding, edgings, pots or rockeries. They make a neat edging for beds of white flowers, and are very effective in masses,being always completely covered with flowers.

Emperor William. A very fine, compact variety with intense blue flowers. One of the best. Half hardy annual........Pkt. 5cts

Queen of Whites. Pure white flowers. Half hardy annual. " 10cts

Crystal Palace. A most desirable variety having bright blue flowers. Half hardy annual.............................Pkt. 5cts

Gracilis. The flowers are dark blue with white centers; fine for baskets, vases, etc., trailing gracefully and blooming profusely. Half hardy annual; six inches high.....................Pkt. 5cts

Cardinalis (*Cardinal Flower*). A native species of very distinctive habit from above; growing about two feet high, with spikes of intensely brilliant scarlet flowers. Hardy perennial. .Pkt.10cts

LONDON PRIDE— (*See Lychnis Chalcedonica*).

LOBELIA EMPEROR WILLIAM.

Larkspur
(*Delphinium*). The Larkspur is one of the handsomest and most useful of plants, and for large gardens is invaluable.

Double Dwarf Rocket, mixed. Produces beautiful spikes of double flowers in many shades. Hardy annual; one foot high.
....Pkt. 5cts

Cardiopetalum. An ornamental, free blooming plant; flowers deep blue, heart-shaped. Hardy annual; one and one-half feet high...Pkt. 5cts

Tall, Stock Flowered, mixed (*Consolida fl. pl.*) Flowers double, borne on spikes about fifteen inches long. Hardy annual; two feet high...Pkt. 5cts

Double Emperor (*Imperiale fl. pl.*) Compact and profuse bloomer, having erect spikes of very double flowers. Hardy annual; one and one-half feet high. *Mixed colors*............,Pkt. 5cts

Consolida Candelabrum fl. pl. Grows in the form of a branched candlestick; flowers double and of various colors. Hardy annual; two feet high...............................Pkt. 5cts

Nudicaule. Scarlet flowers; fine for rockeries, flower borders or pot culture. Hardy perennial; eighteen inches high.Pkt. 10cts

Elatum (*Bee Larkspur*). Flowers are an intense blue color and have hairy petals in the center which give them a fancied resemblance to a bee. Hardy perennial; five feet high.....Pkt. 5cts

Formosum. Flower large, rich blue, with a small, white center. Hardy perennial; three feet high; blooms from July to November...Pkt. 5cts

Cashmerianum. A most floriferous and valuable perennial, flowering the first year from seed sown early in spring. The flowers are dark blue and one to two inches across, and resemble a monk's hood. Height about one and one-half feet...Pkt. 10cts

LATHYRUS LATIFOLIUS—(*See Perennial Peas*).
LATHYRUS ODORATUS—(*See Sweet Peas*).

LANTANA.

MARIGOLD

No flower garden seems complete without this fine old fashioned flower. The African varieties are tall, usually two feet or more, while the French are more dwarf. All are desirable. Hardy annuals; in bloom till frost comes.

African, Double Dwarf, Lemon Colored. Very early and a profuse bloomer of very compact habit. One of the best of this class; about one foot high............Pkt. 5cts

African, Orange Quilled. A double variety with quilled petals; showy and very early. Sixteen inches high.. " 5cts

African, El Dorado, Double. Flowers about three inches in diameter, imbricated and extremely double.. " 5cts

African, Double Mixed.. " 5cts

French, Legion of Honor. A beautiful, single, dwarf, bushy variety, bearing rich golden yellow flowers with garnet blotches in the center of each petal; about one foot high.. " 5cts

French, Double Dwarf, Gold Striped. Brown and golden yellow; very double.. " 5cts

Prince of Orange (*Calendula officinalis fl. pl.*) Large, double, golden yellow flowers, the petals of which are shaded with dark orange; very useful for cutting .... " 5cts

Meteor (*Calendula officinalis fl. pl.*) Large, extremely double, light yellow, passing into orange at the border of each petal.. " 5cts

Cape (*Calendula pluvialis*). Flowers single; white, brown underneath.. " 5cts

Tagetes Signata Pumila. Small, bright yellow flowers; elegant dwarf habit; excellent for borders; about nine inches high.. " 5cts

MARIGOLD FRENCH LEGION OF HONOR.

Mesembryanthemum

Cordifolium Variegatum. The leaves are blotched with light yellow and cream colored spots. Fine for greenhouse and conservatory; half hardy annual; six inches high.......Pkt. 15cts

Tricolor. (*Dew Plant*). Pink with purple center; half hardy annual.. Pkt. 5cts

Love Grass

(*Eragrostis Elegans*) A very pretty species of ornamental grass, growing one foot high; good for winter bouquets. Hardy annual.. Pkt. 5cts

LOVE GROVE—(See Nemophila).

LOVE-IN-A-MIST

(*Nigella*) This singular plant is also known as Lady-in-the-Green and as Devil-in-a-Bush, because the blossoms are partly concealed by the abundance of finely cut foliage. The plant and flower are each handsome and require but little care. Hardy annual:

Damascena fl. pl. Double blue blossoms; one and one-half to two feet high.......................Pkt. 5cts

Damascena Nana fl. pl. Double white and blue blossoms; one foot high.......................... " 5cts

Lophospermum Scandens

Beautiful, rapid growing climbers, reaching a height of ten or twelve feet; excellent for covering trellis work, etc. Tender perennial. Flowers large and bright violet purple.. Pkt. 10cts

LUPIN

Very conspicuous plants with spikes of pea-shaped blossoms of various colors. Looks well as a background to other lower growing annuals. The seed should be planted where they are to remain, in spring, and thinned to one and one-half feet apart. Hardy annual; about three feet high.

Hartwegi. A beautiful species with finely cut foliage and blue blossoms.. Pkt. 5cts

Cruikshanki. Blossoms white, shaded with yellow, blue and purple.. " 5cts

LYCHNIS

The flowers are brilliantly colored, are borne in clusters about three feet high and continue fresh a long time. Hardy perennials.

Chalcedonica. (*London Pride*). Bright scarlet; two feet high.. Pkt. 5cts

The following perennial varieties will blossom the first year:

Haageana. A showy and exceedingly handsome border plant having elegant, large, red blossoms with jagged petals; one foot high.. Pkt. 10cts

Haageana grandiflora gigantea. A tall growing, handsome variety with flowers of varying shades of red and much larger than the preceding.. " 10cts

MALCOMIA MARITIMA—(See Virginian Stock).

Martynia

Formosa. Easily grown, large flowering, half hardy annual; foliage thick, soft and velvety. The seed pods are curiously shaped. Flowers fragrant, delicate rose lilac, blotched and shaded with crimson...........Pkt. 5cts

MARVEL OF PERU—(See Four O'Clock).

MATHIOLA—(See Stocks).

Matricaria

Eximia grandiflora fl.pl. (*Double Feverfew*). White, double, desirable for bedding; half hardy annual.. Pkt. 5cts

Maurandia

Graceful climber for greenhouse, parlor, basket or outdoor purposes. Set out in border with a little frame to which to attach their tendrils, they will be covered all the season with rich purple, white or rose colored, foxglove shaped blossoms. Tender perennial, blooming first season; six feet high. *Choicest kinds mixed*......Pkt. 10cts

MOURNING BRIDE

(*Scabiosa, or Sweet Scabious*). This is one of the most attractive of the old fashioned flowers. Its great abundance and long succession of rich colored, fragrant blossoms borne on long stems make it one of the most useful of the decorative plants of the garden. It has been greatly improved of late years, producing larger and more double flowers of greater variety and brilliancy of color than in the old type. Hardy annual; twelve to eighteen inches high.

Double Dark Maroon. Pkt. 5cts

Double White........ " 5cts

Double Mixed........ " 5cts

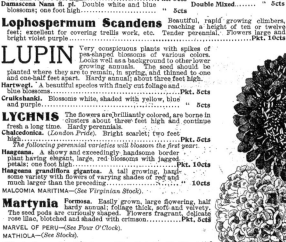

MOURNING BRIDE.

MORNING GLORY

Mignonette

A well known hardy annual, producing dense spikes of exceedingly fragrant flowers. If sown at intervals in spring and early summer it will bloom till killed by frost. Seed sown in autumn will bloom early in the spring. Thrives best in cool temperature. Hardy annual; one foot high.

Golden Queen. Golden yellow, powerfully fragrant...........**Pkt. 5cts**
Victoria. Dark red blossoms, very valuable................. " **10cts**
Crimson Flowered Giant. Of robust habit with very large spikes of handsome crimson flowers....................... " **5cts**
Parson's White. Flowers almost pure white borne on spikes six inches to a foot in length................................ " **5cts**
Dwarf Compact. Forms a dense, semi-globular bush about ten inches high.. " **10cts**
Tall Pyramidal. Tall growing; foliage dark green; flower spikes club shaped; large................................... " **5cts**
Pyramidal Bouquet. Forms a dense, short pyramid, the numerous branches being terminated by large spikes of red flowers. Excellent for pot culture and for the open border................**Pkt. 5cts**
Ruby. A dwarf, compact and vigorous plant producing magnificent coppery red flower spikes. (See Supplement)..........................**Pkt. 15cts**
Machet. Of dwarf and vigorous growth, with numerous stout flower stalks, terminated by massive spikes of red flowers. One of the very best for pot culture..**Pkt. 5cts**
Improved Machet. A highly developed strain; splendid, large, red flower spikes ....**Pkt. 10cts**
Reseda odorata grandiflora, large flowered sweet...............**Pkt. 5cts**

Mimulus

Strikingly handsome flowers of easiest cultivation. Perennial in the greenhouse, annual in the open air. Start under glass.

Moschatus (*Musk Plant*). Cultivated on account of the musky odor of the plant. Flowers pale yellow, lightly dotted and splashed with brown.................**Pkt. 5cts**
Punctatus (*Monkey Flower*). Large, beautifully spotted flowers, having yellow throats with brown dots; blooms first year.......................................**Pkt. 5cts**
Tigrinus duplex, splendid variety, with beautiful, double tubed flowers.................................**Pkt. 10cts**

Morning Glory

(*Convolvulus Major*). A handsome, showy climber of easy culture, suitable for covering arbors, windows, trellises, old stumps, etc., if support be given for the vines. It is so perfectly hardy as to grow in almost any soil, but will bloom earlier if in poor soil. Hardy annual; ten feet high.

Striped....**Pkt. 5cts**	White ....**Pkt. 5cts**		
Blue....... " **5cts**	Purple..... " **5cts**		
Crimson... " **5cts**	Mixed..... " **5cts**		

Giant Japanese Mixed

This strain has been developed to such a state of perfection that it now produces flowers of immense size and almost endless variety of color and markings. Some of the flowers are brilliant red, or rich blue; others are equally brilliant, with broad margins of clear white. Some blossoms are striped and dotted with blue or red on white or lemon yellow ground, others clouded with blue and red; in fact, one may expect to find some new and exquisitely beautiful markings every morning. Not only are the flowers varied but the foliage is equally so; in some plants it comes plain green, in others it is mottled with white and shades of yellow or yellowish-green. The plants do not always produce flowers exactly like those from which the seed came and often give different colored blossoms at different times, so we only offer the seed in mixture. Our seed is the very best it is possible to produce. It is sometimes slow to germinate but if a slight notch is filed or cut in one end and the seed soaked a few hours in lukewarm water the plants will come up more quickly..**Pkt. 5cts**

Aurora This new strain is a result of crossing the common Morning Glory with the Giant Japanese and combines to a remarkable degree the vigor, hardiness and abundant bloom of the vine of the first with the size and rich coloring of the flowers of the second. The flowers are decidedly larger than those of the common Morning Glory and are either a deep, rich blue shading to a white throat, or an exceedingly rich, dark carmine, also with white throat. We consider it the most practically useful strain of convolvulus in cultivation and recommend it as one of the best of summer climbers. The planter is sure to get satisfactory results.................**Pkt. 5cts**

Nasturtium

Dwarf Nasturtiums *(Tropæolum Minor)*.
A bed of dwarf nasturtiums in the yard is very brilliant and attractive, blooming all the season. Hardy annual; about one foot high.

Aurora, light reddish-orange, veined with carmine.	Pkt. 5cts
Bronze colored, bronze-orange	" 5cts
Crimson, rich, dark crimson	" 5cts
Empress of India, small, compact plant, dark scarlet flowers, very dark foliage	" 5cts
King Theodore, dark scarlet-maroon	" 5cts
Pearl, pale yellow	" 5cts
Rose, a warm rose-pink	" 5cts
Scarlet, scarlet-orange	" 5cts
Schilling's Striped, bright yellow, maroon stripes.	" 5cts
Yellow, rich golden yellow	" 5cts
Mixed Dwarf, all of the above colors mixed	" 5cts

Chameleon Nasturtiums
When a plant of this novel sort is in full bloom, one can find upon it flowers of almost every shade of color and form of marking known to nasturtiums. No matter what color a flower may be when it opens, it is continually changing until it fades. Unlike many flowers which are notable because curious, those of the Chameleon Nasturtium are always beautiful and attractive.

Dwarf Chameleon	Pkt. 10cts
Tall Chameleon	" 10cts

Trailing Nasturtiums *(Tropæolum Lobbianum)*.
The Lobbianum differs from the common running nasturtium in being less rank growing, more floriferous, and having richer, more varied colored flowers of many shades, from the richest scarlet to very deep maroon. Fine for covering arbors, trellises and rustic work. Half hardy annual; about ten feet high.

Bright yellow, with carmine stain	Pkt. 5cts
Brilliant, intense deep scarlet red	" 5cts
Cardinal, dark scarlet	" 5cts
Chestnut Brown, rich red maroon	" 5cts
Giant of Battles, sulphur, red blotches	" 5cts
Hemisphaericum, straw color, blotched and suffused with scarlet orange	" 5cts
King of the Blacks, crimson-maroon with darker markings	" 5cts
Light Yellow, with rich maroon stain	" 5cts
Rose, a deep shade, distinct and attractive	" 5cts
Spitfire, bright, fiery scarlet, very floriferous	" 5cts
Mixed Trailing *(Lobbianum varieties)*	" 5cts

Madame Gunter's Hybrid Nasturtiums
Flowers are striped or blotched with shades of red on yellow and orange ground, forming a combination of exceeding brilliancy and beauty. About four feet high. Half hardy annual. ....Pkt. 5cts

(See Nasturtium cover)

Moon Flower
(Ipomœa Grandiflora Alba). This is one of the most vigorous of all the summer climbers. Will grow thirty to forty feet in a single season and be covered with its large, white flowers every evening and cloudy day. The hard, outer coat of the seed should be cut through with a sharp knife, care being taken not to cut any deeper than the hard shell and the seed planted about one inch deep in moist soil in a box or pan and set in a warm place. If the soil be kept moist, germination will take place in ten days to two weeks. After the plants are up tend carefully and plant out doors in a sunny situation when danger from frost is past. Water freely throughout the summer. Rich soil tends to make the plant run to vines and leaves, while poor earth will produce earlier and more abundant flowers. This variety is also known as *Ipomœa Noctiflora*...........................Pkt. 10cts

Momordica
Balsam Pear *(Charantia)*. A curious annual climber, with yellow blossoms and gracefully cut foliage. The fruit, the chief curiosity, is pear-shaped and has a warty skin. When ripe the fruit bursts open and shows a brilliant interior of large, carmine colored seeds. Fine for trellises, etc...........................Pkt. 5cts
Balsam Apple *(Balsamina)*. Like Balsam Pear but the fruit is smaller and nearly round...........................Pkt. 5cts

Nemophila
(Love Grove). The flowers are single, cup-shaped, about an inch in diameter and usually come in delicate shades of blue and white. A delicate and singularly attractive hardy annual about six inches high. *Mixed varieties*.Pkt. 5c

Nicotiana Affinis
Handsome garden plants of the tobacco family, valuable for the freedom and fragrance of their bloom. Half hardy annuals; three feet high. Flowers white, salver-shaped, having long, tubular corollas, and are of exquisite fragrance. Deserve a place in every garden.Pkt. 5c

Nicotiana Sanderae—*(See Supplement)*.
NIGELLA—*(See Love-in-a-Mist)*.

Nolana
Beautiful, trailing plants with prostrate stems. Fine for rock work, pots, baskets and vases, as the branches hang pendulous over the edge of vase or basket. The blossoms are produced abundantly and are convolvulus-shaped, brilliant and of various colors. Hardy trailing annual; six inches high. *Mixed*..........Pkt. 5cts

Nycterinia
Charming little plants, well adapted for rockeries and baskets. The florets are star-shaped, white or tinted with various shades and during the evening are very fragrant. Half hardy annual; six inches high. *Mixed*,...........................Pkt. 5cts
ŒNOTHERA—*(See Primrose)*.

Oleander
(Nerium Oleander). This well known shrub is of easy culture and flowers freely the greater part of the year. In warm, moist climates it requires no protection and attains the proportions of a good sized tree. The flowers have a salver-shaped corolla, with a crown of cut appendages in the center and are white or different shades of red...........Pkt. 5cts

Oxalis
Very pretty, herbaceous plants with richly colored blossoms. They thrive well in a mixture of loam and sand. Desirable for greenhouse decoration, rock work or baskets. Half hardy perennial.

Rosea, rose colored	Pkt. 10cts
Floribunda alba, white	" 10cts

MOON FLOWER.

PAEONY
(Pæonia Herbacea Chinensis). Well known herbaceous perennial plants. They are so gorgeous in their beauty that they should have a place in every yard and are sure to repay the little care required. About three feet in height.
Double, mixed...........................Pkt. 25cts

PALM
The palm is perhaps one of the most ornamental plants in the greenhouse and those varieties that are hardy enough to bear planting out in the lawn during warm weather are sure to command attention. The seed is slow to germinate.
Chamærops Humilis *(Dwarf Fan Palm)*. The most hardy and dwarf of its species, seldom attaining over eight or ten feet in height...........................Pkt. 10cts
Chamærops Excelsa. A greenhouse variety in our climate. As a lawn plant in our southern states, nothing could be more conspicuously attractive. A well grown specimen will attain the height of twenty-five or thirty feet.Pkt. 10c

Pampas Grass
(Gynerium argenteum). Magnificent ornamental grass, producing numerous flower stems surmounted by plumes of silvery inflorescence. Half hardy perennial; ten feet high...........................Pkt. 5cts

Passion Flower
(Passiflora). Most interesting and well known climbers bearing singularly beautiful flowers.
Cœrulea, half hardy deciduous climber with blue and white flowers of remarkable beauty...........................Pkt. 10cts
Coccinea, magnificent greenhouse climber with brilliant scarlet blossoms curiously shaped in the form of a double crown...........................Pkt. 20cts

Petunia

Petunias are unsurpassed for massing in beds. Their richness of color, duration of bloom and easy culture will always render them popular. The modern improved varieties are very choice plants, having been wonderfully brought up from the same species which were in use twenty-five years ago. The full, double petunias do not produce seeds, so that to procure double flowers we must use the seed of single flowers which have been carefully fertilized by pollen from the double ones.

The seed we offer is from the result of careful hybridization, and can be depended upon for giving as large a proportion of double flowers as any.

In some strains the flowers are very large, measuring four or five inches across; in others, they are deeply fringed; still others have star-like markings radiating from the throat and extending nearly or quite to the outer margin of the blossom; again, others have full, double flowers. The colors range from white to deep red-purple and are variously striped and barred.

Plant in a warm, open, sunny place. Seeds may be sown directly in the open ground, or the plants may be started in pots indoors for early results. The plants are tender and should not be trusted in the open until settled weather. Thin to eighteen inches apart. When well started, they grow almost as easily as weeds. They begin to bloom when very small and continue until cut off by frost. Tender perennial, blooming the first year.

Petunias are easily grown under glass in winter. The best method is to sow seeds in late summer or early fall and to grow stocky plants in pots, but old plants can be lifted on the approach of cold weather, cut back and taken inside for winter bloom.

Single Dwarf Compact (*Inimitable Dwarf*). Bushy plants six to eight inches high, covered with beautifully striped and blotched flowers. In many of them the markings are as beautifully star-shaped as in the strains offered as Star Petunia...................................Pkt. 15cts

Countess of Ellesmere. Deep rose, white throat..............................	"	5cts
Finest Striped and Blotched..............	"	5cts
Nyctaginiflora, Pure white...............	"	5cts
Fine mixed................................	"	5cts
Double mixed............................	"	20cts

Phlox Drummondi

Very hardy annuals, unequaled in the magnificent display of their many and brilliantly colored flowers. They will grow even in poor soil, but in order to develop to their highest perfection, must have rich soil and must be given room. Plants from seed sown in open ground in fall or early spring will begin flowering about July 1st and will be literally covered with bloom until autumn. For masses of separate colors, or for cutting for bouquets, they are unsurpassed. One foot high.

LARGE FLOWERING PHLOX

Alba, pure white..........................Pkt.		10cts
Black Warrior, very dark purple.........	"	10cts
Scarlet, black center	"	10cts
Rosea, deep rose..........................	"	10cts
Carmine Red..............................	"	10cts
Kermesina Alba Oculata, rosy crimson, white eye	"	10cts
Splendens, crimson, pure white eye; one of the finest of this strain	"	10cts
Isabellina, creamy yellow; very desirable	"	10cts
Rosy Chamois, beautiful shade of rose..	"	10cts
Stellata Splendens, rich crimson, with star-shaped white eye	"	10cts
Violet, deep violet blue with white eye...	"	10cts
Extra Choicest mixed, best large flowered varieties	"	5cts

Phlox Perennial
The varieties of the Perennial Phlox are among the choicest of our flowers for bedding and border plants. They are hardy and need no protection; will flourish in any soil, succeeding better, however, in deep, rich, rather moist ground. Two to three feet high. Mixed seed saved from splendid sorts.....................Pkt. 10cts

PICOTEE—(*See Carnation*).

Peas, Everlasting   (*Lathyrus Latifolius*).

A perennial climber, producing a succession of clusters of white, rose or purple blossoms. Suitable for trellises, arbors, etc. The plants bloom the second year, but give larger and more abundant flowers as they grow older. Hardy perennial; ten feet high.

Rose ....Pkt.		5cts
White	"	5cts
Mixed.....................................	"	5cts

PELARGONIUM—(*See Geranium*).

LARGE FLOWERING PETUNIAS

Large Flowered mixed....................Pkt. 10cts

Choicest Large Flowered mixed............. " 15cts

Fringed and Stained mixed, large flowered; very desirable.................................. " 20cts

Superbissima mixed. The flowers are of immense size, superbly colored and the open throats are beautifully veined. We have carefully compared other strains sold as Giants of California, etc., and have found none superior and most of them not equal to our strain of this magnificent variety. (*See Supplement*)...............Pkt. 25cts

Brilliant Rose. Exceedingly large, beautiful flowers of the brightest and yet delicate rose color. One of the finest varieties in cultivation and comes true from seed.
Pkt. 25cts

General Dodds. This is a strain of petunia producing large, single flowers that are noticeable because of their exceedingly rich, dark purple color, which is really one of the most striking among petunias. We recommend General Dodds as a vigorous and very persistent bloomer and think there are very few garden plants that will make so good and satisfactory a display ....Pkt. 10cts

Grandiflora Robusta fl. pl. Dwarf, of robust growth, forming a compact, upright, branched bush about ten inches in height and fourteen inches in width, with large, double flowers in all shades of colors existing in petunias.
Pkt. 25cts

Double Fringed Brilliant Rose. Bears large, exceedingly double and fringed flowers of the most brilliant rose color. Very desirable.........Pkt. 25cts

Extra Double Fringed, many colors; beautifully fringed; a good percentage double........Pkt. 25cts

PHLOX DRUMMONDI

Pansies

Pansies are now produced in almost infinite variety of form, color and markings. Their variety of bloom, brilliancy of coloring and long keeping characteristics render them general favorites. We have been interested in the bringing forward of advanced types of large varieties, both in this country and in Europe, and our stocks are the very best obtainable. We spare no pains or expense to satisfy the most critical trade. We every year visit the gardens of the most expert specialists in Europe, and we are in position to give our customers the benefit of their knowledge. The following list comprises the best kinds on the market. Pansies do best in very rich, moist soil and cool, moist atmosphere. A situation sheltered from high winds and exposed to the morning sun is most favorable. Frequent sprinklings are advantageous.

Lord Beaconsfield. The ground color is purple-violet, shading off in top petals only, to a whitish hue; large flowering........**Pkt. 10cts**

Snow Queen, also called Snow Flake; flowers of a delicate, pure white; large flowering.**Pkt.10c**

Emperor William, indigo, dark center; large flowering.....................................**Pkt. 10cts**

King of the Blacks, large flowering, one of the darkest colored flowers grown, being truly black. " **10cts**

Odier, or Large Stained, large, each petal blotched " **15cts**

Pure Yellow, large flowering....................... " **10cts**

Variegated and striped, very varied in color; purple striped with lighter shades and yellow...... " **10cts**

White, large flowering........................... " **10cts**

Gold Margined, rich purple or red with narrow yellow margin.................................. " **10cts**

Mahogany colored............................... " **10cts**

Violet, white edged............................. " **10cts**

Meteor. Large, rich, velvety red or mahogany colored flowers that show to excellent advantage in massing or edgings. It is very hardy... " **10cts**

Peacock. Large flowered variety of English origin, marked with shades of blue and purple, which are suggestive of the spots on a peacock's tail, hence its name........................... " **10cts**

Giant Blue Black (*Trimardeau*). Extra large, very fine dark, rich velvety purple, almost black flowers.................................. " **10cts**

Giant Yellow (*Trimardeau*). Enormous, yellow flowers with large, black centers.............. " **15cts**

Bugnot's Very Large Stained, mixed. An extra large, five blotched race, having immense flowers of fine form and substance. The plants are vigorous with short, stiff stalks bearing flowers well above the foliage. Extra fine............. " **15cts**

Trimardeau, Very Large Flowered, mixed. An entirely distinct and beautiful race with flowers of the richest and most varied shades of color. Plants of vigorous, compact growth, with immense, three blotched flowers................. " **10cts**

Red Flowered, Victoria. The blooms are of good substance and form, and deep claret red color..**Pkt. 10cts**

Ferry's Superbissima Blotched. A magnificent new Pansy, having large, broad, thick, brilliantly colored petals forming most perfectly shaped flowers. These are not only of immense size, but the petals have great substance and are very broad, overlapping one another to such an extent as to give the effect of a somewhat doubled flower. It is distinctly superior, rather than simply different from old strains.......... " **15cts**

Large Flowering Parisian, mixed. Flowers of largest size and finest form, as well as the greatest variety of magnificent colors; are borne on stout stems which show their beauty to perfection. An excellent sort for florists............. " **10cts**

Extra Choice Mixed, from choicest named flowers " **10cts**

Choice Mixed .... " **5cts**

Collection of thirteen splendid varieties.........; **$1.00**

SHIRLEY POPPIES

SEE
OPPOSITE
PAGE

PENTSTEMON

Handsome, half hardy herbaceous perennials, much in favor for bedding out. Flowers bell-shaped or tubular, an inch and a half long, borne in racemes or spikes. The roots should receive some protection in winter.
Mixed, seed saved from collection of best varieties..**Pkt. 10c**

PERILLA
Nankinensis Atropurpurea Laciniata.

Ornamental foliage plants similar to Coleus. They are of easy culture, growing freely in any good, common garden soil. Fine for bedding with silver-leaved plants. Foliage dark metallic bronze, almost black. Half hardy annual; two feet high....................................**Pkt. 5cts**

PERIWINKLE—(See Vinca).

PINKS
(Also see Carnation).

(*Dianthus*). The Dianthus family furnishes many of the most beautiful flowers, including the Carnation, Sweet William, Chinese and Japanese Pinks, in all their varieties. Hardy and half hardy biennials and pe enni s but nearly all blooming the first year from seed; of easy culture. A warm soil is desirable, one where water will not stand, particularly during the winter. Seeds may be sown in the open ground where they are to stand but better results are obtained, at least in the north, if plants are started in the house.

Crimson Belle. Rich, vivid crimson-like color; flowers single and of extraordinary size and substance, evenly and finely laciniated. Half hardy biennial, blooming freely the first season.**Pkt. 10cts**

Eastern Queen. Single flowers beautifully marbled; the broad bands of rich mauve upon the paler surface of the petals are very striking and pretty. Half hardy biennial, blooming freely the first season........................... " 10cts

Heddewig's Single mixed. Flowers of the best shades and beautifully marked; half hardy biennial.............................. " 5cts

Double Brilliant Maroon. This beautiful variety is easily cultivated, and its velvety maroon flowers are very attractive. Very valuable for cut flowers and in bouquets. Half hardy biennial.............................. " 10cts

Double Diadem. Very regular, densely double, and of all tints, from crimson-purple to deep black-purple. Half hardy biennial, blooming freely the first season........................... " 5cts

Double Japan. To be properly appreciated, these should be seen; rich in hue, very double, deeply fringed petals—only lacking fragrance to make them perfect. Half hardy biennial, blooming freely the first season; mixed........ " 5cts

Heddewig's Double. Flowers very large and double, and of various shades of brilliant colors. Half hardy biennial.............................. " 5cts

Double China, mixed. A mixture of the last four strains, sure to give very fine flowers..... " 5cts

Portulaca

There are few flowers in cultivation that make such a dazzling display of color in the bright sunshine as a bed of portulacas. They are in bloom from about the first of July till killed by frost in autumn. The seed requires a moderately high temperature for germination, and should not be sown until settled warm weather. Sometimes they are started indoors but usually are sown directly where the plants are to stand. The soil need not be rich, the plants doing better in hot, rather dry ground. They should have sunny situation; the flowers close in shadow but are open in sunshine. Tender annual; about six to eight inches high.

SINGLE VARIETIES.
Alba, pure white...........**Pkt. 5cts**
Aurea, deep golden........ " 5cts
Caryophylloides, carnation striped.................... " 5cts
Striata, yellow, striped with red.......................... " 5cts
Fine Mixed.................. " 5cts

DOUBLE VARIETIES.
Not all the plants will come double, but the single ones can be pulled out. They will stand any amount of dry weather.

Double white............**Pkt. 10cts**
  " **scarlet**............ " 10cts
  " **sulphur**............ " 10cts
  " **orange**............. " 10cts
  " **rose striped**....... " 10cts
  " **mixed**.............. " 10cts

POPPY

(*Papaver*). Well known hardy annuals and perennials flowering in great profusion throughout the summer.

As early in spring as ground can be worked sow the seed where flowers are to bloom and cover lightly, since if planted too deep the seed will not germinate and the annual varieties do not bear transplanting. To insure a continuous bloom during a long season the flowers should be cut regularly and no seed pods allowed to form.

Iceland, single mixed. The delicate, fragrant flowers are exceedingly beautiful, their long stems make them very suitable for cutting. The colors are white, yellow and orange-red; blooms produced continuously throughout the season. Hardy perennial, blooming the first year from seed...................................**Pkt. 5cts**

Tulip Flowered. Produces large, splendid bright scarlet flowers borne well above the foliage. The petals form a tulip-shaped cup and after a time black spots appear at the base of each petal. Strikingly beautiful, reminding one of a bed of brilliant tulips. Hardy annual; about one foot high...................................**Pkt. 5cts**

Orientale. Large, gorgeous scarlet blossoms; base of petals black. One of our most striking and showy garden perennials................. " 5cts

Umbrosum. Rich vermilion, with a shining black spot on each petal; one of the most showy varieties; hardy annual................. " 5cts

The Shirley. This magnificent strain of Poppies affords during a long season flowers of the most charmingly delicate shades of colors imaginable, ranging from a pure, glistening white through the pinks, reds and scarlets to the deepest crimson, the darker shades frequently being margined with white. Some of the petals are of silky texture, others look like tissue paper; some are plain, some crimped and some wavy. The flowers are exceedingly graceful and airy and lend themselves readily to bouquets which should be cut before the blooms are fully expanded; they will then keep fresh in water for several days. (*See colored plate opposite*)................................... " 5cts

Cardinal. This is a very large and very double poppy, each petal being so cut as to give the blossom the appearance of a large ball of brilliant cardinal colored silk. It is certainly one of the finest poppies in cultivation and a worthy companion to our Double White Fringed Poppy, from which it differs only in color............. " 5cts

Double White Fringed. This is the finest double white poppy. The blooms are from three to four inches in diameter, perfectly double, finely fringed and of the purest white............... " 5cts

Carnation, double white........................ " 5cts

Carnation, double mixed. Large, showy, double flowers of various colors; two feet high....... " 5cts

Bracteatum. Large, orange-crimson flowers; perennial................................... " 5cts

☞ *Papaver Somniferum*, of which the Carnation Poppy is an improved form, is the species used for the extraction of opium.

PORTULACA.

PHYSALIS FRANCHETI

(Lantern Plant). When well grown, plants are about two feet high producing from the axis of each leaf one or more large, brilliant red-colored seed pods which in form and color are suggestive of a Japanese lantern. These contain bright, cherry-like fruit, which is occasionally used for making preserves. A strikingly beautiful, decorative plant. It grows readily to a fruiting size the first year from seed in the warmer latitudes....**Pkt. 10cts**

PLATYCODON JAPONICUS fl. pl.

(Japanese Bell Flower). This is distinctly superior to the ordinary varieties of Platycodon. The flowers are double instead of single and the ten petals, in color a very attractive deep blue, are arranged in the form of an open bell. A hardy perennial; twelve to eighteen inches high and in flower from June to October....................**Pkt. 10cts**

PLATYCODON
JAPONICUS.

Primrose, Evening

(Œnothera). Produces large, showy blossoms which are fully expanded only towards and during evening. Blossoms yellow or white and very freely and constantly produced.

Acaulis Alba. Of prostrate habit, the leaves lying on the ground; produces an abundance of large, white flowers about three inches across. Hardy perennial; six inches high..............**Pkt. 5cts**

Lamarckiana. Superb spikes of large, bright yellow blossoms three to four inches across. Hardy biennial, but blooms the first year; height four feet...**Pkt. 5cts**

PRIMULA JAPONICA

(Japanese Primrose). The beautiful, large, various colored flowers stand in whorls, pyramidically arranged on short flower stems; one foot high. Though perennial, new plants flower more freely and seed should be sown every year. *Mixed varieties*....................**Pkt. 25cts**

After sowing the seeds of Primula Japonica, let them remain in a cool and moist, place for four or five weeks, then place in a frame or house where there is bottom heat and they will grow freely.

Primula Sinensis

(Chinese Primrose). The beautiful, large flowers stand in pyramids arranged on short flower stems. Blossoms of every shade of color, from pure white to deep crimson, and even deep blue are found on different plants. The first week in April is a good time to sow the seed in order to get plants to flower well the following winter, and about the middle of May for a second batch to succeed the first sowing. Sow in well drained, shallow pans. Use finely sifted leaf mold, loam and sand in equal parts. Cover slightly and place the pans, when well watered, in a temperature of about 60° F.

SINGLE FRINGED PRIMULA.

Cœrulea blue..**Pkt. 25cts**	**Mont Blanc,** white..**Pkt. 25cts**		
Scarlet........ " 25cts	**Bright Rose** .... " 25cts		
Alba Magnifica, white........	" 25cts		
Punctata Elegantissima, flowers velvety crimson, fringed and spotted on the edge with white	" 25cts		
Soliel d' Empel, magnificent, fine, white variety.	" 25cts		
Choicest mixed, from choicest of best fringed varieties...........................	" 25cts		
Choicest Fern Leaved, mixed....................	" 25cts		

DOUBLE FRINGED PRIMULA.

The following are very choice and will produce a large percentage of double flowers.

Double crimson..**Pkt. 25cts**	**Double white**....**Pkt. 25cts**		
Double red........ " 25cts	**Double mixed**.... " 25cts		

Pyrethrum

Very ornamental plants both in foliage and flowers. Sow from December to April in shallow boxes, in a temperature of 60°. As soon as the young plants can be handled, transplant singly into small pots or shallow boxes, where they may remain until the time of planting out into the open ground in May. (*See also Matricaria*).

Parthenifolium aureum, *(Golden Feather).* Beautiful, gold leaved bedding plant. Flowers white; height one foot ....**Pkt. 5cts**

Parthenifolium aureum selaginoides. Has finely cut, fern-like leaves of bright golden yellow color. Extra fine for bedding. Half hardy perennial; height one foot..**Pkt. 10c**

Roseum. Flowers large, yellow and rose colored; handsome. Hardy perennial; two feet high..............**Pkt. 10cts**

QUAKING GRASS—(See Briza).

RHODANTHE

One of the most beautiful of the everlastings. The flowers are somewhat bell-shaped, gracefully poised on very slender stems. The blooms should be gathered before fully expanded and dried in the shade. Tender annual; one foot high.

Manglesi, rich rose, with golden center........**Pkt 5cts**			
Maculata alba, white, with yellow disc............ " 5cts			
Mixed .... " 5cts			

RICINUS—(See Castor Bean).

ROCKET

(Hesperis Matronalis). The Sweet Rocket produces clusters of flowers which are very fragrant during the evening. The seed germinates readily in the open ground and with very little care. Hardy perennial; one and a half feet high.

Sweet, purple...................**Pkt. 5cts**　　**Sweet, white**..................**Pkt. 5cts**

Rose

Multiflora Dwarf Perpetual, mixed. A most distinct and valuable addition to our list of flowers, especially so because of the ease with which fine blooming plants can be raised from seed. Plants have been made to bloom within thirty days from the planting of the seed and even under ordinary care they will commence to flower when six inches high and two months old and will continue to grow and bloom until they form compact bushes about sixteen inches high covered with flowers. The different plants will give flowers of varying shades of color. Tender perennial; blooming the first year.

....**Pkt. 15cts**

ROSE CAMPION—(See Agrostemma Coronaria).

ROSE OF HEAVEN—(See Agrostemma Cœli-rosa).

Snapdragon

(Antirrhinum). An old border plant with dark and glossy leaves and long spikes of curiously shaped, brilliantly colored flowers, having finely marked throats. They have been much improved of late years by careful selection. Snapdragons blossom the first season from seed sown in spring, especially under frames and transplanted produce blooming plants the same season. If early bloom is desired sow the seed in August or September and cover the plants with a mulch on the approach of cold weather. These may be transplanted into pots and flowered in the house. Give them the same temperature and treatment as geraniums and carnations. Tender perennial; one and a half to two feet high.

Majus Album. Pure white, tinged with yellow in the throat...............**Pkt. 5cts**			
Majus Brilliant. Crimson, with yellow and white throat................... " 5cts			
Majus Delila. Brilliant crimson, with white throat....................... " 5cts			
Fine mixed. All the best colors................................... " 5cts			

Salpiglossis

Very showy bedding or border plants with richly colored, funnel-shaped flowers which are purple, scarlet, crimson, yellow, buff, blue and almost black, beautifully marbled and penciled. The seed may be sown indoors by the middle of March, or later, or may be sown outdoors in early spring; useful for cutting. Bloom from August to October. Half hardy annual; one and a half to two feet high. **Fine mixed**, *hybrid varieties*.**Pkt. 5c**

Salvia

(*Flowering Sage*). Among the most brilliantly colored of garden flowers and extremely useful for bedding; also valuable for pot culture. Blooms are borne in long spikes well above the foliage and are of fiery red, crimson or blue color, continuing in flower for a long time. Start early in heat and transplant into light soil one to two feet apart. Tender perennials, but bloom the first season; height two to three feet.

Splendens. Brilliant scarlet......................**Pkt. 10cts**
Golden Leaved. This is a variety of Salvia Splendens which comes true from seed and has rich yellow leaves, contrasting beautifully with the brilliant scarlet flowers.**Pkt. 25cts**
Patens. One of the finest blue flowers known... " **15cts**
Lord Fauntleroy. Many strains of Salvia Splendens have been offered under different names with the claim that they are l a r g e r flowered or more floriferous than the old type. We have found none of them more distinctly valuable than this strain in which the plant is more uniformly dwarf and floriferous and the flower spikes longer than in the common stock, so we strongly r e c o m mend it as a decided improvement. The plant is uniformly dwarf,averaging only about twentyinches high. In habit it is exceedingly free blooming, bearing above the dark green foliage brilliant c r i m s o n spikes which are longer than those of the common sorts....**Pkt. 25cts**

Sanvitalia
Procumbens fl. pl.

Very pretty, dwarf, trailing plants; excellent for rock work, borders, or edging of beds. They are so completely covered with flowers as to nearly hide the foliage. Double flowers of a brilliant, golden yellow, resembling a miniature double zinnia. Hardy annual; s i x inches high...**Pkt. 5cts**

Sensitive Plant
(*Mimosa pudica*). An interesting and curious plant with globular heads of small, pink flowers. The plant is chiefly valued because of the extreme irritability of its leaves which close and droop at the slightest touch, or in cloudy, damp weather and during the night. Tender annual; height one and a half feet....................**Pkt. 5cts**

SALPIGLOSSIS.

SALVIA LORD FAUNTLEROY.

Smilax

No twining plant in cultivation surpasses this in graceful beauty of foliage. Indispensable to florists; its hard texture enables it to be kept several days after being cut, without wilting. *The seed germinates very slowly.* The process may be hastened somewhat by soaking the seed in hot water for ten hours before planting but even then it is often six or eight weeks before the plants make their appearance. Tender perennial climber; ten feet high................**Pkt. 5cts**

Solanum
Pseudo Capsicum nanum.

Ornamental, fruit bearing plants, useful for conservatory or drawing room decoration. The foliage is handsome and contrasts finely with the miniature, round, scarlet fruit with which the plant is covered. Tender perennial; about one and a half feet high......................**Pkt. 10cts**

SCABIOSA—(*See Mourning Bride*).

SCARLET FLAX—(*See Linum*)

STIPA PENNATA—(*See Feather Grass*).

SWEET PEAS

Our stocks are **absolutely unsurpassed in selection, purity and vitality.**
Our prices are reasonable, being lower than those of many smaller firms, but were we to charge twice as much the quality of the stocks **could not be improved.**

CULTURE—Early in spring make a trench about six inches deep in rich, mellow soil, so arranged that no water can stand in it and plant the seed in the bottom, covering no more than two inches. Sweet Peas, particularly the white seeded sorts, are often a little difficult to start. If the soil is too dry they will remain a long time without germinating; if it is too wet and cold they will not sprout at all. In soils at all heavy or composed largely of clay put about two inches of sand in the bottom of the trench and sow the seed on this, covering with more sand. Cover the row with a board to shed the rain and protect the soil from the hot sun, but remove this as soon as the young plants appear. When the plants are about five inches high, gradually fill up the trench and furnish some support for the vines to run upon. The blooms should be picked before they form pods or the plants will soon stop flowering.

FORCING AND INDOOR SORTS

Extra Early Blanche Ferry, Mont Blanc, Josephine White and Inconstancy with us have proven most desirable varieties for forcing. These and other sorts marked thus (*) have given the best results in their respective classes of colors when grown indoors.

WHITE

MONT BLANC.* This variety originated in the Extra Early Blanche Ferry and like that sort is of dwarf, slender, very graceful habit with narrow leaves, throwing the blossoms well out from the foliage so that every one is well exposed. Its greatest merit is in its extreme earliness and its consequent fitness for forcing. Flowers of good form and size and very clear white color. **Pkt.5c; Oz.10c; ¼ Lb.25c; Lb.75c.**

JOSEPHINE WHITE.* One of the earliest white Sweet Peas and especially desirable for forcing. Habit like Emily Henderson but earlier and produces flowers during a longer season. Very desirable for cutting. **Pkt. 5c; Oz. 10c; 2 Oz. 20c; ¼ Lb. 30c; Lb. $1.00.**

EMILY HENDERSON. A bold, well formed, clear white flower. Wings broad and well expanded. An early and wonderfully free and persistent bloomer. The flowers have more substance and the plant more vigor than the other whites and it will give good flowers where most sorts fail. **Pkt. 5c; Oz. 10c; ¼ Lb. 20c; Lb. 50c.**

BLANCHE BURPEE. A splendid pure white variety. While not so profuse a bloomer or as hardy a plant as the Emily Henderson, the flowers are fine. **Pkt. 5c; Oz. 10c; ¼ Lb. 20c; Lb. 50c.**

THE BRIDE. Flowers like the Blanche Burpee but stems more slender, more gracefully poised, and attractive for bunching. **Pkt. 5c; Oz. 10c; ¼ Lb. 20c; Lb. 60c.**

LIGHT YELLOW

INCONSTANCY.* Aside from being extremely early is remarkable because the same plant will at one period of growth give pure white flowers and at another period flowers unquestionably primrose. Frequently white and primrose flowers are found on one plant at the same time. **Pkt. 5c; Oz. 10c; 2 Oz. 20c; ¼ Lb. 30c; Lb. $1.00**

MRS. ECKFORD. Plant strong-growing and vigorous; stems three and four flowered; flowers large, of great substance and perfect form. A delicate shade of primrose yellow at first, becoming nearly white at maturity. **Pkt.5c; Oz.10c; ¼ Lb.20c; Lb.55c.**

QUEEN VICTORIA. Light primrose of hooded form showing a pink tint while in the bud but a clear soft primrose when matured. **Pkt. 5c; Oz. 10c; ¼ Lb. 20c; Lb. 60c.**

THE HON. MRS. E. KENYON.* The best of the deeper primrose shades; a beautiful large semi-hooded flower. **Pkt. 5c; Oz. 10c; ¼ Lb. 25c; Lb. 75c.**

LIGHT PINK

MRS. SANKEY. Standard round, very thick; delicate shell-pink, wings a little lighter than standard. Beautiful delicate pink, becoming white as it fades. **Pkt. 5c; Oz. 10c; ¼ Lb. 20c; Lb. 50c.**

LOTTIE HUTCHINS. Standard and wings of light primrose with stripes of light pink. One of the best of the hooded shapes. **Pkt. 5c; Oz. 10c; ¼ Lb. 20c; Lb. 60c.**

STELLA MORSE. The flowers of this variety are of the finest form and a peculiar warm salmon-pink. A combination yellow and pink, which is quite distinct and very attractive. **Pkt. 5c; Oz. 10c; ¼ Lb. 20c; Lb. 60c.**

VENUS. Standard large, of fine form and substance; a brilliant but delicate and soft shade of warm rose-pink and buff; wings similar to the standard. **Pkt. 5c; Oz. 10c; ¼ Lb. 20c; Lb. 50c.**

COQUETTE. Large, finely formed flower. Standard warm primrose shaded purple; wings primrose. **Pkt. 5c; Oz. 10c; ¼ Oz. 20c; Lb. 60c.**

LOVELY.* Flowers very large, fine form. A delicate shell pink tinged with yellow, often four flowers on a stem. **Pkt. 5c; Oz. 10c; ¼ Lb. 20c; Lb. 60c.**

ELIZA ECKFORD. Large flower of rosy pink over white, exceedingly delicate and beautiful. **Pkt. 5c; Oz. 10c; ¼ Lb. 20c; Lb. 50c.**

PRIMA DONNA. The stems bear three or four very large, perfect flowers of a brilliant yet soft shade of pink. **Pkt. 5c; Oz. 10c; ¼ Lb. 20c; Lb. 60c.**

ROYAL ROBE. Bright rose pink. Those who like a hooded, gracefully rolled standard will be pleased with this sort. **Pkt. 5c; Oz. 10c; ¼ Lb. 20c; Lb. 55c.**

KATHERINE TRACY.* The color is a soft but brilliant pink, in wings and standard. Plants vigorous and give a profusion of flowers which continue large and fine until the end of the season. In hardiness, prolific flowering habit, durability and practical usefulness this is greatly superior to most sorts of recent introduction. **Pkt. 5c; Oz. 10c; ¼ Lb. 20c; Lb. 60c.**

SHAHZADA

SWEET PEAS—Continued

ORANGE PINK

LADY MARY CURRIE.* A large, well formed flower of brilliant orange-pink color. Similar to Lady Penzance, but rounder and of more brilliant color. **Pkt. 5c; Oz. 10c; ¼Lb. 20c; Lb. 60c.**

ORIENTAL. The large, finely formed flowers are a primrose or even yellow shade, very striking and attractive. **Pkt. 5c; Oz. 10c; ¼ Lb. 20c; Lb. 60c.**

MISS WILLMOTT.* A fine semi-hooded type; standard orange pink; wings rose tinted with orange. Of very large size, long stems, plant very vigorous. **Pkt. 5c; Oz. 10c; ¼Lb. 25c; Lb. 75c.**

RED STANDARD WITH WHITE WINGS

EXTRA EARLY BLANCHE FERRY. This is the pioneer extra early sweet pea and bears much the same relation to the other sorts of this section that the original Blanche Ferry does to other American sorts, in that it is of vigorous and hardy though dwarf habit, and a wonderfully free and persistent bloomer. It will be found to be one of the first varieties to furnish flowers, either in greenhouse or out of doors, and it will continue to furnish them in great abundance longer than most varieties. **Pkt. 5c; Oz. 10c; ¼ Lb. 20c; Lb. 60c.**

BLANCHE FERRY. Standard medium sized, but of fine form and bright pink color; wings large, rounded and nearly white. **Pkt. 5c; Oz. 10c; ¼ Lb. 20c; Lb. 50c.**

SHADES OF RED

MRS. DUGDALE.* A large, finely formed flower of a peculiar shade of primrose overlaid with crimson-rose. **Pkt. 5c; Oz. 10c; ¼ Lb. 20c; Lb. 60c.**

OVID. A good sized, hooded flower of bright pink overlaid with a darker shade. **Pkt. 5c; Oz. 10c; ¼ Lb. 20c; Lb. 50c.**

LORD KENYON. Magenta rose; wings veined with a deeper shade. Similar to American Queen, but hooded instead of open form. **Pkt. 5c; Oz. 10c; ¼Lb. 20c; Lb. 60c.**

HER MAJESTY. The flowers are very large, and both the standard and wings are beautifully curved and a delicate rose-pink color. **Pkt. 5c; Oz. 10c; ¼Lb. 20c; Lb. 60c.**

PRINCE OF WALES. Flowers very large and a peculiar, brilliant red, distinct in shade from any other sweet pea. Very attractive. **Pkt. 5c; Oz. 10c; ¼Lb. 20c; Lb. 60c.**

COCCINEA. Distinct in color, a bright cherry red and unlike any other we offer. Very pleasing and effective. **Pkt. 5c; Oz.10c; ¼Lb. 25c; Lb. 75c.**

ROYAL ROSE. One of the largest and finest formed flowers yet produced. Standard a deep rose-pink; wings a lighter shade of the same color. **Pkt. 5c; Oz. 10c; ¼ Lb. 20c; Lb. 60c.**

BRILLIANT. Flower of good size and substance. Standard round and inclined to curve forward. Color very brilliant rich red. Mars is similar, but fades purple. **Pkt. 5c; Oz. 10c; ¼ Lb. 20c; Lb. 60c.**

FIREFLY. Very bright and intense crimson-scarlet, of good size and form. **Pkt. 5c; Oz. 10c; ¼ Lb. 20c; Lb. 60c.**

SALOPIAN.* One of the most brilliant and most richly colored sorts yet introduced. The flowers are of faultless form, large and a very rich, brilliant cardinal red. **Pkt. 5c; Oz. 10c; ¼ Lb. 20c; Lb. 60c.**

LAVENDER AND LIGHT BLUE

MAID OF HONOR. Medium sized flower, nearly white, having a distinct edging of blue which gives it a peculiar and very attractive appearance. **Pkt. 5c; Oz. 10c; ¼ Lb. 20c; Lb. 60c.**

BUTTERFLY. Standard a combination of shades of violet and lavender; it is often notched on the sides. Wings white, shaded and edged with blue. **Pkt. 5c; Oz. 10c; ¼ Lb. 20c; Lb. 50c.**

LOTTIE ECKFORD. Standard a peculiar and delicate shade of magenta blue; wings very large, long and shaded lavender deepening to violet at edge. **Pkt. 5c; Oz. 10c; ¼ Lb. 20c; Lb. 50c.**

FASCINATION. Standard lilac, wings blue tinged with lilac; the blossom finally turning to a bright blue. Large size, hooded form. **Pkt. 5c; Oz. 10c; ¼ Lb. 20c; Lb. 60c.**

DOROTHY TENNANT.* Flowers warm violet or mauve, finely formed. Standard broad, incurved or hooded; wings very large, rounded. **Pkt. 5c; Oz. 10c; ¼ Lb. 20c; Lb. 50c.**

COUNTESS OF RADNOR. Self colored in a very distinct and beautiful shade of lavender. **Pkt.5c; Oz.10c; ¼Lb.20c; Lb.60c.**

LADY GRISEL HAMILTON.* A large flower similar in color to Countess of Radnor, but nearer blue. A strong grower, producing an abundance of very fine flowers. Superior to Celestial. **Pkt. 5c; Oz. 10c; ¼ Lb. 20c; Lb. 60c.**

BLUE AND PURPLE

COUNTESS OF CADOGAN.* Stems very long, each bearing three or four flowers, a little darker than Navy Blue. **Pkt.5c; Oz.10c; ¼Lb.20c; Lb.60c.**

WAVERLEY. Wings and standard are a beautiful blending of rose-pink and lavender-blue shades which vary as the flower matures. **Pkt. 5c; Oz. 10c; ¼ Lb. 20c; Lb. 60c.**

CAPTAIN OF THE BLUES. Standard large, broad, bright purple-blue; wings expanded, lighter and brighter blue than standard. **Pk.5c; Oz.10c; ¼Lb.20c; Lb.55c.**

NAVY BLUE. A true blue, quite distinct. **Pkt. 5c; Oz. 10c; ¼ Lb. 20c; Lb. 60c.**

INDIGO KING. Standard very rich purple-maroon; wings more blue. **Pkt.5c; Oz.10c; ¼Lb.20c; Lb.50c.**

EXTRA EARLY BLANCHE FERRY

STELLA MORSE

G.H.H.

Sweet Peas—Continued

PINK AND RED STRIPES

AURORA. Very large and of fine form. The standard and wings are striped and flaked with delicate orange-salmon-pink over white.   Pkt. 5c; Oz. 10c; ¼ Lb. 20c; Lb. 55c.

GOLDEN ROSE. Primrose striped and mottled with light pink. Of semi-hooded form and largest size. One of the most attractive of the newer sorts.   Pkt. 5c; Oz. 15c; 2 Oz. 25c; ¼ Lb. 40c; Lb. $1.25

MRS. JOSEPH CHAMBERLAIN. Very large and perfect shaped flowers; white, striped with bright rose-carmine.   Pkt. 5c; Oz. 10c; ¼ Lb. 20c; Lb. 50c.

AMERICA.* White, nearly covered with splashes, stripes and dots of exceedingly bright carmine. The most brilliant red striped sort.   Pkt. 5c; Oz. 10c; ¼ Lb. 20c; Lb. 50c.

PURPLE STRIPES

GRAY FRIAR.* Very large, finely shaped flowers of delicate heliotrope color, tinged, marbled and dotted with darker shade.   Pkt. 5c; Oz. 10c; ¼ Lb. 20c; Lb. 50c.

PRINCESS OF WALES. Standard broad, flat, striped purple on nearly white ground; wings very large and lighter colored than standard.   Pkt. 5c; Oz. 10c; ¼ Lb. 20c; Lb. 50c.

SENATOR. Standard broad, very large, delicate lavender, nearly covered with stripes and splashes of purple-maroon; wings medium sized, round, striped with a bluer shade than the standard.   Pkt. 5c; Oz. 10c; ¼ Lb. 20c; Lb. 50c.

CLARET AND MAROON

MONARCH. Standard large, fine form, violet-maroon; wings very large and expanded; quite similar in color to the standard, but having a blue shade.   Pkt. 5c; Oz. 10c; ¼ Lb. 20c; Lb. 50c.

DUKE OF CLARENCE. A fine flower with large standard and wings of uniform shade of dark claret.   Pkt. 5c; Oz. 10c; ¼ Lb. 20c; Lb. 50c.

BOREATTON. One of the darkest and richest colored. Standard large, rounded; rich, satin-like maroon; wings are similar in color to the standard. One of the best dark varieties yet produced.   Pkt. 5c; Oz. 10c; ¼ Lb. 20c; Lb. 50c.

STANLEY.* A very beautiful sort. Standard large and flat, color a deep maroon and warmer than Boreatton.   Pkt. 5c; Oz. 10c; ¼ Lb. 20c; Lb. 50c.

BLACK KNIGHT. One of the darkest varieties.   Pkt. 5c; Oz. 10c; ¼ Lb. 20c; Lb. 55c.

SHAHZADA.* This has a very rich, dark maroon standard and deep violet wings. One of the finest dark sorts.   Pkt. 5c; Oz. 10c; ¼ Lb. 20c; Lb. 60c.

OTHELLO. A very dark maroon, practically self colored, with almost black veining. Large size, hooded form.   Pkt. 5c; Oz. 10c; ¼ Lb. 20c; Lb. 60c.

Mixtures of Sweet Peas

Most people obtain more satisfaction from planting Sweet Peas in mixture than from growing named sorts, but to be successful it is necessary that the seed be of the best quality obtainable. Often what is offered as mixed seed is stock harvested from plants that have come up as volunteers on ground where Sweet Peas have been grown before, or a lot of seed which has been grown, saved or handled so carelessly that it cannot be sold as any distinct variety. The use of such seed will not give satisfactory results. However, where the seed is grown from the very best stock that can be produced, is mixed in most carefully studied proportions and then the seeds of desirable but shy seeding sorts are added, there is nothing superior for use in the home garden.

Choice Mixed   We assure our customers the Mixed Sweet Pea seed which we offer is the result of as great care in breeding and selecting as any stock we grow, and as fine flowers are obtained from it as from any seed that can be bought. We invite comparison with any and all others, no matter under what name or at how high a price offered and are certain a trial will demonstrate the superiority of our mixture.   Pkt. 5c; Oz. 10c; ¼ Lb. 15c; Lb. 40c.

Eckford's Hybrids Mixed   This is made up of the best of Eckford's large flowering sorts carefully proportioned. As only Eckford's varieties are used in this mixture, some of our very best sorts are necessarily excluded, but it will give large, finely formed flowers in a great variety of beautiful colors.   Pkt. 5c; Oz. 10c; ¼ Lb. 15c; Lb. 45c.

Cupid, or Dwarf Sweet Peas

When the Cupid Sweet Pea was introduced, it seemed to most people that its distinct habits had so delighted its propagators that they had exaggerated its value, but continued trial demonstrates that in those localities where the conditions of soil and climate are favorable for its best development, it is even more valuable than was claimed. For growing in pots, for edgings and bedding, the Dwarf Sweet Peas are a valuable addition to our flowering plants. They require no support, but form a low, compact bush covered with large, finely formed flowers.

CULTURE—Cupid Sweet Peas require a well drained, rich soil and care should be taken that the seed is not covered to exceed one inch in depth and that the surface soil does not become caked or hard. Sow in a sunny situation somewhat later than other Sweet Peas and give each plant plenty of room. The white seeded varieties are especially liable to rot if exposed to extreme moisture. They germinate best in moist, sandy soil. If such is not available, a little damp sand should be placed in the bottom of a trench and the seed embedded in it and then covered to a depth not exceeding one inch. Place a board over the row, supported two or three inches above the soil, so as to afford protection from rain and sun. Be careful to remove the board as soon as the young plants begin to appear.

ALICE ECKFORD CUPID. Flowers creamy white, blended with shades of pink and borne on stiff stems well above the foliage.   Pkt. 5c; Oz. 10c; ¼ Lb. 25c; Lb. 75c.

APPLE BLOSSOM CUPID. Standard rose on white, with lighter wings.   Pkt. 5c; Oz. 10c; ¼ Lb. 25c; Lb. 75c.

BEAUTY CUPID. An exceedingly large and perfectly formed flower of a beautiful rose color shaded with dark carmine. A very free bloomer.   Pkt. 5c; Oz. 10c; ¼ Lb. 25c; Lb. 75c.

BOREATTON CUPID. Standard large, rounded; dark, rich, satin-like maroon; wings are similar in color to the standard.   Pkt. 5c; Oz. 10c; ¼ Lb. 25c; Lb. 75c.

CAPTAIN OF THE BLUES CUPID. Large, bright purple-blue standard, wings a lighter and brighter shade.   Pkt. 5c; Oz. 10c; ¼ Lb. 25c; Lb. 75c.

COUNTESS OF RADNOR CUPID. A large, beautiful lavender self.   Pkt. 5c; Oz. 10c; ¼ Lb. 25c; Lb. 75c.

EXTRA EARLY BLANCHE FERRY CUPID. The earliest of the dwarf forms. Very attractive and blooms freely.   Pkt. 5c; Oz. 10c; ¼ Lb. 25c; Lb. 75c.

FIREFLY CUPID. Very bright and intense crimson-scarlet; of good size and form.   Pkt. 5c; Oz. 10c; ¼ Lb. 25c; Lb. 75c.

HER MAJESTY CUPID. Large and beautiful rose-pink flowers. Both the standard and wings are beautifully curved.   Pkt. 5c; Oz. 10c; ¼ Lb. 25c; Lb. 75c.

MRS. JOS. CHAMBERLAIN CUPID. Rose, striped on white; of large size and best hooded form.   Pkt. 5c; Oz. 10c; ¼ Lb. 25c; Lb. 75c.

PRIMROSE CUPID. Flowers yellowish-white in front, pronounced primrose-yellow on the back; hold form and color well.   Pkt. 5c; Oz. 10c; ¼ Lb. 25c; Lb. 75c.

PINK CUPID, OR DWARF BLANCHE FERRY. Inheriting the good qualities from the popular Blanche Ferry, the plants are unusually vigorous and floriferous. Blooms are bright, attractive and borne on long stems. Seed being dark is of strong vitality, succeeding where some weaker sorts fail.   Pkt. 5c; Oz. 10c; ¼ Lb. 25c; Lb. 75c.

ROYALTY CUPID. Large standard and wings of a beautiful rose-pink color.   Pkt. 5c; Oz. 10c; ¼ Lb. 25c; Lb. 75c.

WHITE CUPID. Flowers large, clear white, and of fine form.   Pkt 5c; Oz. 10c; ¼ Lb. 25c; Lb. 75c.

CUPID MIXED. This mixture is composed of choice shades of white, yellow and red, from light rose to deep scarlet and maroon.   Pkt. 5c; Oz. 10c; ¼ Lb. 25c; Lb. 75c.

.. Stock ..

(*Mathiola*). The Stocks, though not thriving so well in America as they do in England, are indispensable where a fine display of flowers is wanted. To such perfection has selection brought them that good seed will give a large proportion of exceedingly double flowers. Average height one and a half feet.

Double German Ten Weeks. These favorite summer flowers are excellent for bedding out and afford fine blooms for cutting. *Mixed*······**Pkt. 5cts**
Double German Ten Weeks, Pure White························" **10cts**

INTERMEDIATE, OR AUTUMNAL STOCKS.

The Intermediate Stocks, if sown at the same time as the Ten Weeks, will succeed them in bloom, thus affording flowers continuously until late in the fall. If sown in pots late in the summer they will bloom the following spring.
Intermediate White.Pkt.15c Intermediate Scarlet.Pkt.15c

BROMPTON AND EMPEROR STOCKS.

These Stocks should have the same treatment as the Intermediate. They cannot endure our winters unless protected.
Brompton, mixed, blooms well in winter. Half hardy biennial························**Pkt. 10cts**
Emperor, or Perpetual, mixed, the fine spikes of bloom are rich and attractive. Tender perennial········**Pkt. 10cts**

Sunflower

Valuable as a screen to hide unsightly places and as a background for lawns, also sometimes used to mitigate the evil of adjacent swamp holes. Hardy annual. Sunflowers grow readily in almost any soil but do best on light, rich limestone or alluvial land, well supplied with moisture and not shaded by trees or buildings.

Double Chrysanthemum Flowered. A tall plant, growing seven feet high and blooming profusely all summer. Flowers are double, large, round, golden yellow and resemble chrysanthemums····························**Pkt. 5cts**

Globosus Fistulosus. Produces very large, exceedingly double flowers of bright yellow color; plants about five feet high.**Pkt. 5c**

Large Russian. This variety forms very strong, heavy stems about six feet high, which are sometimes used for fuel. It produces single flowers which often measure eighteen to twenty inches across, and the large seed is used for making oil and for chicken feed·····························**Pkt. 5cts**

Stella. The plant of this fine variety is well branched and busty and attains a height of about three feet. The flowers are golden yellow with black discs and are borne on long stems well above the foliage and are produced in abundance throughout the season·····························**Pkt. 5cts**

SUNFLOWER STELLA.

Sweet William

(*Dianthus Barbatus*). For display in the garden, the Sweet William is unsurpassed. The seed can be planted in the spring, in open ground and will make fine blooming plants for the summer following. Hardy perennial; one and a half feet high. Pure White·············**Pkt. 5cts** Fine mixed·············**Pkt. 5cts**
Black, reddish velvety black " **5cts** Mixed double, many colors. " **5cts**

SWAN RIVER DAISY—(See *Brachycome*).
TAGETES—(See *Marigold*).
TROPÆOLUM CANARIENSE—
            (See *Canary Bird Flower*).
TROPÆOLUM LOBBIANUM—
            (See *Nasturtium Trailing*).
TROPÆOLUM MINOR—
            (See *Nasturtium Dwarf*).

Torenia Fournieri
A fine annual with trumpet shaped, sky blue flowers, each having three spots of dark indigo blue and a yellow stain in the center. Extremely handsome when grown in pots or shaded border··············**Pkt. 10cts**

Tree Cypress
(*Ipomopsis elegans*). A handsome plant with fine, feathery foliage, somewhat like that of the Cypress Vine and with long spikes of beautiful flowers; equally desirable for outdoor or conservatory cultivation. Half hardy biennial; three feet high. *Mixed varieties*··························**Pkt. 5cts**

:: VERBENA ::

The Verbena has been wonderfully improved during the past fifty years in form and size of flower truss and thrives particularly well in American soil. For masses in beds on the lawn, no plant excels it. In the varieties may be found every color from white through lilac and rose to purple and very dark purplish blue. If sown in open ground in May they will bloom in August, but if started in the house in pots in winter they will flower sooner and may be had in constant bloom from June even until after the early, light frosts. Seed should be soaked in lukewarm water before planting and care taken that the soil be very rich. Verbenas can be grown from cuttings but seedlings are more vigorous and produce more flowers. Half hardy perennial trailer which has gained much in popularity through treatment as an annual.

Verbena, Montana (*Drummondi*), hardy; rose changing to lilac························**Pkt. 5cts**
Hybrida, Defiance, seed may be relied upon to produce the *true, deep scarlet, color*············ " **10cts**
Hybrida, blue, all shades of blue·············· " **10cts**
Hybrida, Auriculæflora, various shades, all with distinct eye of white or rose···················· " **10cts**
Mammoth white. The largest trusses of the finest formed and clearest white flowers of any named sort. It comes absolutely true from seed, thus enabling us to secure the greater vigor and more abundant bloom of the seedling, united with the fine flowers of the named varieties·············· " **10cts**

Verbena, Hybrida, white, produces large, pure white flowers; fine for florists; comes true from seed····························**Pkt. 5cts**
Hybrida, Italian striped, beautiful·············· " **10cts**
Fine mixed, embraces all colors···················· " **5cts**
Extra choice mixed····························· " **10cts**
Mammoth mixed, embraces a wide range of colors························· " **15cts**
Hybrida, compacta, mixed, distinct. The plant forms a compact bush about five inches high and eighteen inches across, covered throughout the season with large trusses of white, scarlet and violet flowers····························· " **15cts**

Valerian, Greek *(Polemonium cœruleum).* An old standard border plant, often called Jacob's Ladder from its pinnately cleft leaves. Flowers blue, nodding at the ends of upright stalks. It blooms in June, is of easy cultivation and perfectly hardy and may be increased by dividing the roots. Sow early in spring, in open border and thin to one foot apart. Perennial; two feet high..........................Pkt. 5cts

Vinca A genus of ornamental, free flowering, greenhouse perennials, blooming the first season; glossy, green foliage and handsome flowers. If sown early under glass and transplanted in a warm, sheltered situation, will bloom in summer and autumn and may be potted for the house before frost. About fifteen inches high.

Pure White. Beautiful pure white, circular flowers...Pkt. 5cts
Rosea. Rose with crimson eye.................. " 5cts
Rosea alba. White with crimson eye............. " 5cts

Violet The violets commonly grown by florists are propagated from cuttings. The flowers grown from seed are smaller and more delicately colored, but quite as fragrant as the named sorts. As a rule violets do well in any good, well enriched soil. The best results, however, are obtained from soil prepared from sod taken from a rather heavy, sandy loam that is well drained.

Single, Sweet Scented, mixed.................Pkt.10cts
VIOLA TRICOLOR—(See Pansy).
VIRGINIA CREEPER—(See Ampelopsis).

Virginian Stock *(Cheiranthus Maritimus).* The plants are covered with a dense mass of beautiful blossoms and are very useful for border or edging. A continual succession of blossoms may be kept up the whole season by sowing at intervals through spring and summer. Hardy annual; growing about nine inches high.

Red and White, mixed...........................Pkt. 5cts

Wallflower

(Cheiranthus Cheiri). An old favorite garden flower. The large, massive spikes of the Wallflower are very conspicuous in beds and borders, and are very useful in making bouquets. Sow the seed early in hotbeds and while the plants are small, prick them out into pots and sink the pots in the earth. On approach of cold weather remove the pots to the house and the plants will bloom all winter. Although a woody perennial it is best to renew the plants from seed, for they begin to fail after having bloomed one or two years. Tender perennial; one and one-half feet high.

Early Brown. Brownish-red, fragrant flowers; large, thick spikes; early. Tender biennial..............................Pkt. 5cts
Golden Tom Thumb. Free flowering, of dwarf and compact habit... " 5cts
Mixed Double.. " 10cts

Wigandia Caracasana Very ornamental plants with immense, handsome shaped leaves, the veins and the stems being covered with crimson hair. It grows rapidly and should be formed into a bush. Its large leaves and clusters of lilac flowers which continue to open in succession for a long time give the plant a tropical aspect and make it valuable for garden and lawn decoration. Seeds if sown early in spring in hotbed will produce large plants by the middle of summer.......................Pkt. 10cts

Whitlavia **Grandiflora.** A plant with delicate, handsome foliage, producing a constant succession of beautiful violet-blue, bell-shaped flowers about half an inch long and borne in drooping clusters. In heavy, wet soils it does not succeed well but in light, sandy loam few flowers give more satisfaction. Sow the seed in open border, early in spring. Hardy annual; one foot high......Pkt. 5cts

Wistaria Chinensis One of the most beautiful and rapid growing of hardy climbers. Frequently blooms both in spring and fall. The pale blue, pea-shaped flowers are borne in long, drooping clusters, often over a foot in length. Seeds should be sown in mellow loam early in the spring, or in greenhouse or hotbed in winter and when plants are one foot high, transplanted into situations where they are to remain...........................Pkt. 20cts

Xeranthemum A free flowering everlasting flower of compact habit, and the easiest cultivation. The leaves are covered with a silvery down and the single or double flowers are pure white, deep purple or yellow. If gathered before fully opened and dried in the shade, will retain their beauty for years. Hardy annual; one foot high.
Mixed varieties.................................Pkt. 5cts

Zea Maize *(Striped Japanese Corn). Zea Japonica fol. variegatis.* A variety of corn with ornamental foliage; leaves striped green and white. Half hardy annual; six feet high.....................................Pkt. 5cts

ZINNIA.

Zinnia

Very showy plants, with large, double, imbricated flowers which, when fully expanded, might easily be mistaken for dwarf dahlias. There is much satisfaction in a bed of Zinnias, for when nearly every other flower has been killed by frost this plant is still in full bloom. Few flowers are more easily grown or bloom more abundantly throughout the season. Sow the seed early in spring, in open ground and transplant to one and one-half feet apart in good, rich soil. Half hardy annual; about eighteen inches high.

Double, yellow	Pkt. 5cts	Double, orange		Pkt. 5cts
" scarlet	" 5cts	" white		" 5cts
" deep red	" 5cts	" black purple		" 5cts
" magenta	" 5cts	" dark crimson		" 5cts
" striped, or zebra, flowers striped and mottled with various colors				" 5cts
" choice mixed, very fine				" 5cts

Lilliput, double mixed. This strain grows about one foot high and bears a profusion of comparatively small, very double, globular flowers about one inch in diameter, very brilliant in color............................... " 10cts
Pompon, double mixed. The globular flowers are fully as varied and brilliant in color as the ordinary Zinnia and about half its size........................... " 5cts
Haageana double. Dwarf variety with double flowers of a deep orange color, about one and a quarter inches in diameter; fine for cut flowers; height one foot. " 10cts

A Selected List of Flower Seeds in Bulk

We send, postpaid, at prices annexed, but no discount can be allowed on Flower Seeds by Weight.
Half ounces will not be supplied of kinds which sell for less than 30 cents per ounce.

PER OZ.

Acroclinium, Album $0 20
  Roseum 20
Ageratum Mexicanum, light blue.. 25
  Imperial Dwarf White.. 50
Alyssum, Sweet 25
  Golden 35
  Little Gem 40
Amaranthus tricolor 25
Ampelopsis Veitchii 25
Asparagus Sprengeri...100 seeds, 65 cts.
Aster, Queen of the earliest, white.. 1 25
  Queen of the Market, mixed. 1 00
  Victoria, mixed. 1 25
  Truffaut's Pæony Flowered Perfection, mixed........ 1 25
  Charlotte Roumanille........ 1 50
  Cocardeau, or Crown, mixed 1 25
  Comet, Giant, white 1 50
  Comet Giant, mixed........ 1 50
  Japanese, mixed............ 1 25
  Semple's Branching light blue 1 00
    "   "   pink...... 1 00
    "   "   dark purple 1 00
    "   "   rose pink.. 1 00
    "   "   white...... 1 00
    "   "   mixed...... 90
Balloon Vine..... 15
Balsam Double, Solferino. 60
  Camellia, extra fine mixed..... 50
  Pure White 60
  Dwarf, mixed...... 40
  Tall, mixed...... 40
Calliopsis, fine mixed...... 20
Canary Bird Flower...... 40
Candytuft, fragrant white...... 15
  White Rocket 25
  Giant White (Empress). 40
  Lilac...... 20
  Rose Carmine 30
  Purple...... 25
  Fine mixed, per lb. $1.00 ... 15
Canna, finest large flowering, mx'd. 30
Canterbury Bell, single mixed 35
  double mixed...... 75
Carnation, extra choice, dbl. mxd.. 2 50
  double dwarf mixed....... 1 50
  Marguerite, finest mixed 1 50
Castor Bean Sanguineus........... 15
  Zanzibariensis mixed.. 15
  choice mixed 15
Centaurea gymnocarpa........... 50
  Marguerite, white....... 15
  Cyanus (Bachelor's Button) mixed......
  Cyanus (Bachelor's Button) double mixed...... 20
Chrysanthemum, carinatum, mixed 20
  coronarium, double white...... 20
Chrysanthemum, coronarium, double yellow...... 20
Chrysanthemum, coronarium, double mixed...... 15
Cineraria maritima candidissima .. 30
Cobæa scandens...... 50
Celosia, Dwarf (*Dwarf Cockscomb*) mixed...... 1 75
Columbine Californica hybrida.. 2 50
  cœrulea double........ 2 25
  double mixed...... 30
Convolvulus minor, mixed, per lb., 50cts...... 10
Cosmos, early flowered Dawn...... 40
  mixed...... 30
  Giant, mixed...... 40
Cypress Vine, scarlet...... 25
  white...... 25
  mixed...... 25
Dahlia, finest double mixed 1 50
Daisy, double white, extra........ 2 50
  red, (Longfellow) ... 3 50
  mixed, finest quality. 3 00
Datura Wrighti............ 25
  chlorantha fl. pl........... 25
Eschscholtzia Bush............ 50
  Californica, yellow.. 25
  double white 50

PER OZ.

Eschscholtzia mixed........ ......$0 25
Euphorbia variegata............... 25
Forget-me-not, blue............... 50
Four o'clock, mixed 15
  "   in separate colors.... 15
Foxglove, splendid mixed......... 25
Globe Amaranth, mixed 25
Gourds, Orange............. 25
  Dish Cloth............. 25
  Japanese Nest Egg...... 25
  Siphon, or dipper....... 25
  Hercules' club......... 25
  Apple shaped, striped... 25
  Corsican............. 25
  Pear shaped, ringed 25
  striped 25
  Bottle...... 25
  Powder Horn...... 25
  mixed...... 20
Helichrysum monstrosum, double mixed...... 40
Helichrysum bracteatum (*Golden Eternal Flower*)...... 30
Heliotrope, Dark Varieties, mixed.. 1 25
Hibiscus Africanus............... 20
Hollyhock, Double, Lemon...... 1 25
  Canary yellow.. 1 25
  Pure White ... 1 25
  Purple Red... 1 25
  Deep Rose..... 1 25
  Salmon...... 1 25
  Blood Red... 1 25
  Choicest mixed. 1 00
  mixed...... 75
  Chater's finest mixed.. 2 00
Humulus Japonicus............... 35
Hyacinth Bean, Purple........... 15
  White............ 15
Ice Plant............. 25
Ipomœa, Bona nox............... 15
  Coccinea (Star Ipomœa). 15
  Limbata, mixed......... 20
  Setosa......... 15
Job's Tears............ 15
Lantana, finest French hybrids, mixed............ 25
Larkspur, dbl. dwf. rocket, mxd... 20
  elatum...... 40
Linum grandiflorum rubrum........ 25
Lobelia, Emperor William....... 1 75
Love-in-a-mist, double blue........ 20
Lupin Cruikshanki............ 20
Lychnis Chalcedonica............ 30
Marigold, Cape............ 20
  Meteor............ 20
  Prince of Orange...... 20
  African, double mixed.... 20
  Eldorado...... 40
  French, Legion of Honor. 35
  Tagetes signata pumila.. 35
Maurandia, mixed......... 1 50
Mignonette, Sweet, large flowering......Per lb. 75cts. 15
Mignonette, Machet......... 75
  Ruby......... 50
  Golden Queen...... 30
Mimulus moschatus. 2 00
  punctatus............. 1 75
Momordica balsamina............. 25
Morning Glory, Mixed.Per lb. 50 cts. 10
  Aurora........... 1 25
  Giant Japanese, extra select mixed.......... 30
Mourning Bride, Double, Dark Maroon...... 20
  "   "   White...... 20
  "   "   Mixed'... 20
Nasturtium, Chameleon, Tall:..... 25
  Dwarf.... 25
  Mixed, Trailing (Tropæolum Lobbianum)...... 15
Nasturtium, Dwarf, Mixed...... 15
Nemophila, mixed............ 20
Nicotiana affinis............. 30
Pansy, Emperor William......... 1 25
  King of the Blacks...... 1 25
  Pure Yellow...... 1 35
  Variegated and striped ... 1 50

PER OZ.

Pansy, Odier, or Large Stained.....$4 00
  Meteor. 1 50
  Bugnot's very large stained, mixed ....½ oz. $1.25
Pansy, Lord Beaconsfield..... ... 1 25
  Snow Queen.......... 1 25
  Purple: gold edged.......... 1 00
  Large Flowering Parisian, very large stained, mixed.. 2 50
  Ferry's Superbissima Blotched, 1000 seeds 55c; per ½ oz. $1.50
Pansy, Trimardeau, very large flowered, mixed............ 2 00
Pansy, Extra choice mixed......... 1 50
  Choice mixed 1 00
Peas, Everlasting, White......... 50
  Rose.......... 30
  Mixed.......... 35
Petunia hybrida, finest striped and blotched............. 1 00
Petunia hybrida, fine mixed 50
  large flowered, choicest mixed....1-16 oz. $1.00
  in separate colors...... 90
Phlox Drummondi, large flowered, extra choice mixed 75
Pink, China, double mixed........ 30
  Double Diadem...... 90
  Japan...... 50
  Heddewig's, single mixed.... 50
Poppy, Tulip Flowered 60
  The Shirley 40
  Double White Fringed...... 25
  Cardinal Double......... 15
  Carnation, double white..... 15
  mixed...... 15
Portulaca, single, large flowered, mixed...... 35
Portulaca, single, large flowered, in separate colors............. 40
Portulaca, double, large flowered, mixed............ 2 75
Primrose, Evening, Lamarckiana... 20
  Acaulis Alba...... 90
Primula Sinensis fimbriata, choicest mixed ......¼ oz. $2.50
Pyrethrum Aureum............... 50
Rhodanthe Maculata Alba......... 75
  Manglesi 75
Salpiglossis, extra fine mixed...... 50
Salvia splendens............. 2 00
Sensitive Plant, (Mimosa pudica)... 40
Smilax...... 50
Snapdragon, fine mixed............ 30
Stock, Double, German Ten Weeks, pure white............... 3 00
Stock, Double, German Ten Weeks, large flowered, mixed......... 1 50
Stock, Double German Ten Weeks, mixed............ 1 00
Stock, Brompton, mixed......... 50
  Emperor, or Perpetual, mixed 5 00
Sunflower, Double Chrysanthemum Flowered 30
Sunflower, Stella............ 30
  Golden......... 15
Sweet Peas—See prices on pages 88, 89 and 90.
Sweet William, pure white......... 25
  black.......... 25
  single mixed...... 25
  double mixed...... 50
Tree Cypress, mixed............ 30
Verbena Hybrida Defiance......... 1 25
  Blue............. 75
  White............. 90
  Auricula flowered. 1 00
  Italian striped.... 1 00
  Mammoth mixed.. 1 75
  Extra choice mx'd 1 25
  fine mixed...... 75
Wallflower, Early Brown 25
  double mixed 2 50
Zinnia, double, in separate colors... 35
  choice mixed. Per lb. $3.00 75
  striped or Zebra, mixed...... 60
  Pompon, finest mixed...... 40

BULBS AND ROOTS
FOR SPRING PLANTING

All bulbs and roots will be sent by mail or express, **charges prepaid**, when ordered at single or dozen rates. At the 100 rate they will be sent by express or freight, the purchaser paying the charges, unless otherwise stated. Not less than six of any one variety supplied at dozen rates, and not less than 25 at the 100 rate. Orders with money should be sent us as early as possible, and they will be filled in rotation. Bulbs subject to injury by frost will not be sent until such danger is over.

Included in this class are some of our most showy garden flowers, and their culture is very easy. In the spring, after danger from frost is over, plant in a rich, loamy soil, having a sunny position, and flowers the same season are assured with certainty.

BEGONIA, SINGLE.

Begonia *Tuberous Rooted*

The tubers which we offer are of the very best quality, and with proper care will give a beautiful display early in the summer. For growing in pots or boxes in the house, plant in rich, sandy soil, give good drainage and water freely after the leaves start, but do not let the soil become sour or soggy from over watering. If it is desired to have a bed outdoors, select a shady, moist situation, making the bed rich with thoroughly rotted manure and leaf mold, if obtainable. Plant as soon as danger from frost is over. After the plants start in vigorous growth keep well watered.

			EACH	DOZ.
BEGONIAS,	SINGLE,	Pink	10c	$1.00
"	"	Scarlet	10c	1.00
"	"	White	10c	1.00
"	"	Yellow	10c	1.00
"	"	Mixed	10c	1.00
"	DOUBLE,	Pink	20c	2.00
"	"	Scarlet	20c	2.00
"	"	White	20c	2.00
"	"	Yellow	20c	2.00
"	"	Mixed	20c	2.00

CALADIUM

Esculentum Known as Elephant's Ears. One of the finest tropical plants which can be grown in the open air in the north. It can be made to produce three to ten leaves three to four feet long and nearly as wide, on stalks four to six feet high. The soil best suited to Caladiums is a mixture of fibrous loam, leaf mold, peat and well rotted cow or sheep manure in equal parts, with a sprinkling of sand added. The tubers should be potted at first in as small pots as will conveniently accommodate them, and shifted into larger pots as they require it. But little water must be given to the roots till active growth commences, when, as the plants develop, they require an abundance. A warm, humid atmosphere is necessary for their best development. They must also be shaded from bright sunlight.

	EACH	DOZ.
First Size Bulbs, nine inches and over in circumference	25c	$2.50
Second Size Bulbs, seven to nine inches in circumference	20c	2.00
Third Size Bulbs, under seven inches in circumference	15c	1.50

DAHLIA.

Dahlia

The Dahlia has always been a favorite for autumn flowering. The flowers are so symmetrical and perfect, and the range of colors so large and varied, that they will always be popular where display is wanted. The roots are tender and easily injured by frost; they should be set out three feet apart, after all danger of frost is over, and during winter placed in a cool cellar but not allowed to freeze. The plants should be supported by tying to stakes. Our collection of mixed dahlias is of the best, comprising all the positive colors, in their most striking shades.

			EACH	DOZ.
DAHLIAS,	DOUBLE,	Pink	15c	$1.50
"	"	Scarlet	15c	1.50
"	"	White	15c	1.50
"	"	Yellow	15c	1.50
"	"	Mixed	15c	1.50

CALADIUM, ESCULENTUM.

Gladiolus

No flower has gained more rapidly in public favor than the Gladiolus; this could not well be otherwise, for in addition to the great intrinsic merit of the flower, it is *easy of cultivation, and blooms the first season.* They thrive in almost any good soil except a stiff clay, require full sunlight and are liable to injury only from rank manure. Plant Gladiolus bulbs six to nine inches apart, the large ones four inches and the small ones two inches deep. Make an early planting of the smallest bulbs first as soon as the ground is sufficiently dry and warm. Continue to plant at intervals of two weeks during the spring and early summer; in this way a succession of bloom may be had from mid-summer until frost. In autumn, before freezing, they should be dug up and the tops allowed to dry down, after which the dry tops, earth and old bulbs can be removed. Store in a cool, dry place, secure from frost, until spring.

CHOICE NAMED GLADIOLUS

These named varieties are selected with special reference to beauty of flower, range of color and habit of plant.

	EACH	DOZ.
Ajax, red striped and shaded with white	5c	$0.50
Augusta, lovely pure white, with blue anthers	10c	1.00
Brenchleyensis, rich, dark scarlet; very brilliant	5c	.50
Ceres, white, spotted rose	5c	.50
Doctor Hogg, mauve, suffused with rose, center pure white	10c	1.00
Emma Thursby, white ground, carmine stripes through petals, blotch on the lower division	10c	1.00
Eugene Scribe, flowers very large and wide; perfect, tender rose, blazed with carminate red; beautiful	10c	1.00
Glory of Brightwood, scarlet with lemon throat	10c	1.00
Isaac Buchanan, one of the best yellow sorts	10c	1.00
John Bull, white, slightly tinged with sulphur	5c	.50
Lamarck, cherry colored, lightly tinted with orange, blazed with red, center is very well lighted, with large, pure white stain	10c	1.00
Madam Monneret, bright, clear pink	5c	.50
Martha Washington, pure, light yellow, lower petals slightly tinged with rose; stately and beautiful	10c	1.00
May, a lovely pure white flower, finely flaked with bright rosy crimson; superb spike	5c	.50
Pepita, bright golden yellow, slightly striped carmine at the edges of the petals, toward the end of the flower season; the most freely flowering yellow	10c	1.00
Phœbus, brilliant red, with a large, white stain	10c	1.00
Reine Blanche, pure white, dark carmine blotch	10c	1.00
Shakespeare, white, blazed with rosy-carmine, large, rose colored stain	10c	1.00
Snow White, the best white gladiolus; spike enormous and of the most beautiful shape; flowers large and well opened	20c	1.50
Sylphide, pure white, flamed carmine; extra large and fine	10c	1.00

GLADIOLUS.

GIANT FLOWERED GLADIOLUS

A class of hybrids between Gladiolus Gandevensis and Gladiolus Saundersoni, which, for varied and exquisite beauty, has never been equaled. The flowers are of gigantic size, frequently eight inches across, borne on spikes four to five feet high, the upper two feet being covered with flowers. In color and markings they afford the widest range of any cultivated flower. Every color and shade known among Gladiolus is represented in the mixture, also blues, purple-blacks and whites, mottled with crimson, pink, yellow and white.

Gov. McCormack. Extra large flower and truss, beautiful rose mottled with silvery-gray and with violet; white mottled throat. Very fine, being of unusual beauty and oddity. **Each 10c; doz. $1.00.**

Mohonk. A strong, vigorous grower with flowers of large size and great substance. Deep, dark pink with spotted throat, shaded orange and flaked with maroon. **Each 5c; doz. 50c.**

Mottled Gem. Large, spreading flower, showing an unusually large throat, beautifully mottled white, violet and scarlet. **Each 10c; doz. $1.00.**

Mrs. Beecher. Beautiful, deep rosy-crimson. Large, well opened flower, with pure white throat, freely marked and spotted. **Each 10c; doz. $1.00.**

Nezinscott. Bright blood scarlet, with deep, velvety crimson, black blotches and white mottling in throat. **Each 7c; doz. 75c.**

William Falconer. Spike of great length and flowers of enormous size. Beautiful clear light pink. **Each 7c; doz. 75c.**

Giant Flowered, fine mixed. Each 7c; doz. 75c, postpaid.

BUTTERFLY GLADIOLUS

Lemoine's Large Stained.

A distinct race of this matchless class of plants, characterized by the variety and strength of color of their flowers. They last remarkably well and no collection can be complete without them.

Admiral Pierre. Large flowers, round, very open, dark carmine red, lower divisions clouded maroon-purple. **Each 5c; doz. 50c.**

Incendiary. Fiery red, large blotch of crimson red on lower petals, small gold markings. **Each 5c; doz. 50c.**

Lemoine's Butterfly Varieties mixed. Throats very distinctly marked. **Each 4c; doz. 40c; per 100 $2.25.** *The 100 rate is by express at purchaser's expense.*

GLADIOLUS MIXTURES

These choice assortments must not be confounded with the common mixed sorts. We recommend this stock with perfect confidence, as it is composed only of choice varieties, and u c se s can depend upon having a magnificent variety of colors. *Single and dozen prices include postage. The 100 rate is by express at purchaser's expense.*

	EACH	DOZ.	PER 100
Extra Fine American Hybrids mixed	5c	40c	$2.50
Shades of Pink mixed	5c	40c	2.50
" **Red** "	5c	40c	2.50
" **Yellow** "	5c	50c	4.00
White and Light Varieties	4c	40c	2.25
Striped and Variegated mixed	5c	40c	2.50

Dielytra

(Bleeding Heart). Tuberous rooted plants that bloom in the spring, favorably known almost everywhere. They are a charming, hardy, perennial plant with much cut foliage and flowers of interesting structure. The flowers are delicate pink, very graceful and produced continuously from May to July. They require only the ordinary culture of border plants. Roots planted in spring or autumn flower freely and should be divided every third year. **Each 20c; doz. $2.00.**

Madeira Vine ::

Tuberous rooted climber with glossy green leaves, and delightfully fragrant, white blossoms. Sometimes called Mignonette Vine. It is of rapid growth and from a few tubers, vines will be produced sufficient to cover one side of a cottage in a single season. The tubers are tender and must be protected from frost during winter. **Each 5c; doz. 50c.**

Tritoma

Sometimes called Red Hot Poker. This is a fine, handsome p n. It is hardy, though requiring some protection through winter. The flowers are produced in large spikes of rich, orange-red tinted flower tubes. Plant two feet apart. Tritomas are hardy south of Cincinnati with well covered in winter. In the north it is generally safer to dig up the p n s in November, place them in boxes with dry earth and store them in a cellar in winter. In spring, place them in a warm, sheltered, well-drained spot, preferably with a background of shrubbery to set off the plants. **Each 20c; doz. $2.00.**

Lilies

Lilies have always been regarded as among the most beautiful of garden plants. Of queenly beauty, faultless purity and stately form, too much cannot be said in their praise and we are glad to notice their increasing popularity from year to year. Nearly every variety will with a little care, endure the severity of our winters and many are among the most hardy of our garden flowers.

Bulbs should be planted as soon as the frost is out of the ground—the earlier the better. Select a well drained spot, dig the soil deep and make it fine, enriching it abundantly with well-rotted cow manure, adding a liberal mixture of sand. Set the bulbs from three to five inches deep, according to size. During the winter it is advisable to cover the surface of the bed with a thin layer of manure, which will afford a slight protection to the bulbs and also materially enrich the soil. In spring the manure may be removed or dug in between the rows. Care should be taken that they have proper drainage, no water being allowed to stand around the roots. Once firmly established, they should not be disturbed oftener than once in five years. To produce *extra fine* specimens, plant bulbs in pots early in spring and grow them in the house or under glass.

Lilium Auratum

The glorious, gold-banded lily of Japan, and one of the grandest plants in cultivation. Its immense, ivory-white flowers are thickly studded with yellow and crimson spots, while in the center of each petal is a golden band, fading at its edges into the white. Such choice bulbs as we offer if well cared for will give from five to ten magnificent flowers the first year, and under good cultivation will, after becoming well established, give from ten to fifty. 20cts each; $2.00 per doz.

Jacobean Lily

(*Amaryllis Formosissima*). Each of the five narrow petals of this flower is three to four inches long and a very intense, deep scarlet color of unequaled brilliancy, vividness and purity. The plants are readily grown and although the bulbs are not hardy they can be easily preserved during the winter in a dry cellar and planted in the open ground in the spring. They may be grown in winter like hyacinths. 15cts each; $1.25 per doz.

Lilium Tigrinum, flore pleno

(*Double Tiger Lily*). This magnificent lily is of stately habit, bearing clusters of very large, double flowers on tall, strong stems; color bright orange-red, spotted with black. 15cts each; $1.50 per doz.

Lilium Tigrinum, Splendens

(*Improved Single Tiger Lily*). Has very large flowers of excellent form; color reddish-salmon, with dark spots. 12cts each; $1.25 per doz.

LILIUM AURATUM.

Lilium Longiflorum

A very uniform and exceptionally neat plant. Comes readily into bloom for Memorial Day, being a little later forcing variety than Lilium Harrisii and preferred by some to that, since the flowers are of better substance. Extensively used by florists for cut flowers. When grown in the open ground it blooms in June and July. The pure white flowers resemble the well known Bermuda Easter Lily. 12cts each; $1.25 per doz.

Lilium Speciosum Album

Pure white flowers with a greenish band through the center of each petal. They are of great substance and very fragrant. One of the best for general culture. 15cts each; $1.50 per doz.

DOUBLE TIGER LILY.

Lilium Speciosum Rubrum

No words can overstate the brilliant beauty of these famous Japan Lilies. The six broad white or pink petals are thickly dotted with rose or crimson spots, and the graceful form and brilliant color make them very effective and desirable. Especially thrifty and hardy. One of the best for garden culture. 15cts each; $1.50 per doz.

Tuberose

The flowers of this popular plant are waxy-white, double and exceedingly fragrant. They are useful in buttonhole bouquets, in large bouquets, or as single specimens. A good way to grow Tuberoses is to fill five-inch pots half full of *well rotted* cow manure, and the remainder with good, rich, sandy soil. Plant the bulbs in this, in April, water moderately and hasten growth by putting in a warm light place. When weather has become warm, plunge the pots in the earth out of doors. They will usually flower before cold weather; if they do not, the pots can be brought in and they will bloom in the house.

Double Dwarf Pearl, *extra large bulbs*, 4cts each; 35cts per doz.; $2.00 per 100. We will supply second size bulbs 3 for 10 cents, 30 cents per dozen, $1.50 per 100. *The 100 rates are by express at purchaser's expense.*

TUBEROSE.

☞ About September First next we will issue our Annual Catalogue of CHOICE DUTCH BULBS AND SEEDS FOR FALL PLANTING. It will be sent free to all customers without ordering it, and to others who apply for it.

Matthews New Universal ::: Hand ::: Garden Tools

We Deliver at Depot or Express Office in Detroit, Mich., at Prices Given Herein.

New Universal Model Garden Drill.
Price, $6.50

New Universal Model Hill and Drill Seeder.
Price, $7.25

New Universal Constellation Drill

The Latest Improved and Most Complete Combination upon the Market.

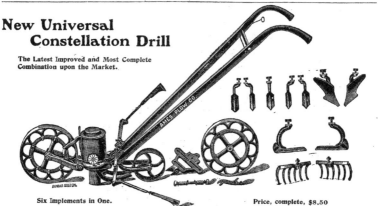

Six Implements in One.

Price, complete, $8.50

New Universal Double Wheel Hoe, Cultivator,
Rake and Plow. Price, complete, $5.50

New Universal Single Wheel Hoe, Cultivator,
Rake and Plow.
Price, Complete, $4.75

New Universal Plain
Double Wheel Hoe,
with one pair
Hoes only.
Price, $3.50

New Universal
Plain Single Wheel
Hoe, with one pair
Hoes, only.
Price, $2.75

MATTHEWS New Universal Hand Garden Tools — Continued.

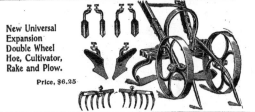

New Universal
Expansion
Double Wheel
Hoe, Cultivator,
Rake and Plow.

Price, $6.25

New Universal
High Arch
Expansion Wheel
Hoe, Cultivator,
Rake and Plow.

Price, $8.00

New Universal No. 2 Single
Wheel Hoe, Cultivator and Plow.

Price, complete, $4.25

Hand Wheel Plow.
Price, $2.00

The **PLANET Jr. Garden Tools**

Space will not permit our showing and describing all the Planet Jr. tools, but we
will send a fully illustrated catalogue free to all who desire it and will ask for it; and
we can supply promptly anything ordered.

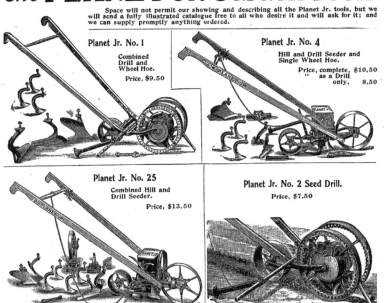

Planet Jr. No. 1

Combined
Drill and
Wheel Hoe.

Price, $9.50

Planet Jr. No. 4

Hill and Drill Seeder and
Single Wheel Hoe.

Price, complete, $10.50
"   as a Drill
only,   8.50

Planet Jr. No. 25

Combined Hill and
Drill Seeder.

Price, $13.50

Planet Jr. No. 2 Seed Drill.

Price, $7.50

Planet Jr. No. 5 Hill and Drill Seeder. $13.00
16½ in. drive wheel. Hopper holds 4 qts.

Planet Jr. No. 21 Hill and Drill Seeder
and
Fertilizer Drill. $17.50

The PLANET JR. GARDEN TOOLS—Continued.

Planet Jr. No. 11

Planet Jr. No. 15

Planet Jr. No. 19

PLANET JR. No. 11 DOUBLE WHEEL HOE $9.00
With 2 pairs hoes, 2 pairs cultivator teeth,
2 pairs rakes, 1 pair plows, and 1 pair leaf lifters.

PLANET JR. No. 12 DOUBLE WHEEL HOE 7.00
With 1 pair hoes, 2 pairs cultivator teeth,
1 pair plows, and 1 pair leaf lifters.

PLANET JR. No. 13 DOUBLE WHEEL HOE 4.75
With 1 pair hoes only.

PLANET JR. No. 15 SINGLE WHEEL HOE 6.50
With 2 pairs hoes, 3 cultivator teeth,
3 rakes, 1 plow, and 1 leaf lifter.

PLANET JR. No. 16 SINGLE WHEEL HOE 5.85
With 1 pair hoes, 3 cultivator teeth,
2 rakes, 1 plow, and 1 leaf lifter.

PLANET JR. No. 17 SINGLE WHEEL HOE 5.00
With 1 pair hoes, 3 cultivator teeth, and 1 plow.

PLANET JR. No. 18 SINGLE WHEEL HOE 3.50
With 1 pair hoes only.

PLANET JR. No. 19 SINGLE WHEEL HOE 3.75
With 1 large garden plow, 1 ten-inch sweep,
1 six-inch sweep, 1 four-inch cultivator tooth,
1 two-inch cultivator tooth.

THE WEED SLAYER A light, strong, inexpensive wheel hoe. **$2.00**
Three in one shipment, $5.00

Brass Greenhouse and Garden Syringes

☞ *Sent only by express at expense of purchaser.*

No. A, one stream and one spray rose $2 25
No. B,   "   "   "   " 2 75
No. C,   "   "   "   " 3 50
No. D,   "   "   "   " 4 50
No. H, length of barrel, 18 in.; diameter 1¼ in.......... 2 25
No. 0, one spray rose, fast ends, large holes 2 50
No. 00,   "   "   "   " 3 00
No. 1,   "   " detachable end.............. 2 75

Plant Bed Cloth

Medium grade, 20 yards or over...............8 cts. per yard
    "   "   60   "   " ....7½ "   "
    At purchaser's expense for transportation.

The Iron King Seed Drill

Sows all kinds of garden seeds in an *exact line*, so that
the cultivator can be worked close up to the row while the
plants are small, and therefore is especially adapted to sowing onion seed. Two patent agitators go with each machine,
which are easily adjusted and act as *force feeds*, thus insuring an even and continuous flow. It
has interchangeable hoppers for dis-
tributing fertilizers and by simply
changing hoppers can be converted
from a seed to a
fertilizer drill.... } **$6.50**
*With Disc coverer, $7.00
With Fertilizer attach-
ment, $10.00*

EXCELSIOR
WEEDING HOOK

Price, 20cts.
Postpaid.

SOLID STEEL FLORISTS' TROWEL
Polished 6-inch Blade.   Price, 50cts., postpaid.

NEVER-BREAK SOLID FORGED
STEEL GARDEN TROWEL
6 inches long. Hardwood Handle.
Superior in Style, Finish and Quality.
Price, 25cts., postpaid.

THE CHRISTY
GARDEN WEEDER   Price, 25cts., postpaid.

HASELTINE HAND WEEDER
AND SCRAPER
Price, 25cts., postpaid.

REFERENCE TABLES

Weight of Various Articles.

Article	Pounds per bush.	
Barley	48	lbs.
Beans	60	"
Buckwheat	48	"
Canary Seed	60	"
Castor Beans	46	"
Clover Seed	60	"
Corn, field, shelled	56	"
" " on ear	70	"
" sweet, sold by measured bushel.		
Flax Seed	56	"
Grass, Rhode Island Bent	14	"
" Creeping Bent	20	"
" Red Top (in chaff)	14	"
" " (cleaned from chaff)	32	"
" Meadow Foxtail	7	"
" Tall Meadow Oat	10	"
" Awnless Brome	14	"
" Orchard	14	"
" Hard Fescue	12	"
" Tall "	14	"
" Sheep's "	12	"
" Meadow Fescue or English Blue Grass	22	"
" Perennial Rye	20	"
" Timothy	45	"
" Wood Meadow	14	"
" Kentucky Blue	14	"
" Fowl Meadow	12	"
" Rough Stalked Meadow	14	"
Hemp Seed	44	"
Hungarian	48	"
Millet, German or Golden	50	"
Millet	50	"
Peach Pits	50	"
Peas, smooth	60	"
" wrinkled	56	"
Rape	50	"
Rye	56	"
Vetches or Tares	60	"

Number of Plants or Trees to the Acre at given Distances.

Dis. apart.	No. plants.	Dis. apart.	No. plants.	Dis. apart.	No. plants.	Dis. apart.	No. plants.
12 x 1 In.	522,720	24 x 24 In.	10,890	36 x 36 In.	4,840	60 x 60 In.	1,743
12 x 3 "	174,240	30 x 1 "	209,088	42 x 12 "	12,446	8 x 1 Ft.	5,445
12 x 12 "	43,560	30 x 6 "	34,848	42 x 24 "	6,223	8 x 3 "	1,815
16 x 1 "	392,040	30 x 12 "	17,424	42 x 36 "	4,148	8 x 8 "	680
18 x 1 "	348,480	30 x 16 "	13,068	48 x 12 "	10,890	10 x 1 "	4,356
18 x 3 "	116,160	30 x 20 "	10,454	48 x 18 "	7,790	10 x 6 "	726
18 x 12 "	29,040	30 x 24 "	8,712	48 x 24 "	5,445	10 x 10 "	435
18 x 18 "	19,360	30 x 30 "	6,970	48 x 30 "	4,356	12 x 1 "	3,630
20 x 1 "	313,635	36 x 3 "	58,080	48 x 36 "	3,630	12 x 5 "	736
20 x 20 "	15,681	36 x 12 "	14,520	48 x 48 "	2,723	12 x 12 "	302
24 x 1 "	261,360	36 x 18 "	9,680	60 x 36 "	2,901	16 x 1 "	2,722
24 x 18 "	15,520	36 x 24 "	7,260	60 x 48 "	2,178	16 x 16 "	170

Quantity of Seed requisite to produce a given number of plants and sow an acre.

	Quantity per acre.	
Artichoke, 1 oz. to 500 plants	6	oz.
Asparagus, 1 oz. to 800 plants	1	lb.
Asparagus Roots	1000 to 7250	
Barley	2½	bu.
Beans, dwarf, 1 pint to 100 ft. of drill	1	"
Beans, pole, 1 pint to 100 hills	½	"
Beet, garden, 1 oz. to 100 feet of drill	7	lbs.
Beet, Mangel, 1 oz. to 100 feet of drill	5	"
Brocoli, 1 oz. to 5,000 plants	2	oz.
Brussels Sprouts, 1 oz. to 5,000 plants	2	"
Buckwheat	½	bu.
Cabbage, 1 oz. to 5,000 plants	2	oz.
Carrot, ¼ oz. to 100 feet of drill	2½	lbs.
Cauliflower, 1 oz. to 5,000 plants	2½	oz.
Celery, 1 oz. to 15,000 plants	2	"
Chicory	4	lbs.
Clover, Alsike and White Dutch	6	"
" Lucerne	15 to 25	"
" Crimson Trefoil	10 to 15	"
" Large Red and Medium	8 to 12	"
Collards, 1 oz. to 5,000 plants	2	oz.
Corn, rice, (*shelled*)	2	qts.
Corn, sweet, ¼ pint to 100 hills	6	"
Cress, ¾ oz. to 100 feet of drill	12	lbs.
Cucumber, 1 oz. to 100 hills	1 to 3	"
Egg Plant, 1 oz. to 2,000 plants	4	oz.
Endive, ¼ oz. to 100 feet of drill	4½	lbs.
Flax, broadcast	½	bu.
Garlic, bulbs, 1 lb. to 10 feet of drill		
Gourd, 2 oz. to 100 hills		
Grass, Blue, Kentucky	2	bu.
" Blue, English	1	"
" Hungarian and Millet	½	"
" Mixed Lawn	3 to 5	"
" Red Top, Fancy Clean	8 to 10	lbs.
" Red Top, in Chaff	20 to 28	"

	Quantity per acre.	
Grass, Timothy	¼	bu.
" Orchard, Perennial Rye, Fowl Meadow and Wood Meadow	2	"
Hemp	½	"
Horse Radish Roots	10000 to 15000	
Kale, 1 oz. to 5,000 plants	2	oz.
Kohl Rabi, ⅓ oz. to 100 feet of drill	4	lbs.
Leek, ⅓ oz. to 100 feet of drill	4	"
Lettuce, ¼ oz. to 100 feet of drill	3	"
Martynia, 1 oz. to 100 feet of drill	5	"
Melon, Musk, 1 oz. to 100 hills	1 to 3	"
" Water, 4 oz. to 100 hills	1½ to 4	"
Nasturtium, 2 oz. to 100 feet of drill	15	"
Okra, 1 oz. to 100 feet of drill	8	"
Onion Seed, ⅓ oz. to 100 ft. of drill	4 to 5	"
" " for Sets	40 to 80	"
Onion Sets, 1 quart to 40 feet of drill	8	bu.
Parsnip, ¼ oz. to 100 feet of drill	3	lbs.
Parsley, ¼ oz. to 100 feet of drill	3	"
Peas, garden, 1 pint to 100 ft. of drill	1 to 3	bu.
" field	2	"
Pepper, 1 oz. to 1,500 plants	3	oz.
Pumpkin, ⅓ quart to 100 hills	3 to 4	lbs.
Radish, ⅔ oz. to 100 ft. of drill	10 to 12	"
Rye	1½	bu.
Salsify, ¾ oz. to 100 feet of drill	8	lbs.
Spinage, ½ oz. to 100 feet of drill	8	"
Spurry	15	"
Summer Savory	¾	"
Sunflower	8	"
Squash, Summer, 4 oz. to 100 hills	2	"
" Winter, 8 oz. to 100 hills	2	"
Tomato, 1 oz. to 4,500 plants	1	oz.
Tobacco, 1 oz. to 5,000 plants	2	"
Turnip, 1 oz. to 250 feet of drill	1 to 3	lbs.
Vetches	2	bu.

FOREIGN NAMES OF VEGETABLES AND HERBS.

ENGLISH.	GERMAN.	FRENCH.	SPANISH.	ITALIAN.	DUTCH.	POLISH.
Anise	Anis, Grüner Anis	Anis	Anis, Matalahuga	Aniso, Anacio	Anijs	Anyz.
Artichoke	Artischoke	Artichaut	Alcachofa	Articiocca	Artisjok	Karczochy.
Asparagus	Spargel	Asperge	Esparrago	Sparagio	Asperge	Szparagi.
Balm	Citronen-Melisse	Melisse citronelle	Toronjil, Citronella	Melissa	Citroen-Melisse	Balsam.
Basil	Basilikum	Basilic grand	Albaca	Basilico	Basilicum	Bazylia.
Beans	Bohnen	Haricots	Habichuela	Fagiuoli	Boonen	Fasola.
Beet	Rübe	Betterave	Remolacha	Barbabietola	Bieten	Buraki.
Borage	Boretsch	Bourrache	Borraja	Boragine	Bernagie	Boraz.
Brocoli	Spargelkohl	Chou Brocoli	Broculi	Brocoli	Broccoli	Brokuly.
Brussels Sprouts	Rosenkohl	Chou de Bruxelles	Bretones de Bruselas	Cavolo di Brusselles	Spruitkool	Latorvil.
Cabbage	Kopfkohl, Kraut	Chou pommé	Col repello	Cavolo cappuccio	Sluitkool	Kapusta.
Cabbage, Savoy	Wirsing	Chou de Milan	Col de Milan	Cavolo di Milano	Savooiekool	Sabaudzka Kapusta.
Caraway	Feld-Kümmel	Cumin des prés	Comino	Carvi	Karwij	Kmin.
Carrot	Carotten, Möhren	Carotte	Zanahoria	Carota	Wortelen	Marchew.
Cauliflower	Blumenkohl	Chou-fleur	Coliflor	Cavolofiore	Bloemkool	Kalafiory.
Celery	Sellerie	Céleri	Apio	Sedano	Selderij	Selery.
Celeriac	Knoll-Sellerie	Céleri-rave	Apio-nabo	Sedano-rapa	Knolselderij	Brukwiana Selera.
Chervil	Kerbel	Cerfeuil	Perifollo	Cerfoglio	Kervel	Czechrzyca.
Chicory	Cichorienwurzel	Chicorée sauvage	Achicoria	Cicoria selvatica	Suikerij	Cukorya.
Coriander	Coriander	Coriandre	Culantro	Coriandorlo	Koriander	Koleder.
Corn Salad	Feldsalat	Mâche	Canonigos	Valeriana	Veldsla	Ziarno Sataty.
Corn	Mais	Mais	Maiz	Mais	Mais	Kukurudza.
Cress	Garten-Kresse	Cresson alénois	Mastuerzo	Agretto	Tuinkers	Rzerzucha.
Cress, Water	Brunnenkresse	Cresson de fontaine	Berro	Nasturzio aquatico	Waterkers	Rezerzucha wodna.
Cucumber	Gurken	Concombre	Cohombro	Cetriolo	Komkommer	Ogorek.
Dandelion	Löwenzahn	Pissenlit	Diente de leon	Dente di leone	Molsla	Papawa.
Dill	Dill	Aneth	Eneldo	Aneto	Dille	Koper.
Egg Plant	Eierpflanze	Aubergine	Berengena	Petonciano	Melanzaan-plant	Jajkowa roslina.
Endive	Endivien	Chicorée Endive	Endivia	Indivia	Andijvie	Endywia.
Fennel	Fenchel	Fenouil	Hinojo	Finocchio	Venkel	Koper.
Garlic	Knoblauch	Ail	Ajo	Aglio	Knoflook	Czosnek.
Horse Radish	Meer Rettig	Raifort sauvage	Taramago	Rafano	Peperwortel	Chrzan.
Hyssop	Isop	Hyssope	Hisopo	Issopo	Hysop	Hyzop.
Kale	Blätterkohl	Chou vert	Breton, Berza	Cavolo verde	Boerenkool	Solanka.
Kohl Rabi	Knollkohl	Chou-rave	Col rabano	Cavolo rapa	Koolrabi	Kalarepa.
Lavender	Lavendel	Lavende	Espliego	Lavanda	Lavendel	Lawenda.
Leek	Porree, Lauch	Poireau	Puerro	Porro	Prei	Pory.

FOREIGN NAMES OF VEGETABLES AND HERBS—Continued.

ENGLISH.	GERMAN.	FRENCH.	SPANISH.	ITALIAN.	DUTCH.	POLISH
Lettuce	Lattich, Kopfsalat.	Laitue	Lechuga	Lattuga	Kropsla	Salata.
Marjoram	Majoran	Marjolaine.	Mejorana	Maggiorana	Marjolijn	Majeranek.
Melon	Melone.	Melon.	Melon	Popone	Meloen.	Melon.
Melon, Water.	Wasser-Melone.	Melon d'eau.	Sandia	Melone d'aqua.	Water Meloen	Melon, wodny.
Mushroom	Schwamm	Champignon.	Seta	Fungo pratajolo.	Kampernoelie	Grzyb.
Nasturtium	Kapuciner Kresse.	Capucine	Capuchina	Nasturzio	Capucine-kers	Nasturcya.
Okra	Ocher.	Gombaud	Gombo.	Ocra		Glinka
						biatozotta.
Onion.	Zwiebel	Ognon.	Cebolla	Cipollo.	Uien.	Cebula.
Parsley	Petersilie.	Persil.	Perejil.	Prezzemolo.	Peterselie	Pietruszka.
Parsnip.	Pastinake.	Panais.	Chirivia.	Pastinaca	Pinksternakel.	Pasternak.
Peas.	Erbsen.	Pois.	Guisante.	Pisello.	Erwten	Groch.
Pepper	Pfeffer	Piment	Pimiento.	Peperone.	Spaansche Peper	Pieprz.
Pumpkin.	Melonen-Kürbiss.	Potiron	Calabaza totanera.	Zucca.	Pompoen	Bania.
Radish.	Radies	Radis.	Rabanito.	Ravanello	Radijs.	Rzodkiew.
Rhubarb.	Rhabarber.	Rhubarbe.	Ruibarbo.	Rabarbaro	Rabarber	Rubarbarum.
Rosemary	Rosmarin	Romarin	Romero	Rosmarino.	Rozemarijn.	Rozmaryn.
Rue	Raute.	Rue.	Ruda.		Wijnruit.	Ruta.
Saffron	Safran.	Safran.	Azafran	Zafferano.	Saffraan.	Szafran.
Sage	Salbei.	Sauge.	Salvia	Salvia	Salie.	Szalwija.
Salsify.	Haferwurzel.	Salsifis.	Salsifi blanco.	Sassefrica.	Salsefy	Jarzynwa.
						ostryga.
Sorrel	Sauerampfer.	Oseille.	Acedern.	Acetosa.	Zuring.	Szczaw.
Summer Savory.	Bohnenkraut.	Sarriette annuelle.	Ajedrea comun.	Santoreggia.	Boonenkruid.	Caber.
						ogrolowy.
Spinage.	Spinat.	Epinard.	Espinaca.	Spinace.	Spinazie.	Szpinak.
Squash.	Kürbiss.	Courge.	Calabaza.	Zucca.	Kalebas.	Mielurcz.
Tansy	GemeinerRainfarn.	Tanaisie.	Tanaceto.	Atanasia.	Wormkruid.	Wrotycz
						pospolity.
Thyme	Thymian	Thym.	Tomillo	Timo.	Tijm.	Macierzanka.
Tomato	Liebesapfel.	Pomme d'Amour.	Tomate	Pomo d'oro.	Tomaat.	Pomidor.
Turnip.	Weisse-Rübe.	Navet.	Nabo	Navone.	Rapen	Rzepa, brukiew.
Wormwood.	Wermuth.	Absinthe.	Ajenjo	Assenzio.	Alsem.	Piotun.

BOOKS

BULBS AND TUBEROUS-ROOTED PLANTS, by C. L. ALLEN. History, description, methods of propagation, and complete directions for their successful culture in the garden, dwelling and greenhouse. Over 300 pages, profusely illustrated. **Price, $1.50**

CELERY GROWING AND MARKETING, by Homer L. Stewart. This valuable book was written by a professional celery grower, and the subject is treated so fully that by its aid any one can grow celery superior to much that may be found on the market. **Price, $1.00**

DAIRYING FOR PROFIT, OR THE POOR MAN'S COW. A practical book by a practical woman, explaining every detail of the best management of a cow to secure the most and best milk, and the care of the milk necessary to produce the best cream and butter. **Price, 50c.**

FIRST BOOK OF FORESTRY, by Filibert Roth, Chief of the Division of Forestry, U. S. Dept. of the Interior. The need for forest protection in America is coming to be generally realized, but the knowledge of the principles underlying forestry is by no means so general. This book has been prepared for this purpose and has been written with special reference to the needs of the library of the country home. Cloth, 291 pages, illustrated. **Price, $1.00**

HOW TO DESTROY INSECTS ON FLOWERS AND HOUSE PLANTS. Tells how to fertilize and stimulate plants, and gives the experience of cultivators in keeping their plants healthy. Among others, there are topics on the following: Red Spider, Aphis, Green Fly, Worms in Pots, Rose Slugs, Rose Bugs, Snails, Caterpillars. It also tells how to destroy ants and all house bugs. **Price, 25c.**

MUSHROOMS, HOW TO GROW THEM. A practical treatise on Mushroom culture by William Falconer. It embodies the experience of the author in this country and in Europe regarding the best methods of making this fascinating occupation a success. Fully illustrated. **Price, $1.00**

MUSHROOM CULTURE. A little book, but full of easily understood directions, which if followed would enable every one to grow his own supply. **Price, 10c.**

TOBACCO LEAF. Its Culture and Cure, Marketing and Manufacture. Every tobacco grower should have this book. We know of no work where the culture of any particular crop is so exhaustively treated and the essentials to success so well presented as in this. It is a model hand book. **Price, $2.00**

WINDOW GARDENING. Written as a help and encouragement to all flower-lovers to assist them in their efforts to make home more beautiful. Nicely bound, about 300 pages and profusely illustrated. By H. T. Williams. **Price, $1.00**

FARM, GARDEN, FRUITS, FLOWERS, ETC.

American Farm Book, by L. F. Allen	$2 00
Broom Corn and Brooms, by Editors Am. Agriculturalist	50
Bulbs and Tuberous-Rooted Plants, by C. L. Allen	1 50
Cabbages, Cauliflower, etc., by C. L. Allen	50
Celery Growing and Marketing, by H. L. Stewart	1 00
Every Woman Her Own Flower Gardener paper	60
Farming with Green Manures, by C. Harlan	1 00
First Book of Forestry, by Filibert Roth	75
Gardening for Profit, by Peter Henderson	1 50
Ginseng, Its Cultivation, Harvesting and Marketing, by M. G. Kains	50
Grape Culturist, The, by A. S. Fuller	1 50
Grasses and How to Grow Them, by Prof. Thos. Shaw	1 50
Gregory on Onion Raising paper	30
Hand Book for Fruit Growers, by F. R. Elliott paper	50
Hop Culture in the United States, by E. Meeker	1 50
How to Destroy Insects on Flowers and House Plants. paper	25
How to Grow Onions on Muck Soil, by C. C. Taylor; paper	10
Irrigation for the Farm, Garden and Orchard, by H. Stewart	1 00

Kalamazoo Celery; Its Cultivation and Secret of Success. paper	$ 50
Method of Making Manures, by Geo. Bommer. paper	25
Mushroom Culture paper	10
Mushrooms, How to Grow Them, by Wm. Falconer	1 00
Onion Culture, by 20 Experienced Growers. paper	20
Our Farm of Four Acres paper	30
Play and Profit in My Garden, by E. P. Roe	1 00
Practical Floriculture, by Peter Henderson	1 50
Robinson's Mushroom Culture.	50
Silos, Ensilage and Silage, by Manly Miles.	50
Small Fruit Culturist, by A. S. Fuller	1 00
Strawberry Culturist, The, Illustrated, by A. S. Fuller.	25
The Rose; Ellwanger.	1 25
Tobacco Culture, by 14 Experienced Cultivators. paper	25
Tobacco Leaf, by J. B. Killebrew and H. Myrick.	2 00
Vegetable Gardening, by S. B. Green, cloth $1.00; paper	50
Weeds, How to Eradicate Them, by Prof. Thos. Shaw.	50
Window Gardening, by H. T. Williams.	1 00

MISCELLANEOUS

Canary Birds paper	$0 50
Dairying for Profit, or the Poor Man's Cow paper	50
Feathered Pets, by Chas. N. Page paper	25
Insects and Insecticides, by C. M. Weed	1 50
Poultry Manual, by F. L. Sewell and I. E. Tilson	50
Quinby's New Bee Keeping, by L. C. Root	1 00

Shepherd's Manual, by Henry Stewart	$1 00
Silk Culture	30
The Language of Flowers, cloth 50c. paper	25
The New Egg Farm (large edition) by H. H. Stoddard.	1 00
Willard's Practical Butter Book, by X. A. Willard.	1 00

ADDRESS ALL ORDERS TO   **D. M. FERRY & CO.,**

All Books sent postpaid on receipt of price.

DETROIT, MICH.

SEED
ANNUAL
1905